D0578342

5344
NEW YORK CENTRAL
SANTA FE

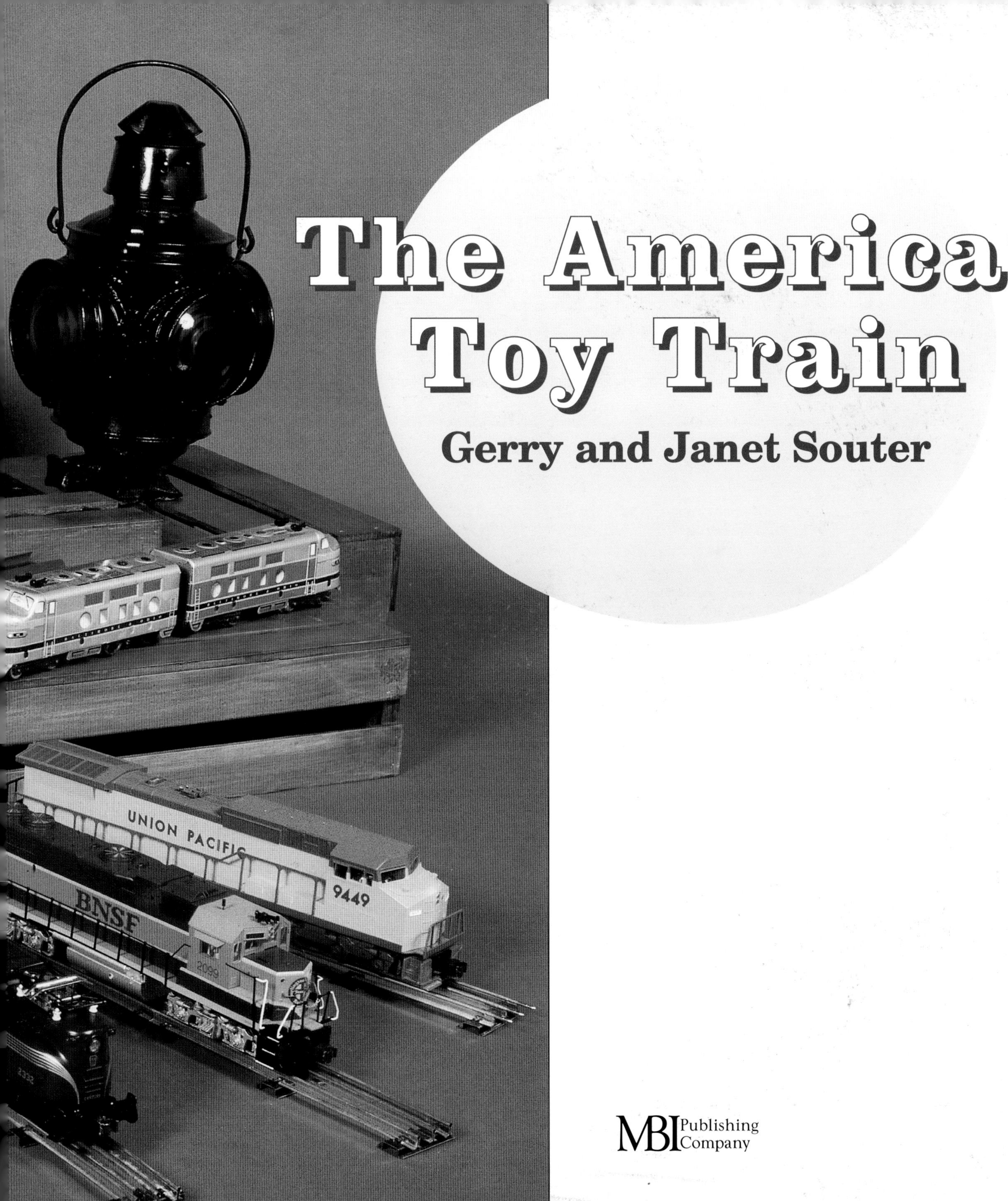

The American Toy Train

Gerry and Janet Souter

MBI Publishing Company

First published in 1999 by MBI Publishing Company, 729 Prospect Avenue, P.O. Box 1, Osceola, WI 54020 USA

Photography by Gerry Souter except as noted.
Book design and layout by Maureene D. Gulbrandsen/Andover Junction Publications, Andover, New Jersey, and Lee, Illinois.
Edited by Mike Schafer/Andover Junction Publications

Library of Congress Cataloging-in-Publication Data Available
ISBN 0-7603-0620-6

On the front cover: Comparison of size from left to right: standard-gauge 408E Lionel reproduction by MTH Rail King, O gauge Lionel F3 in Santa Fe livery, S-gauge Pennsylvania K-5 steamer by American Flyer, and an HO gauge Pacific-type locomotive from Associated Hobby Manufacturers (AHM). *Courtesy MTH-Rail King, Steve Esposito, Jeff Katzner, Gerry Souter*

On the frontispiece: The Wisconsin Standard Gauge Operating Society powers their collection of big trains around a large temporary layout at the Train Fest in Milwaukee, Wisconsin. Both original antiques and reproductions, ablaze with lights, clatter over the indoor-outdoor carpet as kids are mesmerized by the big trains of the 1920s and 30s.*Courtesy, Wisconsin Standard Gauge Operating Society*

On the title page: A group of representative American toy trains from different eras and manufacturers: upper left—a cast-iron pull-toy replica of New York Central & Hudson River Railroad engine 999 from Ideal Toys, circa late nineteenth century; top center—a modern-era reproduction by Mike's Train House (MTH)/Rail King of Lionel's great 408E standard-gauge electric; center—scale model of the New York Central Hudson by MTH/Rail King, an original model designed to run on tinplate track; left-center—a 1948 Lionel F3 diesel A-unit in Santa Fe livery, one of the best selling toy train locomotives of all time; to the right—an American Flyer S-gauge New Haven Railroad EP-5 electric locomotive and the American Flyer Circus Train locomotive; to its right—a Louis Marx electric F3 diesel in lithographed tin; bottom left—the Chicago Transit Authority 'L' train by today's Marx Trains. The three locomotives in the lower right are: the Lionel GG1 electric made for collectors by today's Lionel LLC, K-Line's GP38-2 road diesel—a benchmark for today's O gauge with detail work for moderate cost, and a Union Pacific General Electric Dash-8 diesel by Williams Electric Trains representing low-cost pulling power for today's tinplate O gauge operators. *Collections courtesy Mike McBride, MTH/Rail King, Mike Schafer, Steve Esposito, Marx Trains, Lionel LLC, Williams Electric Trains, and K-Line; lanterns courtesy of Mike McBride*

On this page: A page from a recent Lionel LLC catalog returns to yesteryear when the 1948 Lionel F3 ruled the toy train world; illustrated is the New York Central version. Today's Lionel F3s are loaded with extra features including computer chip Command Control and chatty "crew" radio voices from a sound-effects chip. *Lionel LLC*

On the back cover: Welcome to the world of Lionel and American Flyer! Modeled as a "tribute" to the New York Central's *20th Century Limited*, Lionel's model 400E was the top steam locomotive in its standard-gauge line-up. In royal blue livery, it became the *Blue Comet*, a beautiful and muscular locomotive. *Train Collectors Association Toy Train Museum, Strasburg, Pennsylvania* An American Flyer catalog cover for 1957. This was one of Flyer's best catalogs. The following year saw the start of production shortcuts in catalog presentations as well as in the Flyer line itself. *Mike Schafer collection* In 1954, the father-and-son bond across the tracks of a busy Lionel railroad was emphasized. Inside, new 6464 box cars were introduced and the Fairbanks-Morse Train Master diesel locomotive was a featured player. *Jim Flynn collection* Headed up by the streamlined 353 steam locomotive in deep red livery, this American Flyer Circus Train hauls a circus wagon flatcar and a yellow coach for the performers. Complete sets came with more cars and cut-out performers, a circus tent, and other glitzy accessories. *Mike McBride collection*

Printed in Hong Kong

Contents

Acknowledgments

The authors wish to thank the following people for their generosity in giving their time, materials, and expertise to help us write and produce this book:

Peter J. Cardascia
Hirtech Incorporated
Lancaster, Pennsylvania

Jeffrey L. Cohen
K-Line, Electric Trains
Chapel Hill, North Carolina

Joyce Dearhamer
Lionel LLC
Chesterfield, Michigan

Ed DeRouin
Pixels, Your Image Place
Elmhurst, Illinois

Andy Edleman
MTH Electric Trains
Columbia, Maryland

Brent and Garth Finch
Carlisle & Finch
Cincinnati, Ohio

Jim and Debby Flynn
Marx Trains
Addison, Illinois

Dave Garrigues
Addison, Illinois

Steve Holic
Midwest Chapter president
Train Collectors' Association

Ron Hollander
Newark, New Jersey

Jeff Katzner
Waukesha, Wisconsin

Gary Lavinus
Chairman, Education & Museum Committee
Train Collectors' Association

John Luppino
Operations Manager
Train Collectors' Association

Mike McBride
Dixon, Illinois

Tom McComas
New Buffalo, Michigan

J. P. Miller
Williams Electric Trains
Columbia, Maryland

Mike Moore
Toys and Trains
Morton Grove, Illinois

Gary Moreau
Lionel LLC
Chesterfield, Michigan

Tom Pondek
Severna Park, Maryland

Kelly Rice
Weaver Models
Northumberland, Pennsylvania

Chris Rohlfing
Addison, Illinois

Don Roth
Mount Prospect, Illinois

Stan Roy
Glenview, Illinois

Mike Schafer
Lee, Illinois

Toy Train Operating Society
Pasadena, California

Train Collectors Association
Museum volunteers
Strasburg, Pennsylvania

Bill Van Ramshorst
Lansing, Illinois

A Depression-era ad for Lionel "Multivolt" transformers shows a typical Future master of the Universe (they always wore a shirt and tie to play with Lionel trains) and his faithful dog running a standard-gauge 408E train set towing State passenger cars. The transformer is discreetly hidden inside the "control tower" next to the boy's hand. *Lionel LLC*

Introduction

My grandfather carried me on his shoulders as easily as he hefted the huge two-handed wrenches used in the roundhouse. He was 6 foot, 4 inches of railroad-tempered muscle who had worked his way from gandy-dancer, wielding a shovel at trackside, through mainline fireman to yard engineer and was nearing retirement, finishing out his time in the roundhouse machine shop. His breath almost always smelled of Red Cap Ale because his outings with me were celebrated—out of grandma's sight—with a stop for one schooner at the corner tavern. He was missing parts of three fingers—a badge of honor earned as a brakeman. Earl Nye was a railroad man to his toes. And he would teach me to love trains from the great New York Central steam locomotive towering above me in the misty gloom as it squatted over its grease pit, to the battered old caboose on the yard siding where we had just left his pals slapping down the paste-boards in a game of poker for matchsticks (so they told me).

Earl D. Nye, the author's grandfather, worked as a railroader from his teen years until his retirement in 1952. He is shown in 1910 standing in front of a "bobber" (four-wheel) caboose in the Salamanca, New York, freight yard when he worked for the Buffalo, Rochester & Pittsburgh Railroad. He was responsible for the author's early love of trains and railroading. *Gerry Souter collection*

I was seven years old when that roundhouse tour took place. It was Christmas Eve in Buffalo, New York, and I woke up the next morning in my grandparents' house with the smell of coal smoke and hot grease still in my nostrils to find myself transformed from a little kid of small accomplishments to a Captain of Industry, owner of a railroad. It was an O-27 Lionel, a steamer with a Sunoco tank car, Baby Ruth boxcar, gondola, and the obligatory red caboose. The track was an oval with hand-thrown switches at each end to allow an alternate route down the center. Next to the transformer was a real 1947 New York Central operational rules handbook.

Today, kids are pretty much out of the loop. The tinplate train hobby is largely for grown-ups who collect the old trains, operate both old and new ones on vast layouts, and count their hobby as a dollar investment as much as a pleasant pastime. There are still the railroad dreamers who share their love of trains with kids busy battling Evil Empires with Nintendo's and Sega's computer battery of weapons. Tough competition. Railroads are so retro and space aliens are so cool.

At train shows, however, the kids watch in wide-eyed silence as incredibly realistic HO gauge trains roll at prototype slow speeds around sweeping two-rail curves past painstakingly modeled scenery. But over at the tinplate displays where big Williams, K-Line, Lionel, and MTH O- and reproduction standard-gauge locomotives thunder past, air horns blasting, brakes squealing, and engines grinding with strings of freight and passenger cars whirring and clicking along behind, there is laughter, shouting, and a lot of activity. The track has three rails, the turns are too sharp, and the locomotive speeds are off the prototype speedometer by 100 miles per hour, but there is action, and they are so much fun to watch. *That's* tinplate toy-train railroading. From the simple and charming steel shapes of the Marx trains with their details lithographed onto sheet metal to a beautiful MTH Rail King Hudson gliding along on "hi-rail" track with every rivet and pipe and cross-head bolt accounted for, there is something for everyone. These big model trains are never dull.

We approached this book as a history project—to tell the story of these miniature railroads from the nineteenth century, when they were truly toy trains for kids, to its current adult hobby status. Janet, my wife and co-author, didn't know toy trains from deep center field. In the era when she and I grew up, trains were a guy thing. Girls were always admiring observers of toy trains, but they weren't supposed to touch them (according to us boys anyway). They got the toy stove, Baby-Wetty dolls, and Barbie ad nauseum while Junior got the locomotive and the character-building responsibility of mastering the high iron under the approving gaze of his all-knowing father.

Now it's the 1990s, and I urged Janet to touch the trains. She felt the considerable heft of a 1914 Carlisle & Finch Model 34 steam locomotive and the white-gloved fragility of a Mickey and Minnie Mouse Lionel handcar of 1935. She carefully fitted Ives and Dorfan cars on their tracks and lugged an armload of Lionel 763E Hudson to its place in front of the camera. You can't set up the very same American Flyer mechanical train that a kid in the 1920s wound up and sent around

its oval of two-rail track without feeling the magic where the paint is worn or the plating has been rubbed off the couplers.

While some books require a great deal of hard searching for facts, the history of the toy train is supported by almost too much research material. Every car, locomotive, section of track, accessory, and piece of relevant paper has been cataloged, photographed, and its provenance deeply detailed. Battalions of tinplate railroad hobbyists and archivists have filled shelves with well-written books laying out the arcane bits of the story, layered with descriptions and spiced with serial number variations. For collectors and investors, this material is invaluable. Our hardest job has been editing. This accumulated body of work has been both friend and fiend throughout our efforts to include a non-immersed, general audience in our story. The experts behind these books have been generous helping us make what we have chosen to write as accurate as possible. Any errors in the minutiae are ours and ours alone.

Toy trains did not exist in a vacuum at their inception, nor do they today. They reflected the evolution in children's play as well as the time in history when they were brought home and unwrapped. To understand the lure of the toy train, it's important to place it in the

Nothing draws a crowd like a working tinplate railroad. This setup is the Rampant Rusty Rail layout at the WISE (Wisconsin Southeastern) Division–National Model Railroad Association Train Fest held annually in Milwaukee. Fred Rampant runs the show as kids, dads, and granddads watch with rapt fascination while log, milk, and coal unloaders respond to remote-control commands. A 681 steam turbine tows its working cars around a complex set of O gauge sidings as son Richard (plaid shirt) mans the remote switches. *Fred Rampant collection*

context of events and social values that affected its purchase. Toy buying was—and is—a serious business. Small characters are molded by their playthings, shaped to the demands of their period in history. The toy train industry was built on the marketing premise that the lad's hand that successfully operated a toy train might one day pen national policies or manage great industries. Dads were goaded to buy a toy train in order to bond with their sons and teach them responsible values.

Toy train manufacturers followed national events closely. Unlike selling the necessities of life—food, shelter, or transportation—they were selling toys, and relatively expensive ones at that. The market economy for disposable income has always been both fragile and fickle. During the early days of toy trains, these sellers spun fantasies based on the fastest and most powerful mode of transportation—the railroad. They were tied to the railroad industry's dominance, and when it faded before better technology and other factors, they faded.

Stan Roy's famous Lionel layout has been celebrated in videos by Tom McComas as well as numerous magazine articles. Stan's basement pike can keep as many as 32 trains operating at the same time. His training in relay logic at IBM is key to his complex operational success. He also runs the road off a separate eight-amp power supply! The huge lift bridge in the center dates from 1995, while the oil derrick in the foreground was offered in 1950. *Stan Roy*

Today, the rebirth of the toy train industry is based not on the child's fantasy to one day be a locomotive engineer, but the adult's memory of those dreams and fascination with the latest hobby technology that has helped keep those dreams alive.

Our railroads today have enjoyed a growth period since President Carter signed the Staggers Act in 1980, cutting away draconian interstate commerce regulations. Many modelers are serious fans of the real thing. As computers control real railroad dispatching and locomotive functions, computer chips are now providing prototype simulations in the toy and scale models. Where once cartoon engines pulled strings of cartoon cars on tinplate tracks, today long trains of grain and coal cars are seen snaking behind near-scale double-headed road locomotives. And often, hanging on the end of the last car, is the flashing rear-end device (FRED) instead of the romantic, old-time caboose. Tinplate prototype modeling is no longer an oxymoron.

Capitalizing on childhood memories, love of nostalgia, the joy of modeling, and realistic train operation—whatever the motivation—toy train manufacturers are experiencing a vigorous growth. Price tags for the latest computer-driven technology have risen, but not without giving good value for those dollars.

Janet and I visited a Lionel railroad club to observe one of their Friday-night operating sessions. Janet was just getting into this subject and was standing off to one side trying to make sense of what was going on. Next to her elbow, lights came on in the cab of a large black Dash-8-type diesel locomotive. Its engines cranked over and settled into an idling "thrum, thrum, thrum." She stared at it. In a moment, the locomotive began to shoulder its way forward, the engine revs rising accordingly. With a hiss and squeal of brakes, it stopped just past a siding switch. The switch frog clicked and the big diesel's engine revs climbed again and its rear light came on as it backed into the siding, knuckle-coupled onto a string of coal hoppers, and came to a hissing halt. The horn gave a couple of blasts and, with electric bell chiming, this "toy train" eased its power into the coal train hanging on its drawbar and thrummed its way through the yard and out onto the main line.

She looked at me as I came up to her side next to the tracks.

"I kept waiting for the little engineer to come out and wave at me," she said.

"For the big guy with the mustache on the other side of the layout operating that locomotive's remote control," I answered, "the little guy did come out. And that load of coal is heading for a power plant in a distant city, not just circling the main line tracks ten times. That's what model railroading is all about."

She made a few notes on her pad. "Do you want me to interview the engineer?"

The big diesel rumbled past, its dynamic brakes whistling as it came down a slight grade. I looked up after it had passed.

"Which one?" I asked.

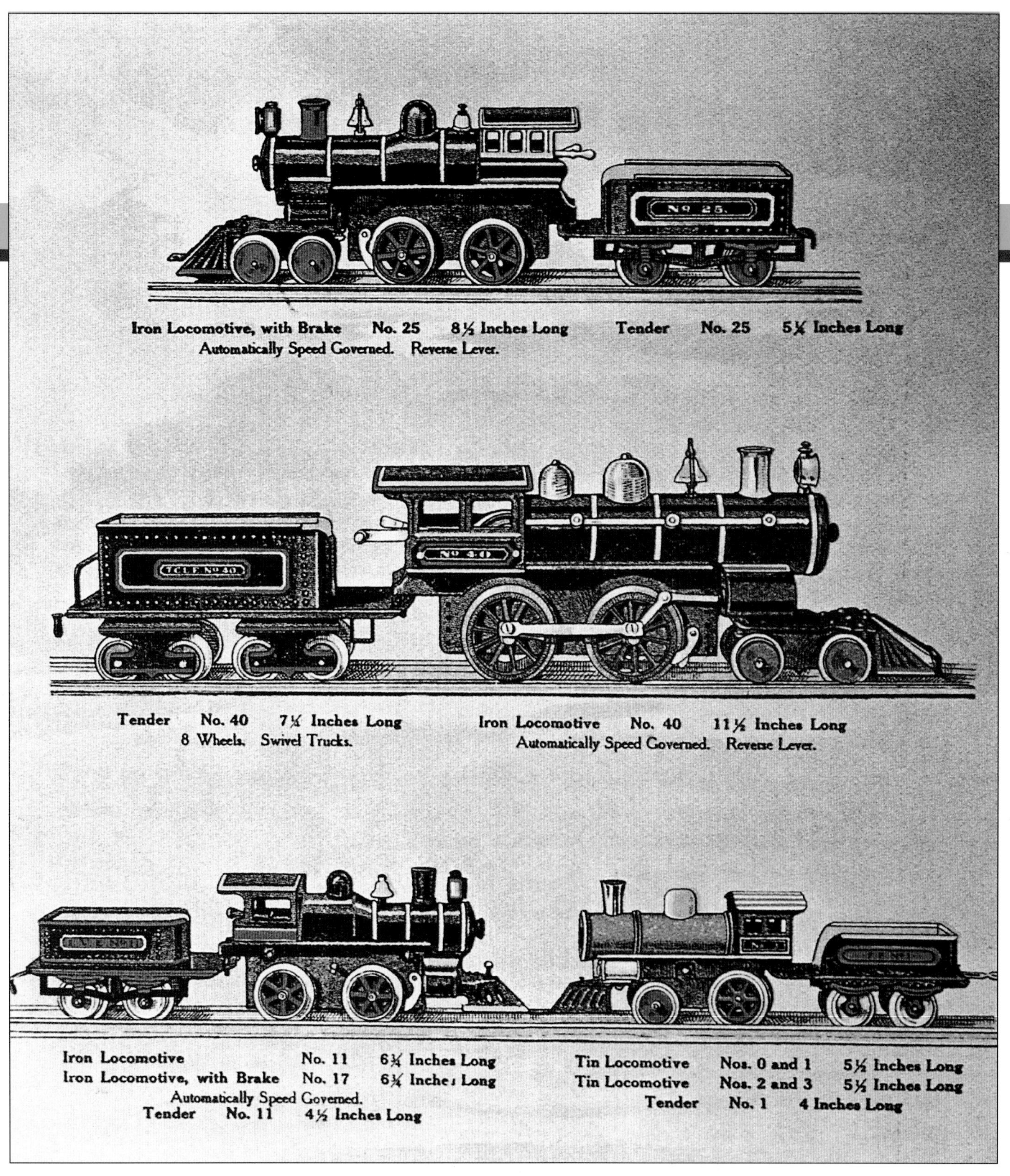

The Ives Miniature Railway System featured wind-up mechanisms in cast-iron locomotives as illustrated in the company's catalog for 1906. *Courtesy Train Collectors Association, Toy Train Museum, Strasburg, Pennsylvania*

"World's Columbian Palace Car" floor toy from 1893 made of wood with lithographed paper sides. This wonderfully detailed car, which mimics a Pullman Palace sleeping car—the ultimate in travel luxury during the late 1800s—was manufactured to coincide with the 1893 World Columbian Exposition held in Chicago. It represents an interesting marketing approach for a boy's toy in those years of strict social separation of the sexes, since its passengers are all girls. *Don Roth collection*

Chapter 1

The Pull, Ignite, and Key-wind Era

First You Had to Have a Real Train

Its name was *Puffing Billy*, and it was a plumber's nightmare. But all the right pieces were there to make it move: a horizontal boiler laid on a frame above ten wheels, with steam-driven pistons turning the gear that meshed with the other gears which turned the wheels. A tall smokestack rose from one end of the boiler where the engineer stood. The fireman stoked the furnace at the other end. It rode on cast-iron plate rails hauling coal cars for the Wylam Colliery west of Newcastle, England. The year was 1815, and it was not the first steam locomotive, but its design was so successful that, with some modifications, several more like it were built. The Wylam Railway lasted until 1862.

Imagine, however, the young children who worked in the depths of that mine breaking coal slabs into fist-size chunks, stepping from the lift at the shaft's head and seeing this thrashing, gear-grinding, steam-blowing beast for the first time. The *Puffing Billy* represented power and great natural forces under the control of the man at the throttle. It groaned and clanked up the rails until its towing chain was connected to the string of coal cars. Then, with steam blowing and blasts of smoke belching skyward in churning clouds of soot and cinders, the train rumbled away. How many of those work-stooped kids with blackened faces and hands were mesmerized by that vision of controlled steam power doing the work of a stable of horses day after day? What a marvel it was.

American youngsters would have to wait 14 years until a steam locomotive appeared on home soil. In 1829, the *Stourbridge Lion*, built by George Stephenson, became the first locomotive to pull a train in America, on the Delaware & Hudson Canal Company's railway. A year later, Peter Cooper's *Tom Thumb* appeared as the sole motive power of the Baltimore & Ohio Railroad. Baltimore, Maryland, could not participate in the canal-building boom of the 1820s because of an encircling range of hills, so to extend trade and grow, its only choice was a "rail road." In 1829, track had been laid, beginning with a ceremony that included the aged Charles Carroll of Carrollton, Maryland, the last surviving member of those who signed the Declaration of Independence. He

RIGHT: One of America's first successful steam locomotives was Peter Cooper's *Tom Thumb,* a replica of which is shown barnstorming along the Baltimore & Ohio Railroad in 1980. It had a vertical boiler that produced a modest amount of power and was hardly a speed demon by present standards, but in 1829 it was the hottest technology around. In its most famous race, this one-horsepower scorcher lost to . . . one horse. *Jim Boyd*

BELOW: One of the most significant of primordial steam locomotives was the *John Bull* of 1831, considered the first locomotive to feature the right elements in the right proportions and in the traditional arrangement: horizontal boiler, cab behind the firebox, smokestack at the forward end, a "cowcatcher," and—supporting the cowcatcher—pilot wheels. This *John Bull* replica was built by the Pennsylvania Railroad in 1924 (the real one still exists, too) and is shown touring the Strasburg Rail Road in southeastern Pennsylvania in 1983. *Jim Boyd*

gave a short speech and said the act of laying the first foundation stone was as important to him as his signing of the Declaration.

The *Tom Thumb* was a little locomotive, weighing about a ton and developing one horsepower from a single cylinder. In 1830 it hauled a trainload of B&O directors over the first 13 miles of line. It was a sensation, even though later it lost a race to a horse and wagon because its belt-driven blower fan broke down.

Caring parents kept kids well away from the new rash of locomotives that began to appear. Steam was not to be trusted because of frequent boiler explosions, causing great carnage. Also, people had been run down or trampled by stampeding horses terrified by the cast-iron monsters. However, the great pioneer locomotives eventually proved the capability and safety of steam power: the *De Witt Clinton*, George Stephenson's *Rocket,* and, in particular, the *John Bull*—the first locomotive with the proper elements arranged in the right proportions that would set the standard for nearly all future steam locomotives: horizontal boiler, covered cab behind the firebox, crude pilot wheels, and a "cow catcher." Some designs were less than successful such as the *South Carolina* of 1831 that ran on track being laid between Charleston and Hamburg. It was two single-cylinder locomotives bolted together facing in opposite directions to avoid having to turn around at end of track—a sort of a mechanical "Push-Me-Pull-You" from Dr. Doolittle. Its inventor, Horatio Allen, prophesied,

> "In the future, there is no reason to expect any material improvement in the breed of horses, while, in my judgment, the man is not living who knows what the breed of locomotive is to command."

If his design was silly, his prophesy was right, and rails began to snake across the western wilderness, bringing the whistle whoop and clouds of smoke to dirt-street settlements and brick cities alike. The power and speed—10 to 15 miles per hour—amazed onlookers. More and more adventurous souls climbed aboard the open carriages or trusted their wheat crops to the wood gondolas. Empires were being built, and by the mid 1800s railroads were the darlings of the stock market—investments as legitimate as shipping or steel-making. Their ribbons of rails represented movement and, to many, escape to faraway places. In rural America, people lived and died within 20 miles of where they were born. Now, distant horizons beckoned. The real possibility of speedy travel encouraged fantasies. For the young, that fantasy was now embodied in the tireless, mysterious steam locomotives. Kids couldn't own a real locomotive, but they could own a toy.

In middle-class mid-nineteenth century homes, playthings were thoughtfully chosen. Children were considered a notch above live-in laborers and caretakers on the family farm or city sweatshop contributors to the family purse. But families were growing smaller. As the economy developed and educational requirements increased, large families became too expensive. Between 1800 and 1851, a white American mother's average childbirth count dropped from seven kids to five and a half. That drop meant fewer siblings, less competition within the household, and more time alone for playing with toys.

Life on the streets and public places during this settlement period could be rough and rowdy, so the raising of middle-class children turned inward to the home where family values could be taught in nurseries and playrooms. To organize the learning process, appropriate age-specific activities, books, and toys were chosen. Kids did not get a dozen presents for Christmas. They got one gift. That toy had to possess at least two attributes: durability and character-building significance. Child rearing was firmly channeled into paths that were essential for their success as adults, so toy manufacturers stressed the learning and family bonding factors inherent in each product. Boys were "little men" and girls were "little women." For the most part, girls got dolls complete with little tea sets that taught manners and gentility of style and etiquette. Boys got rocking horses, miniature weapons, boats . . . and trains.

Draggers and Dribblers

The earliest toy trains arrived in two forms: draggers, designed to be pulled with a string across the floor, and "dribblers," actual self-propelled steam-powered locomotives. Draggers were caricatures of the real thing. Mostly, they were made of wood or tin and had exaggerated, storybook features. Tin trains often had little wheels, huge smokestacks, tiny crew cabs, and were painted in bright primary colors. Wooden models appeared as carved locomotive and passenger- or freight-car shapes with colorful details lithographed on paper that was glued to the sides. The live steamers—dribblers—were toys only in

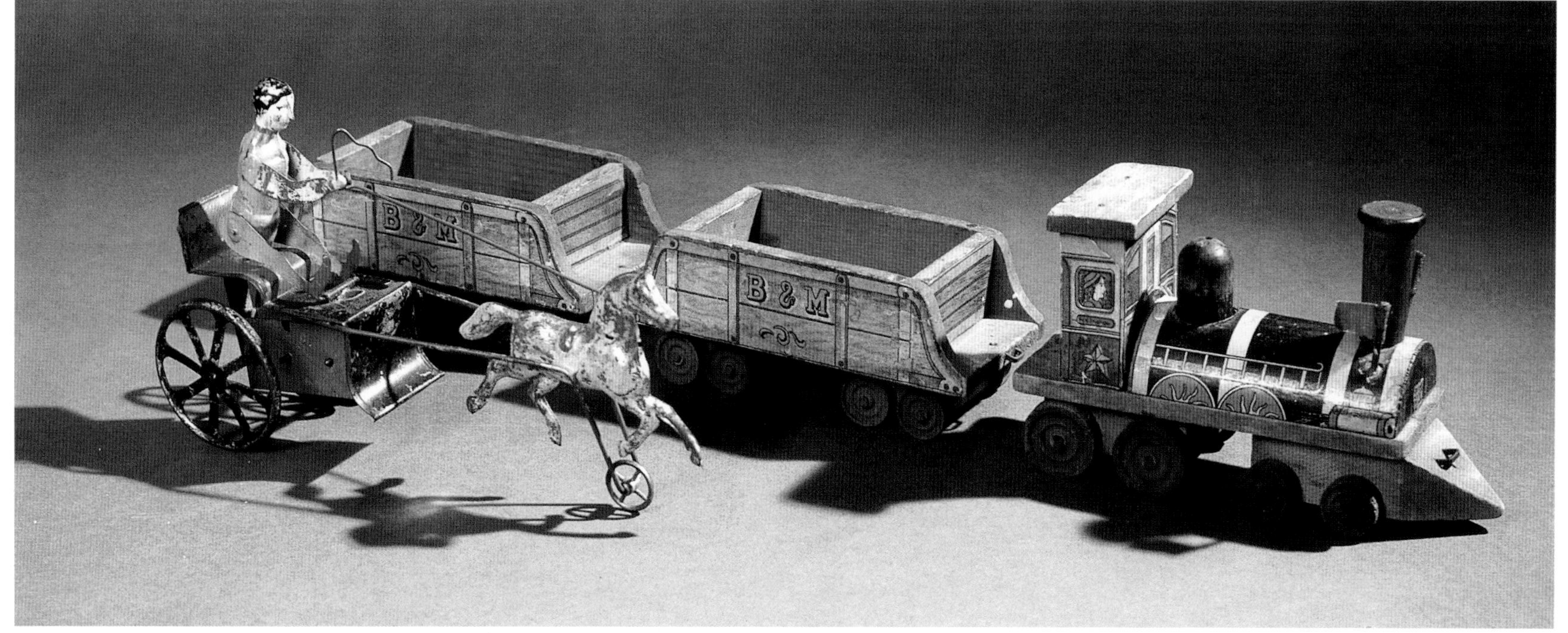

Wooden steam train floor dragger from either Bradley or Bliss races a hand-painted tin horse and buggy. Both are nineteenth century toys that were very popular since they represented "speed" to boys of that time. *Don Roth collection*

the sense that they were marketed to parents as "learning toys" for young railroad engineers. They were, essentially, very realistic, well-made fire hazards on wheels.

From the 1830s to the 1840s the demand for toys had grown to a point whereby almost every town had some kind of store that sold playthings. Most of the better toys came from Europe where toy-making had a long head start. One of the pioneers who jump-started American toy-making in the 1830s was Charles M. Crandall of New York. He was in tune with the learning aspects of child rearing and became famous for recognizing how tongue-and-groove construction used in carpentry could be applied to wooden building blocks embossed with the ABCs or numbers that made learning fun for the insulated kids from affluent and middle-class homes. His line of wooden toys also included trains, boats, and other string draggers that rumbled across the playroom or parlor floor. The best known of his pine railroad novelties was a locomotive that whistled as the young engineer snaked it across the Brussels carpet through the treacherous mountain pass between the ottoman and Father's wingback chair. Eventually, there were no less than seven Crandalls working at toy design. Cousin Jesse invented the combination go-cart, sleigh, swing, hammock, baby jumper, step ladder, and rocking chair. This kind of innovation kept the firm in business until 1929.

By the 1850s there were at least 50 toy manufacturers in the United States. Though the tinplate process was available to Europeans, American toy-makers were first to exploit the mass-production capabilities of this new medium. "Tin" actually refers to sheet iron or steel plated with tin. The toys were stamped out of sheets

An assortment of wood and tin pull-toy trains. The top train comes from Charles M. Crandall, and the car reads: "This is the car in which good little boys and girls may ride." It was manufactured in the late nineteenth century. The center cars are from the "Chicago Limited Vestibule" train from the 1860s, manufacturer unknown. Off to the right is a tin toy carrying the impressive name *Hero,* typical of the fanciful approach to locomotives in the mid-1870s. At the bottom is an 1880 tin locomotive and cars from Fallow. *Train Collectors Association Toy Train Museum, Strasburg, Pennsylvania*

Live steamers that ran with or without track were offered shortly after the real locomotives began running. These toys required patience and care in following directions to get them running without torching the carpet or "spoiling" the locomotive when the boiler ran dry. At top is the brass Weeden Dart from 1887. Center is a steamer made by Beggs in 1903 with a cardboard body and tin boiler. The bottom locomotive is an early Stevens from 1840. Very few were made because they didn't cool down fast enough. *Train Collectors Association Toy Train Museum, Strasburg, Pennsylvania*

with a die. The blanks were then folded and shaped into their final form and either tabbed or soldered together at the joints. A base coat of paint was applied, and details were added by free-hand artists. As mass production really caught its stride, stencils were used on the assembly line for finer details.

The earliest known American-made tin toy—a fire engine pulled by a brace of white horses—was made by the Philadelphia Tin Toy Manufactory and dates from 1840. Most "action toys" of this period were string-pulled floor draggers and involved horses. Twenty years after that little pull-toy charmed children, the Civil War introduced to the populace mass transport of troops and goods by railroad, and the "tin men" began punching out tin trains to meet the new demand.

These early tin pull-toys were simple, featuring only the main parts that identified a steam locomotive: boiler, smokestack, steam dome, wheels, and crew cab. The fact that many resembled designs dating back to the 1840s didn't faze the youngsters. Painted in gold letters on their colorful boilers were names that stirred the blood: *Hero*, *Union*, *General Grant*, *Vigilant*, *Hercules*, *Rocket,* and *Lightning*.

Since the Civil War was the first American war to be covered by toy-makers, toy weapons were soon rolling off the punch presses and wood lathes. Little kids in Northern cities and Southern farms could stage their own slaughters racing from the parlor to the back porch with their string-pulled troop trains to arrive in time for the big battle against Johnny Reb or Billy Yank. By the time the golden spike was driven home near Promontory, Utah, in 1869, joining the Central Pacific and Union Pacific railroads to create America's first transcontinental railroad, string-hauled toy trains of wood and tin were being cranked out by the thousands.

The dribblers were something completely different. The term "dribbler" came from Britain where live-steam toy trains had been built since old *Puffing Billy* hauled its first string of coal cars. These miniature puffers were called dribblers because that's what they did. The boiler and firebox seams were neither robust nor properly sealed, allowing both water and alcohol to dribble onto the floor during operations. A live-steam toy train consisted of a boiler that held water, a kerosene or alcohol lamp that heated the water, and a steam chest that stored the pressurized power source. It was a real locomotive placed in the hands of a 10-year-old. They were very popular.

Not to be outdone, two American firms produced live steamers that could dribble with the best of them. Locomotives built by Eugene Beggs of Patterson, New Jersey, and the Weeden Manufacturing Company of New Bedford, Massachusetts, are good examples.

Eugene Beggs wanted to build real, full-scale locomotives, but when his father's shop, the firm of Paul & Beggs, burned down in 1835, taking with it their prototype engine, the senior Beggs sold out what remained and settled for making locomotive parts and supplies. His son would go on to make more locomotives than all the other firms in Patterson combined. Eugene went on to work as a foreman on the Marietta & Cincinnati Railroad in Ohio and then toiled in the locomotive factory of Danforth & Cooke. When he finally decided to patent his own toy steamer, he faced a market owned by the Europeans. These models were tinplate and were cranked out by the thousands for shipment to America. During the period from 1860 to the 1880s, these cheap and crude trains represented ancient prototypes long gone on the Continent and were distinctly European in design.

No live steam locomotives were being manufactured in America when, in September 1871, Eugene filed a patent for "An Improvement in Toy Locomotives." Together with his associate Jehu Garlick, Beggs began producing steamers that were of better quality than the European imports and, naturally, cost more to buy. But these locomotives looked like American motive power. Their workmanship was impeccable, and dribbles were kept to a minimum. The cylinders acted as the safety valves and were held hard against the frame by springs. When steam pressure exceeded safe margins, it forced the cylinders away from the frame to release the excess steam and avoid bursting the boiler seams.

Eugene's locomotives were long on quality, but some had curious design features. These locomotives were built with their wheels fixed in a turning radius, which meant the trains could only be operated on Beggs track, running in a predetermined circle. The track consisted of metal strips pressed into slots that ran the length of pre-cut sections of wood that dictated the correct radius. The upside of the design—from a parent's point of view—was if the locomotive was run without track, it would still circle and remain in a safe, confined, collision-free area. The play value of these early trains seemed limited to achieving

The famous and popular Weeden Dart set. This small live-steam engine was fueled using the little tin cup beneath the cab to pour alcohol into the heater that boiled the water to make steam. The Dart is made of brass and tin and ran on special coil steel strip track laid on wood roadbed. Passenger cars and a coal tender were also offered. *Courtesy Train Collectors Association Toy Train Museum, Strasburg, Pennsylvania*

movement through manipulation of fire and water, then watching it puff around in a little circle. Beggs continued making live-steam models of a variety of locomotive prototypes long after electric trains had come on the market in the early years of the twentieth century. Their prices averaged $10, a considerable sum for a turn-of-the-century bread-winner to pay for a toy.

Other American manufacturers emerged such as Stevens, which produced a really hot dribbler in 1872 that had been patented by a Stevens employee, R. Frisbie, in 1871. Very few were made due to their slowness in cooling down after a hard day on the rug or rails. J. A. Pierce of Chicago offered steam locomotives along with ". . . Steamboats, Steam Engines, Mechanical Toys and Working Models."

Today, we shudder at the imagined nightmare scenario of watching Little Tommy being blasted through the living room window wrapped in a sheet of flame, smoke, and shards of tin as his toy train detonates. It wasn't considered a big deal back in the nineteenth century when learning the mechanics of live steam operation took precedent over niggling safety considerations. Besides, according to contemporary accounts, the worse that could happen was ". . . a small alcohol blaze," or a meltdown of the locomotive into little balls of solder on the rug when the boiler went dry. It was character-building for Young Tom to accept the responsibility for not torching the homestead with his toy train.

The Weeden Manufacturing Company produced what has become one of America's most famous live steamers, the Weeden Dart of 1888. William Weeden was an inventor and a good mechanic whose first invention, a little cone-shaped pencil sharpener, saved him and his cousin from starvation in a Boston attic. He went on to invent the rolled thread screw for metal workers and graduated to stationary steam engines that were still being manufactured by his company 50 years later. Following a huge success with a glow-in-the-dark match safe for home owners who could now locate their matches in a darkened room, he turned to toy trains.

558 THE YOUTH'S COMPANION. No Premiums forwarded unless Postage is sent.

Horizontal Steam Engine, with Solid Brass Boiler.

Weeden's Horizontal Engine is a miniature type of the engine commonly found in manufacturing establishments throughout the country. Has all the parts for generating steam and converting its power into work. Has boiler and casing, steam dome, whistle, safety valve, cylinder, steam chest, slide valve, eccentric, eccentric rod, piston, cross head, pitman, driving shaft and fly wheel, and a solid brass boiler. The base and boiler casing are of strong Russia iron. It is both a fascinating toy and an instructive piece of scientific apparatus. Size of Engine 3½ x 4½ x 5¼ inches

The Engine given only to Companion subscribers for one new subscriber and 25 cents additional, with 30 cents for postage and packing. Engine sold for $1.25, postage and packing 30 cents extra.

Electric Motor and Battery, Complete.

This Motor is run by an electric current generated in its base. It develops a high rate of speed, and can be used for running light toy machinery. We give with the Motor sufficient chemicals for running it a number of times. The 4-inch Aluminum Fan is not given with the Electric Motor, but will be sent for **25 cents extra.** Notice "Village Blacksmith" offer below. Why not order it?

Given only to Companion subscribers for one new subscriber and 15 cents additional, with 40 cents for postage and packing. Motor and Battery sold for $1.00, postage and packing 40 cents extra.

The Leclanche Electric Bell Outfit.

All modern houses are supplied with electric door bells and call bells. They are easily put up, and not expensive in use.

The Outfit consists of a large Leclanché Battery, with Chemicals, a nickel-plated Electric Bell, mounted on a maple base and having a maple cover; a Push Button with porcelain knob; 50 feet insulated Copper Wire, Clamp Tacks, and full Directions for putting up.

Given, complete, only to Companion subscribers for two new subscribers; or for one new subscriber and 50 cents additional. See Conditions, page 522. Sold for $1.50. Sent by express, charges paid by receiver. Shipping weight of the Outfit 10 lbs.

Model Motor.

This Motor is 2½ inches high, has a 3-pole armature with no dead centres, adjustable brushes, small pulley for running toys. We furnish all the parts for putting the motor together, including the castings, wire and explicit directions for winding.

Materials only given to Companion subscribers for one new subscriber and 15 cents for postage. Sold for $1.00, postage and packing 15 cents extra. The Motor wound, and ready to run, for one new subscriber and 25 cents additional, with 15 cents for postage. Price, $1.50, postage and packing 15 cents extra. Carbon, zinc and package of salts for battery, by mail for 25 cents

Locomotive, with Tender, Car, Track and Station.

Description.

This is a perfect steam Locomotive. The Train, 22 inches in length, is made entirely of metal and very handsome in appearance. The Engine alone is 7½ inches long, and uses alcohol for fuel. The Car has swivelled trucks. The Track, when put together, forms a 12-foot circular railroad. The Station, Trackmen, etc., are lithographed in colors on paper for pasting on wood.

This Locomotive, together with a Tender, Car, Track and Station, given only to Companion subscribers for four new subscribers; or for one new subscriber and $1.50 additional. See Conditions, page 522. Sold for $2.75. Sent by express, charges paid by receiver. Shipping weight 5 lbs.

"Village Blacksmith."

This toy is designed to be set in motion by an electric motor or steam engine. This is easily done by simply connecting the two with a belt or cord. When in motion the "Village Blacksmith" hammers away at his anvil, while a boy at his side operates the bellows, as natural as life. We will include the "Village Blacksmith" with a motor or steam engine for **50 cents extra**, post-paid.

Price-List of Steam Toys. We can supply an Illustrated Price-List of Steam Toys which range in price from $1.00 to $10.00. These Toys are made by the well-known Weeden Manufacturing Co. This Price-List will be sent to any address on receipt of a two-cent stamp.

William Weeden's company produced a number of steam- and electrical-powered products aside from his famous 1888 Weeden Dart live steam train as shown in this ad appearing in The *Youth's Companion* Magazine. *Train Collectors Association Toy Train Museum,, Strasburg, Pennsylvania*

A 4-4-0 American-type steam locomotive with a diamond stack and kerosene lamp. This was the most common type of locomotive used in the nineteenth century. Its distinctive shape was reproduced in both tin and cast iron for floor trains. This short Civil War-era train appeared at the Chicago Railroad Fair in 1948–50 to represent President Abraham Lincoln's funeral train of 1865. *Chicago Museum of Science and Industry*

Like Beggs' models, Weeden's beautifully proportioned little locomotive and passenger car ran on track and was very well made. Weeden affixed a small stationary boiler to a frame and added four flanged drive wheels, side rods, and cylinders. A circle of track made of rolled-top metal strips pressed into wooden ties and the locomotive without coal tender or a car sold for $2.50. It was an instant success, selling over 1,100 units in three weeks after going on display at the A. G. Spaulding store in New York City.

Louis Hertz, in his evocative 1944 volume, *Riding the Tinplate Rails*, notes a stirring quote from a Weeden announcement of the little Dart in an 1888 issue of *Youth's Companion*.

The King of Toys

> Three years ago we began a series of experiments and investigations. A steam locomotive was what we were after. We first imported models of the English, or the French and of the German Toy Steam Locomotive, all of which were very costly and very clumsy-looking, about as much like our new locomotive as a dump cart resembles a fine coach.
>
> As the foreign locomotives were of no use to us, and the only American locomotives then made cost from $6 to $10 each, we decided to have a locomotive designed for us, and made after our superb American models. By means of special tools and large orders, we hoped to be able to offer our subscribers this king of toys at a low price.

A Railroad President

> America is the home of the great railroad kings and managers. Now, every boy who obtains one of these locomotives can, no doubt, work up from Engineer to President of his own road, providing, of course, that he owns the controlling interest.

This "young lad becoming president of his own railroad" was the first of the toy train ads stressing this imaginary rise to power. After all, the late 1800s was the "Rail Baron" era of American railroading, and the Cornelius Vanderbilts and Jay Goulds were busy gouging one another in the race to create rail empires that would rule into late twentieth century. Other companies would pick up on this theme in their catalogs—as would parents who were directing their offspring's future into a turn-of-the-century world that seemed boundless with opportunity.

If one wished to expand his Dart empire, a tin passenger car with cast wheels and labeled *City of Bedford* could be had along with a coal tender and "special track" built along the lines of Beggs' strips of slotted wood. Unlike Beggs, this track had straight sections so Young Tom, Railroad President, could pilot his steam-puffing Dart from the playroom, down the hall, and to the distant wilds of the dining room.

Weeden was a tireless promoter of the Dart and tried to make sure the play experience was a good one. As stated in its direction sheet,

> We have studied to closely imitate a large "Loco." and have everything strong, light and well-arranged, so that our "Young Engineer" may readily generate steam of the required pressure to take his Engine smoothly around the Track with the Tender and Car attached . . . when carefully set up, properly used, and well taken care of, will prove to be an unfailing source of instruction and amusement, to old and young alike.

Then follows a rigorous set of explicit instructions spelling out that any deviation will result in a "spoiled" locomotive. One can imagine father reading the two pages of directions in a stentorious voice as Tommy measures his alcohol level, is certain the boiler is only two thirds full, applies a match to the alcohol-sodden wick, and watches expectantly as this little pressure cooker works up steam for its first run. Finally, it begins to percolate and the directions bid him to give it a push.

No movement? The directions anticipated this temporary puzzlement . . .

> Wait a few seconds for steam pressure to increase, then give it a gentle push again. Don't wait too long as the pressure increases *rapidly*.

The italics are Weeden's. Fun in the playroom could get a little edgy in these early toy train days.

European manufacturers hurriedly cobbled together "American" versions of their live steamers by removing their coupling buffers from the front end and substituting a "cow-catcher." They also added a steam dome and covered cab plus some passenger cars labeled with American railroad names. The steamer from Georges Carette & Co. of Nuremberg, Germany, was well made, running on track that closely approximated what would later be the American "O" gauge, or 1$^1/_4$ inches between the rails. Its small size made it a popular little performer. But live-steam tinplate trains would always be the playthings of the prosperous. Co-existing with steam was a sturdy pull-toy for the masses that was made possible by another technology break-through: cast iron.

True cast iron was very difficult to drill or file because of its hardness, but heat-treated, smelted iron was more malleable and elastic. This process adopted the name "cast iron" and was the plastic of its day, adaptable to a variety of shapes and thickness. The molds were created by first building the locomotive, tender, and cars to be replicated in brass or wood. Then a cast was made of the models from very fine sand or silicon combined with a binder, one mold for each side of the finished piece. Made from remelted pig iron ingots and containing two to six percent carbon, cast iron was poured from a crucible into the molds. The gray iron cooled and shrunk, allowing the halves to be extricated and joined together by heat brazing.

When applied to toy pull-trains, cast iron made the toys virtually impervious to youthful frolic and diabolical imaginations. The castings were pierced with axles for the locomotive drive and pilot wheels, also of cast iron. Black or primary color paint was applied with gold free-hand trim on the fancier models. Maybe a bell was hung in a little spring frame atop the boiler, and out the factory door it went .

Hubley, Ideal, Harris Toy Company, Grey Iron, Dent, and Ives—the number of manufacturers grew steadily after the first patents for cast-iron toy trains were issued in 1880.

The "American Standard" 4-4-0 wheel configuration locomotive was the favorite prototype. Four pilot wheels followed by four tall drivers beneath a slim boiler made for a graceful design. Strings of iron passenger cars clanked after the locomotive, coupled together with wire clips or cast hooks. There was a size and style for any kid or purse. On some there were working drive rods that added action to the ride across the hallway throw-rug. Bells dinged and the cast wheels made a suitable rumble on wood floors. Of course, the smaller the castings, the fewer details emerged as the 4-4-0 became a 2-2-0, and finely spoked wheels became solid buttons like those on the Ives *Hero* cast in 1889 and sold by Montgomery Ward for $4 a dozen. They were impervious to rough play and proved to be a good bargain.

To keep the going price competitive and stifle foreign competition at the same time, good old American protectionism called together 37 manufacturers into the National Novelty Corporation in 1903. By interchanging parts and patterns for cast and wood toys, costs among the anointed could be controlled and unwanted competition shut out. The group came to be called the Toy

Carette live steamers like this small locomotive towing two passenger vans were made in Germany for American export. Unlike many foreign imports, this little dribbler was very well made and was only slightly dangerous. *Don Roth collection*

RIGHT: Scooping water from a "track pan" to replenish her tender's supply, famous New York Central & Hudson River Railroad No. 999 wheels along with a four-car passenger train—possibly the *Empire State Express* between New York City and Buffalo—around the turn of the century. On May 10, 1893, this 4-4-0 "American"-type locomotive broke the speed record by purportedly being the first to achieve 112 miles per hour. Models of the then-modern 999 thus became the most prolific of all cast-iron pull-toy trains. *New York Central, Jim Boyd collection*

BELOW: A cast-iron floor dragger model of famous NYC&HRR 999. This one is believed to be by Ideal Toys, circa early 1900s. *Courtesy, Mike McBride collection*

Trust. The Trust only lasted four years; its demise and eventual bankruptcy caused a shake-up and merging of many manufacturers. Under the Trust, individual creativity was replaced by volume production of the shared patterns. Collectors of these trains note that the best cast-iron pull trains were made before 1903.

The way toy trains were sold was also affected. Although the manufacturer's name appeared on the catalog used by jobbers and dealers, it did not appear on the locomotive or cars. A few iron foundries poured the castings for most of the manufacturers who then painted and assembled the final product. According to Rick Ralston in his exhaustive book, *Cast Iron Floor Trains. . .*

> . . . Castings from the period [of the Toy Trust], are nearly identical from one toy company to the next. But, fortunately for collectors, most bear small traces of individuality, much like twins with different fingerprints. A number added to the side of a locomotive. A style variation in a wheel. The way the peen was hammered on the end of an axle. From its infancy, the history of the American toy train has been a marketing story as well as a look at the advance of technology. Often, a shrewd marketing plan has triumphed over superior technology.

Cast-iron floor draggers continued to be made through the 1940s, modeled after the latest real-life prototypes. From old No. 999, the New York Central 4-4-0 that broke the 100 mile per hour speed record at the turn of the century while hauling the *Empire State Express*, to 4-4-2 Atlantic-type and 4-6-2 "Pacific" steamers, the high-stepping passenger locomotives of the 1920s and 1930s, a kid could have a railroad wherever he wanted it; inside, outside, no plugs in the wall, no track, no "adult supervision."

A vast number of cast-iron floor draggers exist in collections today. As recent as the 1990s, molds have been made from the original toys and were being sold as "antique" toys by artisans such as John Wright of Wrightsville, Pennsylvania. While these "second generation" cast pieces may not have the sharp edges or subtle details of the originals, they are charming in their own right and bring back the days when imagination was the motive power and a blown computer chip couldn't bring the play to an end.

A Key to Power: Wind-up Trains

Horologically speaking, clockwork-powered toys date their source back to Peter Heinlein in the year 1500. He was a German clock-maker and was the first to use a spring-driven mechanism that could be wound with a key. His small clocks only had an hour hand, but they were portable. The minute hand was added 170 years later and it was 362 years following his benchmark design that the first patent for a clockwork toy was issued in the United States.

In 1862, Enoch Rich Morrison created the "Autoperipatetikos." This was his catchy name for a "Walking Doll." Turn the key in her back and your very own Autoperipatetikos would traipse across the floor on her tiny tin feet.

Wonderfully intricate and expensive clockwork toys had been available for the European aristocracy for a hundred years, but tin toys for American kids had to wait for the explosion of toy-making following the Civil War. Even then, industrialists using the latest mass-production methods still charged from $1 to $3 for some of these self-propelled wonders, the equivalent of several days wages for working-class adults.

The earliest clockwork trains were floor toys marketed to middle-class parents as miniature systems used by adults for acquainting their male offspring with this mode of transportation. Kids were repositories for adult traditions and what an adult considered fun. If the knee-high recipient of this wind-up toy managed a covert a fantasy or two, these lapses from preparation for adulthood were tolerated with prejudice.

As with the tin pull-toys, clockwork-powered trains were colorful, fanciful, and bore scant relation to the diamond-stack, wood-burning locomotives racing at a blistering 30 miles per hour on tall drive wheels with a mustachioed engineer at the throttle. These steam engines appeared from some distant location where the rails ended, traveled through town as curious faces peered from the windows of ornate wooden coaches, then hurried on to disappear again, leaving only a smudge of smoke drifting on the wind. Young imaginations must have secretly run wild as they watched their tin train chatter unaided across the length of the porch and disappear over the edge of the stairs.

Like the steam-powered toys, some tin locomotives were fixed so the train traveled in a circle on the floor. Eventually, two-rail tracks were created

Ives *Hero* cast-iron floor train. Traces of the original paint are visible. Cast iron had great durability ensuring many of these little draggers would endure to become collectibles. *Don Roth collection*

ABOVE: The Kenton 600 is a rare cast-iron floor train because it modeled an unusual locomotive type—the "Camelback"—favored by some Eastern railroads, such as Lehigh Valley Railroad No. 798 illustrated in the top photo. Camelback locomotives had cabs that straddled the boiler to allow for a huge firebox that burned anthracite (hard) coal. *Kenton model courtesy Train Collectors Association Toy Train Museum, Strasburg, Pennsylvania; LV photo, Andover Junction Publications Archives*

and flanged wheels were pinned to the axles, guiding the wind-up through a controlled environment.

It was Riley Ives and his son, Edward, who turned their metal-stamping shop to toy-making in 1868 that brought the spring-powered train up to a new level of sophistication. Having moved their operation to Bridgeport, Connecticut, in 1870, their fertile imaginings for wind-up tin train designs began. By the 1880s they had come up with a "smoking" locomotive. This little tin steamer had room in its stack for a lit cigarette. A piston connected to a moving drive wheel forced air through a tube and caused puffs of smoke to billow from the stack in synchronization with the speed of the drivers. A "whistling" locomotive joined the smoker, and for the more sanguine youth, Ives provided the ultimate thrill for $3. The "Rocket," patented by William D. Hardin and Joseph P. White in 1886 and marketed by Ives, clattered along the floor until the wind-up mechanism caused a paper cap to explode with a bang. The cab roof, boiler, and stack flew off, simulating a boiler explosion. Replace the pieces, slip in a new cap and the young tad could turn his locomotive to scrap once again. And you thought violence in the playtime arena was something new.

Ives created the first cast-iron pull-toy train in the 1880s and followed that with its "Mechanical Iron Locomotive" which appeared in the 1892 Ives, Blakeslee & Williams catalog. Cast-iron trains were almost exclusively floor draggers. The weight of the locomotive and the additional weight of its towed cars put a strain on the early brass spring-wound mechanisms. The Ives mechanisms were particularly durable and long-lasting. Some springs allowed a half hour of continuous running on one wind-up.

A distinction must be made here between true "clockwork" and spring "wind-up" trains. Clockwork mechanisms employing heavy springs,

RIGHT: A shiny green locomotive from Johann Andreas Issmeyer tows its tender and a blue tin coach. This 1885 wind-up train is typical of the virtually hand-built tinwork from Nuremburg that flowed into the U.S. before the turn of the century. Considering the robust steamers that were plying America's rails at the time, this little putt-putt is very old fashioned, but sold well. *Don Roth collection*

heavy-duty brass gears, and precision internal parts were the products of clockmakers who turned their talents to toys. Their most productive period occurred between 1860 and 1880. After that era, cheaper spring-wound wind-up devices began to replace the more precise clockwork mechanisms. Low-cost mechanical trains used the wind-up system, sometimes employing a brake to hold the spring tension until released by a lever. Although these wind-ups achieved long running times and great durability, the term "clockwork" does not apply.

As the turn-of-the-century approached, all the modes of toy train power co-existed. Wood, tin, and cast-iron floor trains thumped and clattered behind their string tethers. Keys churned in the sides of tin choo-choos, independently ticking away with their cars in tow down the long hall runner or circling obediently on crude loops of track. In the playrooms of the affluent, Beggs and Weeden live steamers percolated and hissed their way forward on tracks made of thin strip steel pressed into wood roadbed.

Gaining on these methods of motive power was the invisible force that leaked from the ends of wires and caused copper-wound armatures to spin between two magnets. Clear glass bulbs burned magically and brighter than gas. This new "electricity" came into the house from poles on the street, or could be made right on the kitchen table with some metal plates and chemicals. Inventors and toy-makers were quick to seize its potential.

ABOVE: The large and the small of wind-up locomotives. At top is a large key-winder built for Montgomery Ward to sell through its catalogs. The lower engine is the first wind-up locomotive built by Ives in the 1890s. *Train Collectors Association Toy Train Museum, Strasburg, Pennsylvania*

LEFT: A shiny tin Ives wind-up from 1905-1907 pulls two little cartoon-like passenger cars from 1903. *Don Roth collection*

Lionel "Multivolt" Transformers—For 110 and 220 Volts—60, 40 and 25 Cycles

Power Houses for Transformers

THIS illustration shows transformer contained within the new Lionel Power Station, made in two sizes to accommodate every type of Lionel "Multivolt" Transformer. Full description of this desirable new accessory will be found on Page 39.

The Lionel Power Station is placed over the Transformer, and you can manipulate the controlling switch by simply raising the grating on the roof.

LIONEL "Multivolt" Transformers have been on the market for a great many years and operate all makes of Electric Trains. We justly claim they are best. Don't experiment with other makes of doubtful value. Remember, that all transformers look alike outside, but their imperfections will only be discovered after they are in actual use for a length of time. Lionel "Multivolt" Transformers will last indefinitely and are guaranteed unconditionally as long as they are used on the current for which they are intended. They are absolutely safe and will give steady, even power.

For Greatest Efficiency Always Use a Lionel "Multivolt" Transformer with a Lionel Train

Lionel "Multivolt" Transformers Are For Use Only on Alternating Current. Do Not Use Them on Direct Current.

Type "A" Transformer will operate any "O" gauge outfit.

For 110 volts, 60 cycles. 40 watts capacity.

Gives 15 volts in following steps: 4, 7, 10, 13, 15.

Size: 4¼ by 2¾ by 4¼ inches. Sub-base: 3¾ by 4¾ inches.

Price $3.75

Code Word "STRONG"

NOTE: Type "A" Transformer is recommended for use with the train outfits shown on Page 12.

Type "B" Transformer will operate any "O" gauge outfit, and in addition the extra binding posts enable the user to light up lamp-posts, semaphores and other electrically illuminated accessories.

For 110 volts, 60 cycles. 50 watts capacity.

Gives 25 volts in following steps:
Permanent: 7, 8, 15.
Variable: 2, 4, 6, 8, 9, 10, 11, 12, 13, 17, 19, 21, 23, 25.

Size: 4½ by 3¾ by 3 inches. Sub-base: 5 by 4¼ inches.

Price $5.00

Code Word "BRADLEY"

A fully guaranteed transformer at a very popular price.

Type "T" Transformer will operate any "O" gauge or "Lionel Standard" outfit; also has extra binding posts for attaching illuminated electrical accessories.

For 110 volts, 60 cycles. 100 watts capacity.

Gives 25 volts in following steps:
Permanent: 2, 4, 6, 7, 8, 10, 12, 14, 15, 16, 17, 18, 19, 21, 23, 25.
Variable: 2, 6, 8, 10, 12, 14, 16, 17, 18, 19, 21, 23, 25.

Size: 5 by 4 by 3¾ inches. Sub-base 4½ by 5½ inches.

Price $7.50

Code Word "BIRCH"

Type "K" Transformer will operate any outfit as well as illuminated accessories. This transformer has sufficient wattage capacity to operate two trains at once.

Size: 5 by 4 by 4½ inches. Sub-base 4½ by 5½ inches.

"K"—For 110 volts, 60 cycles. 150 watts capacity. Specifications same as Type "T," but has higher wattage capacity. Price . $11.00

Code Word (110 V.) "BINGHAM"

"K"—For 220 volts, 60 cycles. 150 watts capacity. Specifications same as Type "T," but is for use on 220-volt circuit.

Price $14.50

Code Word (220 V.) "BROOK"

Type "C" Transformer will operate any outfit and illuminated accessories on 25 or 40 cycle current.

For 110 volts, 25 to 40 cycles. 75 watts capacity. Specifications same as Type "T," but is for use on 25 or 40 cycle current.

Size: 5 by 4 by 4½ inches. Sub-base: 4½ by 5½ inches.

Price $7.50

Code Word "LAWRENCE"

This transformer is the best obtainable for use on 25 or 40 cycle current.

33

MAIN PHOTO: Voltamp stamped-steel locomotive with a passenger car resting on Voltamp track with a solid wood roadbed and tubular strip track. Next to the locomotive is a Voltamp stepped transformer. Each brass button raises or lowers speed when touched by the metal arm—a crude rheostat. To the right of the transformer is a solenoid circuit breaker. Two interesting notes: the lamp in the background is very rare and the locomotive set, made for the 1930 catalog, was never produced. INSET PHOTO: A Lionel catalog from 1931 devoted a whole page to its highly regarded "Multivolt" transformers. Note that instead of today's more familiar plug arrangement, these transformers had cords that screwed into lamp sockets. In homes of the period, there were usually more built-in lamp fixtures than wall sockets.

Chapter 2

Hot Wiring Early Electric Trains

Coming up with a train that ran on electricity was no mean feat in an era when the technology was just barely understood. Except for the illumination capability courtesy of Thomas Edison, electricity was a novelty. Quack doctors sold mail order "electrical belts" that cured everything from gout to sciatica. Parlor games existed that would generate a "small electrical charge that can be regulated in strength of shock from amusing a small child to surprising a strong man." It was a cinch to make a strong man's eyeballs stand out from his head, but it was another challenge to get juice into those two skinny rails and make a locomotive go 'round and 'round.

According to tinplate railroad scholar Louis Hertz, the first model electric train in America is credited to Thomas Davenport in 1835, a Vermont blacksmith. Power came from three wet-plate batteries at the center of a circle of elevated track. The battery cables went directly to the connectors on the motor in an open gondola car rather than to the track. The car circled the batteries at the end of this wire tether with four wheels on two rails. Davenport's idea was to build a model to show to a gathering of scientists at Troy, New York, that electricity was the wave of the future for real railroads. His demonstration of the model on October 14, 1835, was hooted by the scientists who had not yet even passed judgment on the viability of the steam locomotive. He went back to shoeing horses and played with his little train when he wasn't hammering iron.

In 1884, an electric toy train patent was given to Murray Bacon who assigned it to the Novelty Electric Company where it languished without ever being built. Plans for making an electric train exist in a book called *Electric Toy Making for Amateurs,* published by T. O'Connor Sloane in 1891. By 1895, Jehu Garlick, the associate of Eugene Beggs, builder of model live-steam trains, had an idea for an electric model. He had observed operation of the Baltimore & Ohio electric locomotives in the Howard Street Tunnel at Baltimore and built a working model. His direct-current (DC) motor was powered by batteries through wires to an overhead trolley pole. The little car ran on track with rails 1 7/8 inches apart, borrowing the gauge from Beggs. Filled with enthusiasm for his invention, he had 200 built.

Carlisle & Finch built this electric trolley in 1900. Two models are shown, one with the sheet brass shell removed to show the motor and the other fully assembled for play. This model ran on two-rail, strip-steel track. The trolley was very well made . . . and expensive at $3.50—a week's wages for an average worker. *Courtesy Train Collectors Association Toy Train Museum, Strasburg, Pennsylvania*

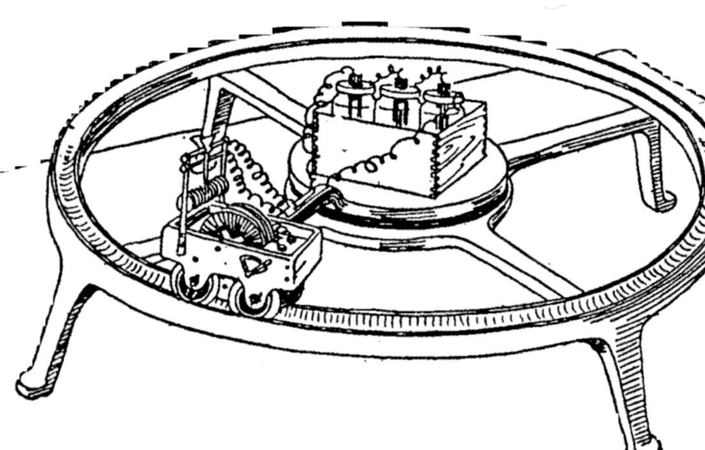

Thomas Davenport is credited with creating the first electric train. He presented his three-wet-plate, battery-driven car to scientists at a meeting in Troy, New York, on October 14, 1835. Since he wasn't a card-carrying scientist himself, the academic community hooted him out of the hall, and he returned to his blacksmith shop. *Courtesy Train Collectors Association*

Unfortunately, buyers were slow to recognize his genius, and the line was discontinued.

It could be that either Morton Carlisle or Robert Finch saw one of Garlick's electric cars or coincidence struck. In 1893 these two young men had started a company in Cincinnati, Ohio, to repair electrical motors and other devices. As Brent Finch, the grandson of Robert Finch, tells it:

> "We started by buying out a little branch of General Electric, repairing generators and motors, but very quickly we realized that if we were going to grow, we needed a product. For some reason, we got interested in mechanical and wind-up toys."

Both American and German wind-up trains were dueling for market share, and the boys decided they could build a model train powered by electricity flowing to the track for pick-up by a small motor in the locomotive.

"Since we already knew about electricity," says Brent, "why not make toys that ran on electricity? And that just took off like wildfire."

Using sheet brass and a small DC motor, they cobbled together a chunky little four-wheel trolley car that ran on three-rail track to sell for three dollars. Estimating the market as uncertain, they ordered 500 built in 1896 and placed their first ad in the March 22,1897, issue of *Scientific American* magazine. It read:

> Complete Electric Railway with battery and track. Car made of polished brass. A perfect working model. Weight 5 pounds. Will run 9 miles on 1 quart solution. Sent on receipt of price $3.

In no time, 1,000 orders were received. Carlisle & Finch were now railroad builders.

Their choice of three-rail track with a pickup shoe riding under the car for positive charge electrical contact predated what would become the standard tinplate track configuration for the next 100-plus years. It was simple and avoided insulation problems caused by using two-rail track where the positive electrical charge is picked up by the wheels from one rail, passed through the motor, and returned through the wheels on the other side of the locomotive. All wheels on one side must therefore be insulated from those on the other. At the time of its design, three-rail track was being considered as standard by full-size electric trains according to an article and drawing in *Harpers* magazine.

In that same year, when C&F's fall model was announced, three-rail had been abandoned in favor of more the more realistic two-rail track. These tracks were made from lengths of strip steel pressed into slotted wooden ties; the slots were two inches apart. By Christmas, they had two models of trolley cars, using four-wheel and eight-wheel configurations. Their first crack at insulating the wheels eliminated the steel axle that joined the wheels. The cast-iron wheels, one inch in diameter, were simply nailed to part of the wood frame. With the eight-wheel cars, each of four wheels was nailed to a block of wood that turned on a wood screw into the bottom of the wood frame, thus forming a four-wheel "truck"—two trucks per car. On the trolleys, where spur gears and pulleys connected the motor to the wheels, fiber tubes split the steel axles. Eventually this fiber insulation between the wheels was used on the rest of the line and by other two-rail manufacturers as well.

Carlisle & Finch continued to use wood frames on its steam locomotives until the release of its model No. 45, one of the most beautifully proportioned electric steam engines ever built. According to W. Graham Claytor Jr., former president of the Southern Railway and Amtrak and author of "An Introduction to Carlisle & Finch" in the *Greenberg Guide to Early American Toy Trains*, "Its top-of-the-line No. 45 locomotive of 1903-1908 is the only engine not using a wood frame, and here the same result is achieved by having a two-piece cast-bronze frame with the two parts insulated from each other."

Both the No. 1 (four-wheel) and No. 2 (eight-wheel) trolley cars used both two-pole motors connected to one set of drive wheels by a rubber band or pulley. Having only two poles means that at startup, the motor armature is not near the magnetized pole, or has a "dead" center. This state requires the "engineer" to give the car a gentle nudge to get the armature to pass the magnet and begin the power transfer. The eight-wheeler had two of these two-pole motors, so the odds that one of the motors was in contact with the pole were good and the car would start without a push. In 1899, Carlisle & Finch installed three-pole motors on its locomotives that would easily self start and could be reversed as well.

If our friend of chapter 1, Little Tommy, managed to survive live steam locomotives without self-immolation, torching the varnish off the hardwood floor, or turning his $10 toy into a lump of melted tin, he now faced dealing with the electrical distribution systems of the day.

First of all, many homes did not have electricity at the turn-of-the-century. If they were wired up, there was no safe way to reduce the direct 110- or 220-volt current to the low wattage needed to run the train. There were few wall plugs, and those were used by lamps with screw-in Edison light bulbs. One of Carlisle & Finch's trolleys, model No. 2-S, had its motor wound so it could use household current as long as the hook-up was in series with a light bulb. This model was designed to run in store windows for long periods of time. All other models bore a warning against this practice. Tommy did have some other choices.

Between 1897 and 1902, C&F suggested using the Chromite wet battery. Chromite (FeCr2O4) is a naturally occurring mineral, an oxide of iron and chromium. In its "B" catalog of 1900, C&F explains how to move the trolley along at a speed of 150 feet per minute around a three-foot-diameter circle:

> The battery consists of three zinc-carbon elements and one 10-ounce bottle of Chromite. We do not furnish battery jars . . . The purchaser may use ordinary tumblers, or jelly jars. NO ACID—The use of Chromite does away with all acids. To operate the battery, dissolve the 10 ounces of Chromite in one quart of water. This makes enough solution for two charges.

At this point, the three elements attached to a bar were immersed in the Chromite. Wires were attached to each end of the bar and then to each rail of the track. Electricity was now flowing, and the car (after a nudge) started running. Lift the bar and dripping elements from their jelly jars and the car stopped. Slowing the car was done by partially removing the zinc-carbon elements.

For the No. 2 electric railway locomotive with its dual motors, Tommy needed five jelly jars and

No. 42. Electric Railway.

Price, $4.70.

4 to 5 VOLTS. **½ AMPERE.**

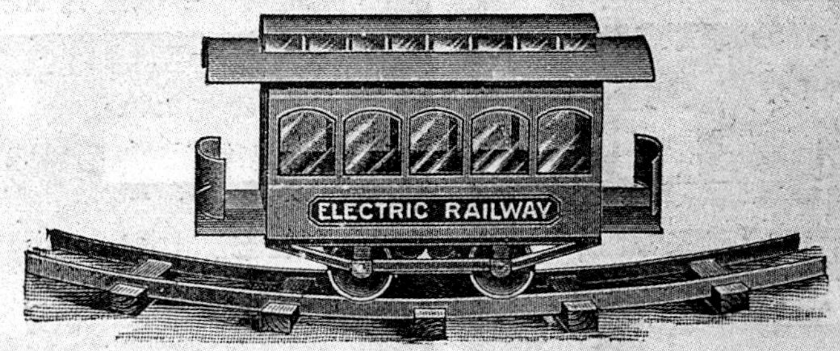

This model is an entirely new and improved design and is without doubt the most perfect and complete car that has ever been sold in the way of a toy. It has trucks the same as a large trolley car. The motor is connected to the axle by means of brass spur gearing—machine cut. The motor is reversible and has strong and substantial bearings, brushes and commutator. It is provided with a 3-pole self-starting armature.

A reversing switch enables the operator to run the car backwards or forwards, or start and stop it at will.

The car is 8 inches long, 5 inches high; has brass wheels 1¼ inch in diameter. It will fit our standard 2 inch gauge track.

Speed of car, 150 to 200 feet per minute.

The complete equipment consists of car, 9 feet of strip steel track and 4 cells of dry battery.

Weight, boxed, 12½ lbs.

Motor car only, $3.35.

Track and ties strip steel in 9 ft. lengths, 35 cents. By mail 50 cents.

Extra dry batteries, per cell, 25 cents.

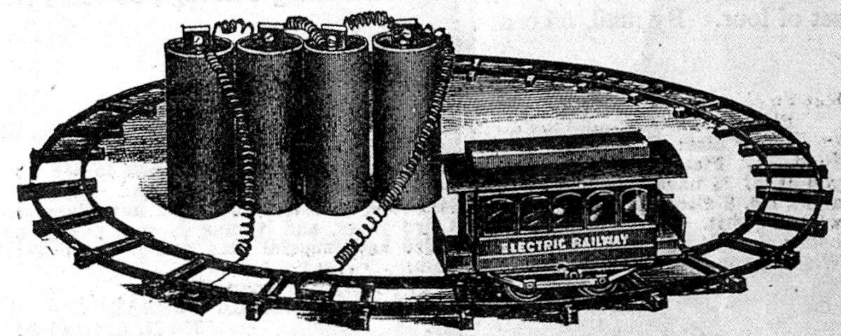

This illustration shows the complete No. 42 Railway with battery.

—5—

Carlisle & Finch catalog featuring their small trolley running off four chromite dry batteries. While better—and less dangerous—than wet acid batteries, these power sources had to be stacked like cordwood to last through the winter holidays.

RIGHT: The somewhat demonic electro-chemical procedure needed to send current to the tracks as pictured in the Lionel 1903 catalog. Obvious care was needed so as not to send the current through Little Tommy or bathe him in the sulfuric acid and water mixture. Imagine this set-up featured in Toy Mart today. *All illustrations this page courtesy Train Collectors Association Toy Train Museum, Strasburg, Pennsylvania*

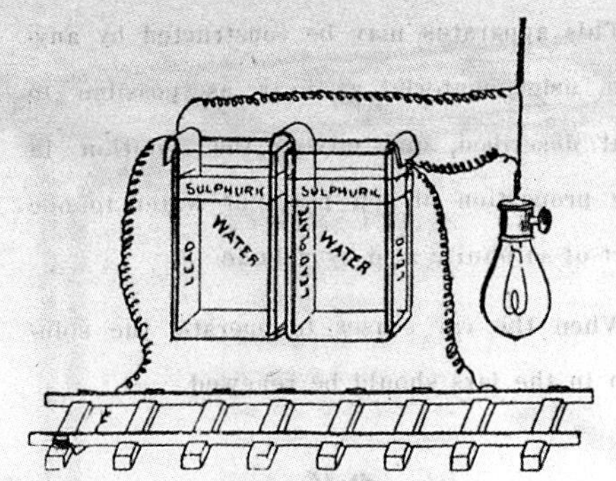

Diagram showing the proper way to operate our cars when utilizing direct electric current.

(Catalogue No. 370.)

The outfit supplied by us consists of two glass jars 2x1 1-4x3 1-2 inches, and plates of lead 1 inch wide and 1-16 inch thick.

The cells are filled with water to the first line from the bottom, and a sufficient amount of sulphuric acid is added to bring it up to the second mark. **NEVER ADD WATER TO THE ACID IN ANY EVENT, BUT POUR THE ACID ON TOP OF THE WATER.**

The glass jars are placed with their narrow sides together, and the lead plates inserted, as shown above. The plates must not touch each other. They should be placed apart as far

BELOW: Lionel 1902 catalog showing how to attach a set of batteries to the track. Note how the instructions educate the child about which terminal is for the carbon core and which connects to the zinc wrapper, instead of dumbing down to "A" and "B."

ABOUT BATTERIES.

(Catalogue No. 301.)

We have found it advisable when making up outfits complete with battery, to supply four dry cells, which work satisfactorily when used intermittently for from ten to fifteen hours; allowing the battery to rest is very beneficial to them as it prolongs their usefulness.

Price of four dry cells, with wire and full directions for connecting, $1.20.

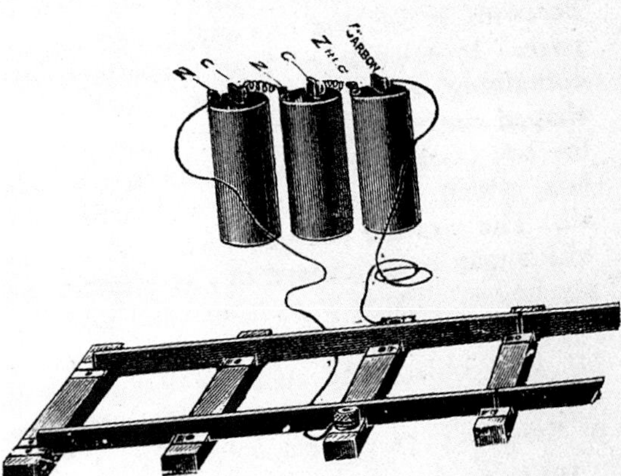

This illustrates the proper way to connect battery to track.

7

RIGHT: Carlisle & Finch water-powered dynamo. Hooked to the kitchen sink, this compact water wheel drove C&F trains until Mom needed to make dinner.

The Carlisle & Finch Co., Cincinnati, O. 13

No. 8. Complete Water Power Plant.

Price, $8.00.

Wherever water of forty pounds pressure or over is available we recommend the use of one of these little machines for supplying current for operating toys, miniature lamps, etc. You can obtain electric current at actually no expense, the amount of water used being so small that it costs nothing. It can be attached to any faucet by means of the rubber hose and clamps furnished with it.

With fifty pounds pressure enough current is obtained to light a ten candle power, ten volt incandescent lamp. The output is 8 to 10 volts and 1 to 2 amperes. With greater pressure more current can be obtained.

This is the nicest way of running our electric toys that we know of. No battery, no trouble, no renewals of zinc, etc. NO EXPENSE.

For show window displays it is the best and cheapest method of operating. . The motors on the cars will last longer and give better power than when run from electric light current. Wires may be run any distance from the dynamo, and with perfect safety, because the voltage is so low that no dangerous shocks can be felt, nor can the sparks set fire to inflammable material.

Weight, packed ready for shipment, 16 lbs. Dimensions of box $7\frac{3}{4}$ x $8\frac{1}{4}$ x $8\frac{1}{4}$ inches.

For ordinary experimenting and for lighting incandescent lamps we recommend the series wound dynamo.

(OVER)

20 ounces of Chromite. This locomotive was guaranteed to be able to haul other cars and climb steep grades. For heavy-duty operation, a five-pound jar of Chromite could be purchased.

If this sounds like fun, Tommy has an even better alternative. On page 13 of the 1900 catalog, C&F explains how he can run his railway by means of direct electric light current.

> Provide two glass or earthenware jars of about two quart capacity (each) for the No. 1 or No. 3 Railways (single motor), or three jars for the No. 2 (dual motor) or No. 4 (Steamer) Railways. Fill the jars three-fourths full with water—10 parts and sulphuric [sic] acid—one part by volume. Take some sheet lead about 1/16 of an inch thick and cut plates as shown in the sketch. Make connections with lamp cord, plates and track as shown. Be careful to cut only one strand of the lamp cord and connect the wires exactly as shown. . . A 20 candle power or 32 candle power incandescent lamp must be used.

So, there sits Tommy next to his railway and three earthenware jars of sulfuric acid mixture connected to 110 volts of direct current. This is the kind of sweaty-palmed, character-building responsibility that either makes or breaks future captains of industry.

One direction has been inadvertently left out of the catalog instructions, one that could definitely affect Tommy's future as the good looking lad he is. In 1903, when Joshua Lionel Cowen supplied similar instructions for making a wet cell battery, he warned in vigorous capitals:

> NEVER ADD WATER TO THE ACID IN ANY EVENT, BUT POUR THE ACID ON TOP OF THE WATER.

If done the wrong way, sulfuric acid hisses, spatters, and burns big holes in whatever it touches.

From 1903 to 1915, C&F recommended using dry-cell batteries to run its railway locomotives. There was no risk of spilling Chromite solution or slopping sulfuric acid mixture all over a freshly pressed pair of knickers and the bare wires of the lamp cord. When the dry cells were used up, they could be discarded. What was not pointed out, unfortunately, was the duration of these early dry cells. In 1903, when the large No. 45 locomotive was introduced, C&F recommended eight of these batteries—each the size of a small artillery shell—be wired up to the track. Later on, the number was increased to 10. Apparently, it was assumed, if Tommy's dad could afford that huge locomotive, the outlay for batteries should not be a problem.

Carlisle & Finch produced a number of electric products, from toy trains to toy automobiles and boats. They also built various sizes of electric motors and dynamos. Two of its products were very useful to households that had no electricity whatsoever which was the rule rather than the exception in 1900. The No. 7 Hand-Power Dynamo would . . .

> . . . light a 10 candlepower lamp, 12 volt incandescent lamp, furnish current to run any of our electrical toys, or perform any electrical experiment. . . When used with any of our railways, it makes an ideal miniature power plant . . . the speed of the car can be varied by changing the speed of the dynamo.

Here, Tommy can recruit little brother, Bobby, with promise of either (A) pain or (B) candy, to be Dynamo Man for the session. Bobby can turn the dynamo crank until the *Express* slides neatly to a stop at the station after a record run, or until he blacks out.

If Tommy can't find Bobby, there is another option, the Carlisle & Finch No. 8 Complete Water-Power Plant. The dynamo is clamped to the sink, a hose is connected to the faucet, and—with 50 pounds of water pressure—8 to 10 volts and 1 ampere of electricity is produced. To speed up the *Fast Mail Express* to Kansas City, Tommy just increases the water pressure or shouts to Mom in the kitchen for more speed. The instructions guarantee that, ". . . no dangerous shocks can be felt, nor can the sparks set fire to inflammable material."

With these options available in the early days of electric trains, it's no wonder many families stayed with wind-up locomotives.

Carlisle & Finch included track accessories such as crossings with gapped rails to avoid short circuits and switches that created track sidings and more complex layouts. The company offered bridges and a passenger station with two semaphore signals that were wired in line with the batteries and operated by means of electromagnets. C&F's "No. 3 Coal Mining Locomotive and Train" of little dump cars was the first American electric train "set." The wedge-shaped locomotive was

Continued on page 34

Power to the Locomotives

The earliest electric train built by Thomas Davenport in 1835 tethered the moving locomotive to a central battery by wires while the little four-wheeler circled around its power source on a raised loop of track. Not much play value there.

Sending electricity into the tracks as with Lionel's earliest Electric Express, or Carlisle & Finch's second trolley car (the first used an overhead wire) allowed for greater flexibility and realistic operation. However, this advance came at a price. Getting electricity to the track around the turn of the century was an edgy proposition. The delicate operation combined direct current wired to lead plates hand dipped into a sulfuric acid bath, creating a "wet-cell" battery. The "dry" battery supplanted the dangerous wet-cell, but these power sources were expensive and had to be bought by the carton for a weekend of play.

Eventually, direct current was harnessed and reduced to a safe amperage through heavy iron wire-wrapped converters, then transformers with separate circuit breakers and finally with modern transformers including all the safety devices.

Today, tinplate operators can use computer chip-controlled, hand-held, walk-around throttles that manage full train operation, uncoupling and a variety of railroad sounds. For very realistic railroading, more than one train can operate independently on the same track. No more sweaty palms from dipping electrified lead plates in and out of an acid bath in order to roll your express train smoothly into the Toy Trainville station.

12 *The Carlisle & Finch Co., Cincinnati, O.*

No. 7. Hand Power Dynamo.

Price, $6.50.

This is a powerful hand dynamo, operated by gearing. It is very compact and gives a large current for a machine of such small size. It is the most neatly designed and finished small dynamo that has ever been put on the market. Is mounted on hardwood base, has tool steel shaft and babbitted bearings, and is neatly painted.

It will light a ten candle power, ten volt incandescent lamp, furnish current to run several of our electrical toys at once, or perform any electrical experiment. Among other things it will decompose water, electroplate metals, fire blasting fuses, etc.

When used with any of the railways it makes an ideal miniature power plant. There are no batteries to be considered and the power is ever ready, and the speed of the car can be varied by changing the speed of the dynamo.

Weight of dynamo, packed in wooden box, 16½ pounds. Box measures 6¾ x 9⅜ x 9¾ inches.

We can also furnish this dynamo without hand wheel and pinion, but provided with pulley, so as to be run by a belt. When furnished in this shape the price is $6.00. The weight is about two pounds less.

Description of No. 7 Hand Powered dynamo from Carlisle & Finch. Run your train while developing incredibly strong wrists. *Train Collectors Association Toy Train Museum, Strasburg, Pennsylvania*

RIGHT: Dorfan electrical products were of high quality manufacture in the mid to late 1920's and rivaled any of the hardware offered by Lionel, American Flyer, and Ives. *Train Collectors Association Toy Train Museum, Strasburg, Pennsylvania*

An Electric Motor You Can Build Yourself

DORFAN MOTO-BUILDER MOTOR, No. 1002 (*Left*)

Dorfan originated this powerful "take-apart" motor. This type of motor is also used in the Dorfan Loco-Builder narrow gauge engine. Will run toy lathes, drills, saws and other mechanical toys. A popular favorite because it affords an opportunity to study motors in a thorough, yet enjoyable manner. Housing made of famous Dorfan-Alloy, the practically unbreakable metal. An all-around useful motor. Price, complete, $2.50.

DORFAN MOTO-BUILDER OUTFIT, No. 1004 (*Below*)

Consists of "housing" and parts for building the Dorfan Motor. Parts are sturdily constructed, carefully tested and will give long service. Handsomely finished. Complete with assembly instructions. Price, $3.00

A Good Transformer is Essential

Dorfan Electric Trains are designed to operate on a current of 6 to 8 volts. In most homes the electric lighting system operates on a current of 110 volts. Therefore, to use the house current for running your electric train it is necessary to reduce the strength of that current to the proper voltage.

For this purpose a Transformer is used when the current is *Alternating Current*, the kind supplied to most homes. The company that supplies your home with electricity will gladly inform you what kind of current you have.

For Alternating Current

The Transformer connected with your house current produces the current required to operate your train. So you can see that it is important to know that your transformer is a good one; that it will not get hot, that its wiring is correctly and carefully done, so there will be no danger of burning out your engine's motor by turning on too strong a current. It must be made of the best steel and other materials.

We supply two kinds of transformers, as shown on this page, and guarantee both of them to be reliable in every way. They are well made, of best materials and are *air-cooled* to prevent overheating.

FOR DIRECT CURRENT

In homes supplied with Direct Current a different method of reducing voltage is required to run Dorfan trains. A Direct Current reducer may be used—but we recommend use of a radio or automobile battery. It is advisable to use a charging device such as a "trickle charger" with batteries.

DORFAN TRANSFORMER No. 442

For 110 volt—60 cycle Alternating Current. 50 watts capacity. Has a range of five "steps" or different strengths of current, ranging from 5½ to 10½ volts. Each step is one volt. Two outlet connections. Air-cooled. Strong metal case. Wire cord, 6¼ feet long, with two-piece plug to prevent kinking of cord. Fully guaranteed. Must NOT be used with Direct Current. Full directions for use. Price, $3.50

DORFAN TRANSFORMER No. 443

DORFAN TRANSFORMER, No. 443

For reducing 110 volt-60 cycle Alternating Current for use with Dorfan engines. 75 watts capacity. Seven "steps" of ¾ volts each. Range 5½ to 23 volts. Five outlet connections. Air cooled. Strong metal case. 6¼ feet of cord; two-piece plug. Must not be used with Direct Current. Fully guaranteed. Price, $6.50.

DORFAN TRANSFORMER, No. 444

For 110 volt-25 cycle Alternating Current. Not illustrated. Price, $7.50.

DORFAN TRANSFORMER, No. 442

American Flyer offered a variety of transformer sizes from single- to dual-train control in 1957, and all featured "circuit breakers" to avoid overloads and short circuits. The models with the red-handled levers mimicked the 'dead-man's control" of real railroad locomotives. If the engineer let go of the handle, the train stopped. At a hefty $34.95, the 30B transformer—complete with volt meters—at upper left in this catalog page was Flyer's answer to Lionel's ZW. *Mike Schafer collection*

American Flyer "Safety-First" TRANSFORMERS

No. 30B DUAL TRAIN POWER CONTROLLER, WITH DOUBLE CIRCUIT BREAKERS
OUTPUT: 300 WATTS, 110-120 VOLTS, 60 CYCLES, A. C.

The finest electric train power controller you can buy! Has features never before incorporated in transformers and with its giant capacity you can run two trains at different speeds on separate loops of track, or FOUR trains (two running at same speed) on four separate layouts. Has full directional control; when train stops it will start up again without going into reverse first. Two panel meters indicate voltage—one for each control. Has green power-on light and two red warning lights that indicate a short circuit. Transformer has "Dead Man's Control" a real railroad feature. When throttle is let go, train halts! Operation is guarded by two circuit breakers—one for each controller—which shut off power if over-load or short occurs. Case is high impact material.

No. 18B DUAL TRAIN POWER CONTROLLER, WITH DOUBLE CIRCUIT BREAKERS
OUTPUT: 190 WATTS, 110-120 VOLTS, 60 CYCLES, A. C.

Two circuit breakers guard transformer against short circuit damage or overload. Has exclusive "Dead Man's Control" and permits full directional operation. Can run two trains on separate track loops at different speeds. Transformer case is high impact material.

No. 18B *$24.95*

No. 19B *$29.95*

No. 30B - *$34.95*

No. 19B TRAIN POWER CONTROLLER, WITH CIRCUIT BREAKER
OUTPUT: 300 WATTS, 110-120 VOLTS, 60 CYCLES, A. C.

It's more than a transformer—it's a real model rail-

No. 4B *$9.95*

No. 15B *$15.95*

No. 13 *$1.75*

No. 15B TRAIN POWER CONTROLLER, WITH CIRCUIT BREAKER
OUTPUT: 110 WATTS, 110-120 VOLTS, 60 CYCLES, A. C.

Has ample output to operate a train set plus small quantity of remote control and automatic accessories. New features provide full directional control: when train stops, it will re-start without going into reverse first. Built-in Circuit Breaker prevents transformer burn-outs due to over-load or shorts. Green light indicates power-on; red light warns of a short circuit. Like real railroads it has exclusive "Dead Man's Control"—if throttle is released, train halts. Case is high impact molded material.

No. 4B TRANSFORMER, WITH CIRCUIT BREAKER
OUTPUT: 100 WATTS, 110-120 VOLTS, 60 CYCLES, A. C.

Powerful enough to operate a set of trains plus quantity of automatic and remote control accessories. Automatic Thermostatic Circuit Breaker, built-in, protects Transformer from burn-outs. Has three binding posts for simplified wiring. Case is heavy pressed steel.

No. 13 CIRCUIT BREAKER

If your transformer does not now have a Circuit Breaker you can provide one quickly with this accessory. Suitable for any transformer without a circuit breaker. Prevents transformer burn-outs and overloading.

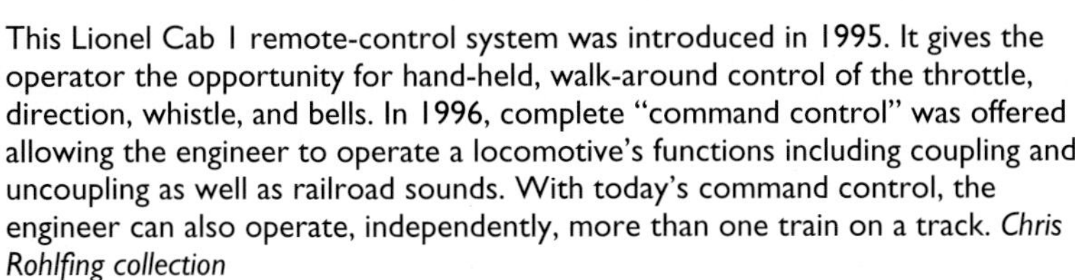

This Lionel Cab 1 remote-control system was introduced in 1995. It gives the operator the opportunity for hand-held, walk-around control of the throttle, direction, whistle, and bells. In 1996, complete "command control" was offered allowing the engineer to operate a locomotive's functions including coupling and uncoupling as well as railroad sounds. With today's command control, the engineer can also operate, independently, more than one train on a track. *Chris Rohlfing collection*

The MTH Z-4000 transformer is the latest in computer-chip-controlled power sources for today's toy train railroads. Based on the famous Lionel ZW transformer design in looks only, this powerhouse delivers 180 RMS watts for each control handle and has full Underwriters Laboratory approval. It offers computer-style menus to scroll through for locomotives equipped with MTH ProtoSound™, accessing any of some 30 commands in seconds. MTH's Mike Wolf claims a half million dollars were spent in developing the Z-4000, but only a portion of those costs are passed on to MTH customers. *MTH Electric Trains, Inc.*

Carlisle & Finch's coal-mine train was modeled after an actual prototype and was the first American electric train "set." This is the model with cars that dump their contents with a tip of the finger. The tin station shown is a C&F product but does not have the operating semaphore signals in the roof. *Train Collectors Association Toy Train Museum, Strasburg, Pennsylvania*

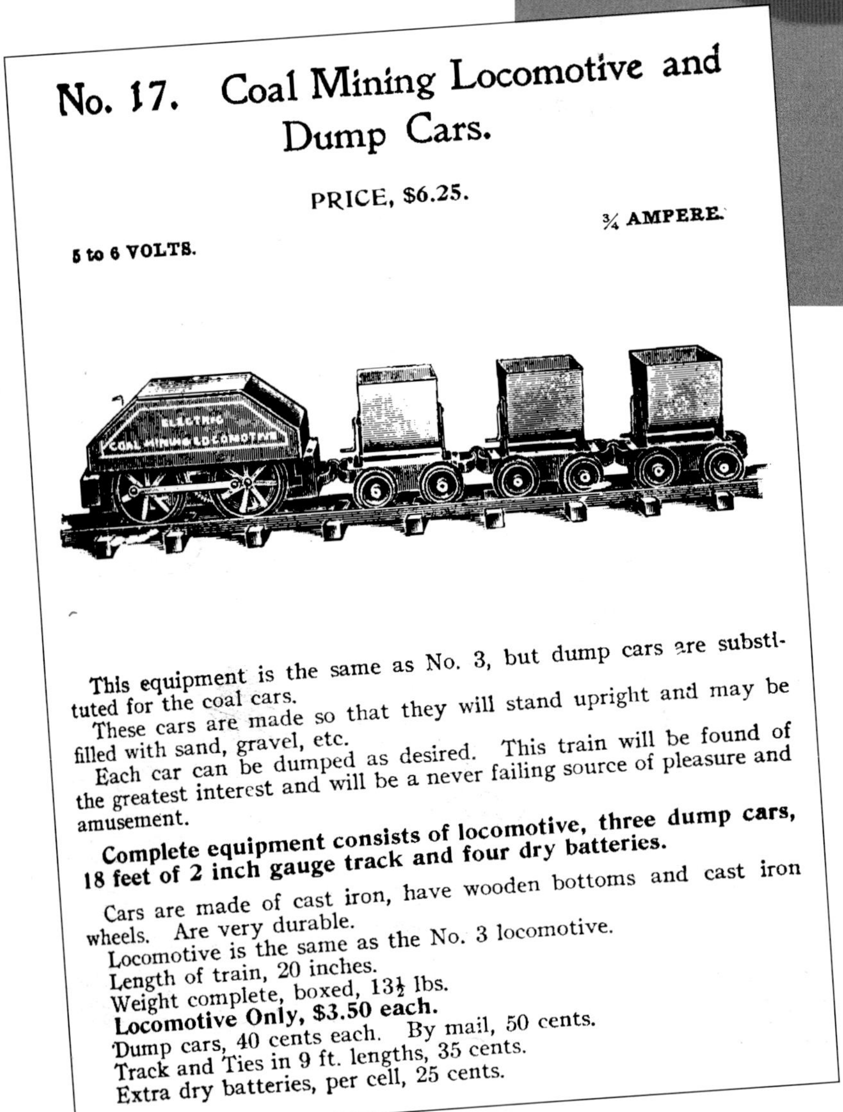

No. 17. Coal Mining Locomotive and Dump Cars.

PRICE, $6.25.

5 to 6 VOLTS. **¾ AMPERE.**

This equipment is the same as No. 3, but dump cars are substituted for the coal cars.

These cars are made so that they will stand upright and may be filled with sand, gravel, etc.

Each car can be dumped as desired. This train will be found of the greatest interest and will be a never failing source of pleasure and amusement.

Complete equipment consists of locomotive, three dump cars, 18 feet of 2 inch gauge track and four dry batteries.

Cars are made of cast iron, have wooden bottoms and cast iron wheels. Are very durable.

Locomotive is the same as the No. 3 locomotive.

Length of train, 20 inches.

Weight complete, boxed, 13½ lbs.

Locomotive Only, $3.50 each.

Dump cars, 40 cents each. By mail, 50 cents.

Track and Ties in 9 ft. lengths, 35 cents.

Extra dry batteries, per cell, 25 cents.

LEFT: The first "train" offered by Carlisle & Finch in the early 1900s was modeled from a prototype coal-mining locomotive. It ran off a reversible three-pole motor and could pull 10 to 12 loaded cars on level track. The cars shown tipped to dump their load. *Train Collectors Association*

Continued from page 31

based on an actual prototype and had a manual reverse lever.

C&F's crowning glory in this first year of the twentieth century was its No. 4 electric locomotive and freight train. This was a "steam outline" electric locomotive. Collectors use the "outline" terminology to designate the prototype from which the electrically run model is based. An "electric outline" locomotive would resemble a full-size prototype that ran actually did run on electricity from an overhead wire or third rail.

This No. 4 0-4-0 locomotive was very realistic, beautifully proportioned, and came with a gondola and boxcar—later to be joined by a caboose. The logo of the Lake Shore & Michigan Southern Railway (a component railroad of the then-growing New York Central System empire) is on the coal tender. All wheels were iron and flanged for the 2-inch-wide track and the locomotive featured a manual reverse lever. The length of the engine and tender was 18 inches and the cars added

A Carlisle & Finch No. 4 switcher of the 0-4-0 configuration. This model underwent at least five different variations from its release in 1899 until 1916 when the C&F toy train product line was shut down for good. It had a reversing three-pole motor with the manual lever beneath the right side of the cab. Its boiler is sheet metal mounted on a wood frame. This variation is an early one with a dummy kerosene headlight. These locomotives ran only in the houses of the well-to-do because of their $6.50 price tag. *Carlisle & Finch collection, Cincinnati, Ohio*

another 21 inches. The entire train weighed in at 16 pounds. A brass passenger coach and baggage car were also offered. In effect, this was a complete electric railroad with no competition in the marketplace. So, why weren't later generations of Little Tommys playing with Carlisle & Finch trains?

To own a complete C&F railroad—locomotive, freight or passenger cars, track, station, bridge, and a stack of dry cell batteries—cost upwards of $20 in the early 1900s. Wages at this time for an office worker's 64-hour week were about $12. Factory workers earned an average of $9.42 for six day's labor. The child labor force numbered over a million kids earning about 25 cents a day. Even the cheapest C&F Motor Car No. 1 cost over $5 with track, zinc plates, and Chromite. Setting aside almost a week's wages for a toy at a time when a kid's income-producing capability was more important than his character-building play, wage-earners opted for food in the pot and clothes on the back rather than a toy electric train on a track. Until the cost of producing toy electric trains was brought down after World War I, all these toys were very expensive gifts, bestowed on the privileged few at Christmas—the time for such largess. This seasonal association would continue through the decades.

Carlisle & Finch motive power, rolling stock, and accessories were largely handmade requiring considerable soldering and fitting. Manufacturing costs kept their prices high and dictated their market. C&F's later No. 45 steam-outline, 4-4-2 Atlantic-type locomotive that was built between 1903 and 1915 stood head and shoulders above any other toy train of its time. It is an almost-scale representation of the type of New York Central & Hudson River Railroad locomotives assigned to the New York–Chicago *20th Century Limited*. Twenty-seven inches long, 5½ inches wide at the cylinders and 6½ inches high at the cab, it is a high-stepping brute. A string of matching brass baggage and open-vestibule passenger cars—each 15½ inches long—could be coupled behind it. But only the affluent would ever see it run.

An elegantly proportioned steam locomotive, the Carlisle & Finch No. 34 is modeled after an "Atlantic"-type 4-4-2 passenger hauler, specifically one belonging to the mighty Pennsylvania Railroad. This C&F version was produced from 1908 to 1915. It is 23 inches long including the tender and 6½ inches high at the cab. *Carlisle & Finch collection, Cincinnati, Ohio*

December, 1917 33

Oh, Boy! You Talk About FUN!

Get a Lionel Train

Lionel Electric Trains May Now Be Had *for as* Low As $5

Lionel Trains range in price from $5 up by easy steps to wonderful de luxe Pullmans at $40. All are operated by the now noted Lionel Electric Motor. This motor has a special, high-power wiring that gives great speed on a minimum of current. Has genuine self-lubricating brushes. More than a toy—an instrument of really scientific construction that will give years of joy and service. Remember this when you buy trains.

Be Sure It's a LIONEL!

NEW YORK CENTRAL LINES 42

PULLMAN

PULLMAN

OBSERVATION

Just What You Want For Christmas!

You turn on the current. Away she dashes! Out of the station, down the main line, past electric-lighted semaphores, through tunnels, over bridges—just like a long, overland limited. Starts and stops at a touch of your hand, from any place in the room. *Say!* Get a Lionel Train if you want a jolly Christmas. And—be sure it *is* a "Lionel."

Lionel Trains are big, businesslike, heavy gauge steel structures, with Lionel special, high-power motors. They are designed after the regular electric trains seen on the great railway systems. The weight is close to the track—turn on the highest speed; they can't derail. Operated very economically on batteries or with the Transformer described below. Beautifully finished in bright, non-chipping enamels. Good for years of fun. Seats inside for little "passengers," which I can furnish if desired.

LIONEL ELECTRIC TOY TRAINS & Multivolt Transformers

Something new! A Lionel "Multivolt" Transformer at $3.40. Your dealer should have it. If not, don't take a "just as good." Get him to order from me or *you* order direct; I'll ship, charges prepaid, upon receipt of price. This transformer attached to your house current not only does away with batteries but uses much less current. Speed is controlled by the switch on top. The mechanism is entirely enclosed in a handsome steel case, so no harm can come to the user. 2 to 30 volts. 15 variable and 2 permanent voltages.

This "Multivolt" Transformer Runs Any Make of Electric Train

$3.40

with great efficiency and economy—as well as all kinds of electric toys. Also operates scores of small electric apparatuses that ordinarily require batteries, such as induction coils, annunciators, bells, burglar alarms, wireless sets and medical appliances.

We manufacture other models up to $8.00 retail

Boys! Get My Xmas Catalog

—a handsome book done in colors with over a hundred pictures. It shows the entire Lionel line, which includes electric locomotives, electric steam-type locomotives, passenger cars, observation cars, sleeping cars, and scores of freight cars, such as cattle cars, oil tanks, flat cars, etc. Also electric-lighted semaphores, switches, tunnels, stations and everything necessary to set up a complete railroad system. It's FREE. Get it *now*—don't wait till Christmas is almost here.

J. LIONEL COWEN, *Friend of the Boys*
Pres. THE LIONEL MFG. CO.
48 A, East 21st Street, New York City

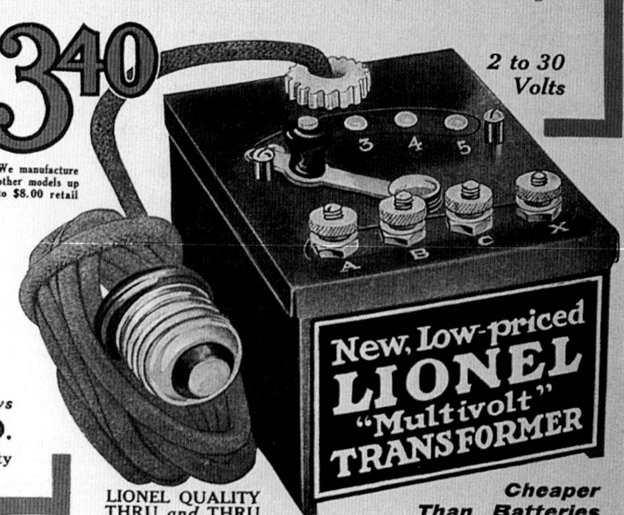

LIONEL QUALITY THRU *and* THRU

Lionel ad in *American Boy* magazine, November-December 1917. Lawrence Cowen posed for the artist who created the kneeling boy in knickers that became part of many Lionel advertising campaigns. *Train Collectors Association Toy Train Museum, Strasburg, Pennsylvania*

Chapter 3

Highballing Into the Twentieth Century

As the calendar ticked over to the twentieth century, a combination of events occurred that would determine the destiny of the American toy train in the growing toy marketplace for decades to come. Shrewd and clever young men were stepping forward during those first years.

Hafner Company Enters the Toy Train Market

William Hafner was born in Chicago in 1870, and after discovering the packing-crate business was not his cup of tea, he put his mechanical energies into developing a wind-up motor that was both simple and reliable. In 1901, the young mechanic formed the Hafner Company and put his motor into toy trucks, tiny doll swings, and a sheet metal automobile called the "Hafner Roundabout." This sturdy toy resembled the gas buggy built by auto pioneer Ransome Olds. It was seven inches long, had a tiller for steering, and a cloth seat; its rubber-tired wheels could be set into any one of 19 grooves to run in a circle. Hafner's powerful motor could drive it in a straight line for 100 feet on one wind-up.

From this model auto, he went on to design other wheeled vehicles that sold well, but still beneath his expectations. Finally, in 1905, after seeing buyer interest rising for toy trains, he put his wind-up motor into a cast-iron locomotive shell and never looked back. This experiment guaranteed the existence of the wind-up train well into the 1950s and, a few years later, established the name American Flyer in the turbulent history of the American toy train.

Lionel Is Born

In the closing weeks of 1900, a 23-year-old inventor named Joshua Cowen began searching for another product that could be electrified—the technology of the future. He had passed many store windows in Manhattan when he came upon Robert Ingersoll's toy shop window and peered in. Toys filled the Christmas display space, but there was no action, no buzz, no attraction other than the fixed stares of the dolls, the toy soldiers frozen

The Buffalo train station by Carlisle & Finch was offered in different versions from 1897 to 1915. The brick exterior is glued-on paper over tin. Its most unique feature was a pair of semaphore flags that rose whenever a train passed over the track approaching the station. They were operated off track power, and electromagnets raised the flags when the passing train drew current off the solenoid coil. One of the earliest "action" accessories, the Buffalo station cost 69 cents in 1897. *Carlisle & Finch collection, Cincinnati, Ohio*

ABOVE: William F. Hafner, founder of the Hafner Company, a longtime maker of wind-up locomotives. His son John took over the company and continued production into the 1950s. *Train Collectors Association Toy Train Museum, Strasburg, Pennsylvania*

RIGHT: A slight smile making him look particularly benevolent, Joshua Lionel Cowen had become a near-deity in the world of toy electric trains. When this portrait was made, his toy trains had become the most well-known and collected in the world. *Lionel LLC*

in postures, the tin wind-up toys arrested in their brief mechanical lives. From some part of his accumulated experiences came the idea for a box of toys that could move in a small circle, attracting the stares of the curious. Only an electric motor could supply the motive power for hours on end. He went inside to talk to Ingersoll.

His idea was to construct a foot-long narrow box that rode on a motorized four-wheel truck. The clunky-looking hardwood gondola would be lettered ELECTRIC EXPRESS and could easily carry a squad of toy soldiers, building blocks, or maybe a small doll. Cowen bet his future on the idea that this battery-powered electric novelty circling on a two-rail strip steel track would attract buyers to otherwise static window displays of a few New York shops.

The motor that powered the *Express* was a simple affair he had used for a failed electric fan design. The fan design was a dud, and besides, nobody needed fans in the fall and winter. Cowen and his mechanically inclined partner Harry Grant ran around town collecting the wheels, axles, metal frames, and bodies jobbed out to small backshops and fabricators. Cowen's circle of strip track was the same kind used by Carlisle & Finch, strips of thin steel pressed into slotted wood ties to form rails 2⅞ inches apart.

At this time, C&F was manufacturing much more elegant-looking electric trains for the affluent. Cast-iron and wood pull-toy trains had catered to smaller pocketbooks for 20 years, and expensive live-steam trains sputtered and hissed around circles of track in the playrooms of the rich. The major part of the toy train market was dominated by German companies—notably Maerklin, Bing, and Carette—that also featured full lines of colorful accessories to collect even more American dollars.

Joshua had two things going for him. He was in New York where Thomas Edison built the first electrical power-distribution center and electrical goods flowed in volumes greater than any other American city. Second, he wasn't competing strictly for the toy train market. He was selling his boxy little train primarily to retailers to add action to their store windows, not to people looking for a toy train.

When Cowen found that his homely little motorized cigar box was actually being sold from those shop windows at $4 a pop and there was that much of a demand for electric trains, he shifted gears. In 1901 he went to work designing a toy open trolley car that resembled the ubiquitous trolleys that plied Manhattan's busy thoroughfares and published his first catalog. He and Grant worked out of a third floor loft at 24 Murray Street down the street from City Hall. By this time, Ingersol had ordered a half dozen copies of the Electric Express. A Rhode Island firm ordered two dozen and got the right to exclusive distribution in New England.

Cowen's second catalog, published in 1902, described "Miniature electric cars with full accessories for window display and holiday gifts." Featured in the center of the catalog's cover was a picture of the electric trolley car. At the bottom of the cover was the name of Cowen's new firm, incorporating his middle name: Lionel Manufacturing Company. Inside, on page 5, he still featured his original *Electric Express* gondola with an unmotored trailer attached and six little barrels for a miniature load. Ever the businessman with an eye on moving the inventory, Cowen added the reference: "As a toy, [the *Electric Express*] will afford the user much greater pleasure than the trolley car, as it may be loaded and unloaded."

Had he been focusing entirely on the toy train market, he might have become just another also-ran. Instead, he built a practical, durable product that could run for hours at a time and, when he realized the toy market potential, followed up that small success with a toy of equal quality.

Trolleys clattered and clanged up and down the

Joshua Lionel Cowen's *Electric Express* gondola of 1902 was of wood construction—a "cigar box on wheels." Wire steps and "grab irons" were hammered into the wood. The box rode on a four-wheel frame powered by one of Cowen's electric fan motors. The steel track was sold in strips and pressed into slots 2⁷/₈ inches apart in the wood ties. *Train Collectors Association Toy Train Museum, Strasburg, Pennsylvania*

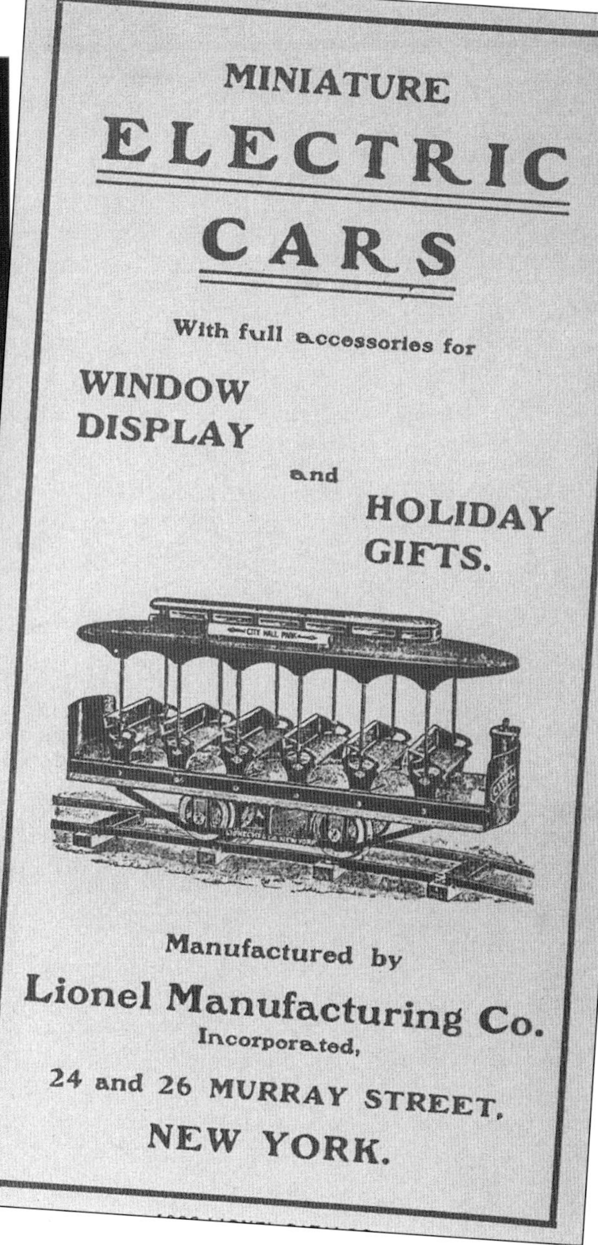

Lionel's 1902 catalog featuring its trolley for "window display" or "holiday gifts." *Train Collectors Association Toy Train Museum, Strasburg, Pennsylvania*

streets near his loft. The cars were open to accommodate women in billowing full skirts and picture hats as well as offering a cooler ride in summer. Lionel's model version of these popular cars featured a 15-inch long trolley body was built by the Morton E. Converse Company of Wichendon, Massachusetts, which had been building them for pull-toy and wind-up applications. Its large size favored keeping the wide 2⁷/₈-inch track. Harry Grant designed the new reversible, three-pole motor whose cleverly placed reverse lever looked like the trolley engineer's tiller. Grant would team up with Cowen full time in 1903 and remain as plant superintendent until 1910.

Also offered in that 1902 catalog was a two-foot-long suspension bridge for $1.50 in kit form—meaning Lionel didn't have to build it, just stock the parts. There were track switches for creating more complex layouts and a bumper for the end of a siding. Drawings showed how to hook up horrific electric-wire-and-sulfuric-acid power plants not unlike the contraptions in the Carlisle & Finch pages. Also shown were dry-cell batteries lashed together illustrating how four of them could run a trolley or *Electric Express* for 10 to 15 hours.

The alternative to purchased dry cells was a sorcerer's dream called the "Plunge Battery," described thus on page eight:

> . . . It consists of four glass jars, each containing a carbon cylinder and pencil-shaped zinc, similar to those commonly used for bellwork. They are put in a wooden box which measures 9 x 12 x 8 inches overall. The jars are charged with electric sand which may be purchased at any electrical supply house. Three pounds of sand added to three quarts of water make a full charge for the four cells. Cells are connected in series, that is, the carbon of one to the zinc of the other, as per cut on page seven. When battery is not in use, zincs should be lifted from the solution and the deposit on them wiped off with a wet cloth. If they are allowed to remain in the solution, they will be consumed. The jars must not touch, they should be kept apart. When the battery is connected, no metal whatsoever should be placed across the rails.

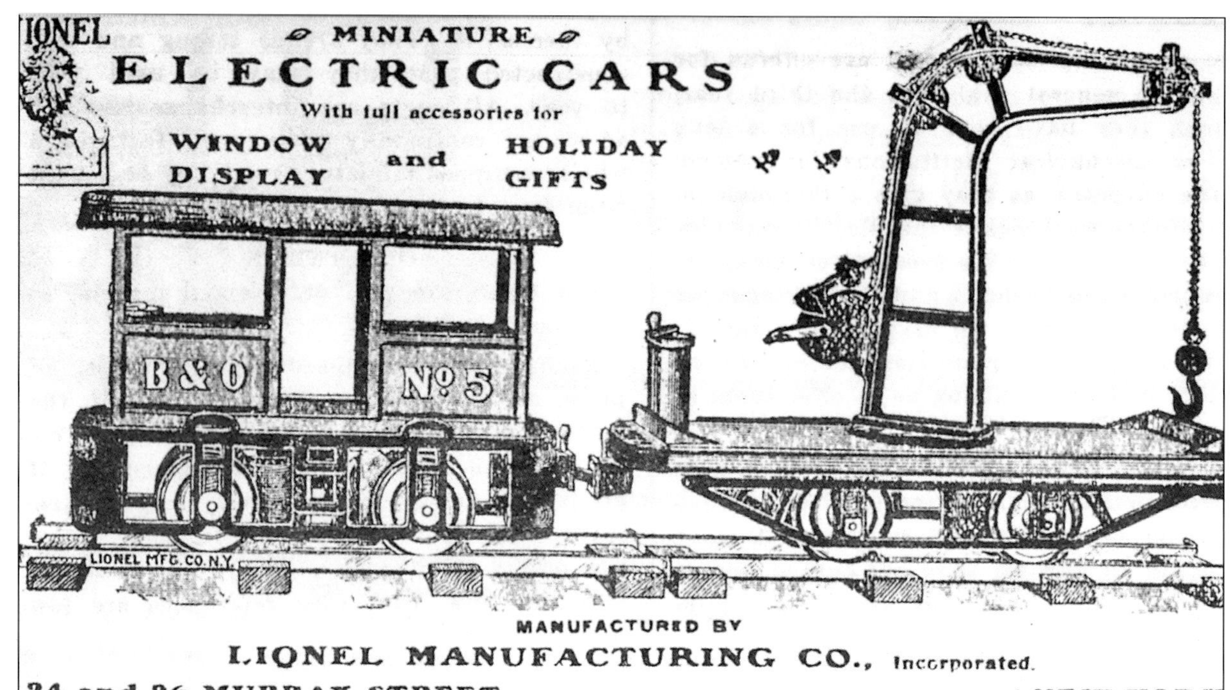

A reproduction of a page from the Lionel 1903 catalog showing Lionel's first locomotive together with the crane car that added "play value" to the line. *Train Collectors Association Toy Train Museum, Strasburg, Pennsylvania*

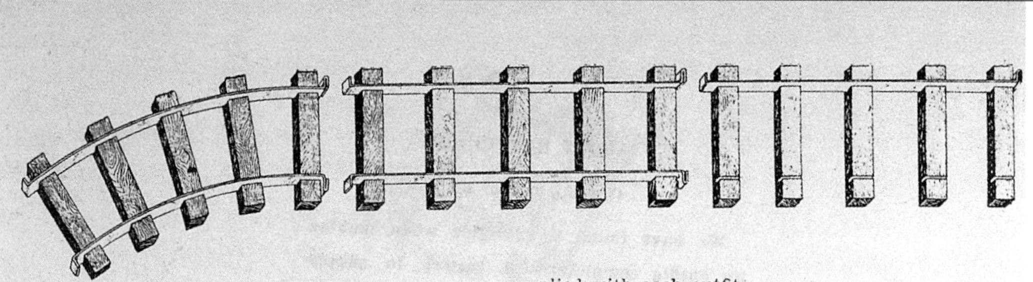

THE TRACK.

(Catalogue No. 310.)

The rails are cut in two lengths. To form a straight track, they should be used in pairs. To form a curve one of the shorter rails is used on the inside and the longer one on the outside. A complete circle is formed by using 8 sections of track. Twelve sections are supplied with each outfit.

The offsets on the ends of the rails should be turned outward and the ties spaced as per illustration. The rails must protrude about 1-8 inch beyond the ties. The sections are joined by sliding the "L" shaped end of one into the hook shaped end of the other.

Price of sets of track, including 30 feet of rail and 60 ties $1.50

Lionel track as described in the 1903 Lionel catalog. The rails were made of steel strips pressed into slots 2 ⅞ inches apart in the wood ties. *Train Collectors Association Toy Train Museum, Strasburg, Pennsylvania*

Later on, on page 15, a further alternative is described for lads who had electric current in the house and/or could not lay hands on sufficient quantities of "electric sand" to build the four-jar battery. This set of instructions is almost identical to the one provided the boys who put together a Carlisle & Finch outfit described earlier. It has enterprising boys with inquiring minds carving one-inch wide plates from sheets of lead, stringing 110-volt wires from lamp sockets, and lugging about large, sloppy glass jars of sulfuric acid and water.

By 1903, Cowen had the bit in his teeth and offered a locomotive based on the 1,800-horsepower Baltimore & Ohio electric locomotive that hauled cars though the Camden-Waverly Tunnel in Baltimore. Sweeping forward with his usual hooplah, Cowen's hype called the locomotive an "exact replica." Actually, it was shy four wheels of the prototype, rendering it more of a "homage" to the B&O prototype, but to pump up sales it was also nickel-plated. A beefed-up motor was installed in a special store deluxe window model that could run all day without eating itself alive.

The boxy gondolas were now made of metal and you could get a working crane car to couple onto your gondola train as well as 30 feet of strip rail and 60 ties. All of this could be had for a grand total of $7. Real train layouts with considerable play value could now be assembled by young engineers with the help of their local chemical supply shop.

In keeping with this expanding market, Cowen swiveled his gaze onto his competitors like a battleship turret and began lobbing hyperbolic vitriol on them—a technique very much in keeping with the rampant Yellow Journalism of that era. William Randolph Hearst had delivered up the

Spanish American War on a plate to readers of his newspapers with bombastic, jingoistic headlines and half-truth stories. Now, Cowen thundered forth about how these "unscrupulous manufacturers" had ineffectively tried to ". . . duplicate our outfits and sell the goods at lower prices." He continued this sniping throughout the days of Lionel's ascendancy.

Cowen's Lionel Manufacturing Company would become a giant as its founder continued to innovate, exercise his true gift as a merchandiser, and hire the best men for the eventual design studio, manufacturing plant, and the front office.

Ives Emerges

In 1900, a devastating fire ripped through the Ives Company plant at Bridgeport, Connecticut, burning it to the ground. Everything was destroyed: the inventory of cast iron pull-toys, toy components, tooling, dies, patterns—everything. The all-consuming blaze was actually a stroke of luck.

Harry and Edward Riley Ives started the company in 1868 at Plymouth, Connecticut. Their toy business grew rapidly, so the plant was moved to larger quarters in the industrial town of Bridgeport in 1870. Ten years later, Edward filed their first patents for cast-iron floor trains. Two other men, Jerome Secor and Francis Carpenter, were first at the patent office desk, but E. R. relentlessly either controlled or owned both their patents in a very short time.

Ives cast-iron floor trains were high-quality sets ranging in size from the 14-inch Hero trains including an engine, tender, and two passenger cars, to the 55-inch-long Cannonball Train, the largest (by Ives declaration) iron passenger train ever built. In 1893 it cost about $7.

By 1884, tin wind-up toys were the rage, and the Ives boys took out patents for their seven-inch Small Iron Locomotive with a wind-up motor powering the high-stepping red drive wheels. It was good-looking, it was powered, and it was still a floor train.

The big fire of 1900 and subsequent insurance payback allowed Ives to start with a clean slate. All around Ives new manufacturers were setting up shop. Carlisle & Finch was an established electric toy train builders, sending its expensive locomotives around complex layouts of steel strip track. A start-up down in New York City called Lionel was running electrified cigar boxes on strip track. And then there was the foreign competition. Maerklin and Bing offered both electric and wind-up trains for the American market. Their two-rail track was sectional, using pins in one track to join into hollow rail ends of the next section. Strip track had thin rails, providing extremely narrow points of electrical contact with the locomotive's wheels. Also, once the coil of strip track had been pressed into slotted ties to create a circle, it was very difficult to re-form those curves into straight track.

Ives was familiar with tracked trains. Ives had distributed Eugene Beggs' steamers that ran on track. Ives had also been involved with the Novelty

An Ives 1906 catalog cover featured the company's wind-up train, a dreamy lad watching it buzz past, and Spot, the faithful dog that always seemed to be hanging around train ads. *Train Collectors Association Toy Train Museum, Strasburg, Pennsylvania*

Electric Company in 1883 and had built toy electric motors in the 1880s. When it came to the crunch of competition, the elder Edward Ives decided on prudence and chose to adapt only one innovation at a time. Ives produced a wind-up train that ran on new sectional track in 1901. Edward's 32-year-old son Harry must have chafed at that decision, but his time would come nine years later when Edward relented, and Ives produced its first electric trains. By 1910, however, the competition had blossomed.

Of course, there was that noisy Cowen person with his clunky store display models and trolleys. Edward and Harry Ives were even making money off the newcomer, selling lithographed metal train stations to Lionel for resale. No real competition there.

Fuld's Voltamp Trains

Manes E. Fuld, founder of the Voltamp Manufacturing Company of Baltimore (an apt name in that era of burgeoning electrical products) built a model electric train for his son. On viewing the result and also becoming aware of the successes achieved by both Carlisle & Finch and Lionel, Fuld ordered a line of electric trains into production in 1903. Not hiding his lamp under a bushel, Fuld created steam-outline electric locomotives including a 4-4-0 steamer and a coal tender that measured 25 inches long and an 0-4-0 switcher with a four-wheel tender. His other steam locomotive was a very realistic 4-4-2 (Pacific type) that weighed in at 11 pounds and was 31 inches long. The prototype Pacific was just coming into use by major railroads for high-speed passenger service.

The model locomotive had a working headlight and built-in reverse lever, and its motor could haul a dozen of the 18-inch-long, 6-inch-high, 8-wheel wood and tinplate Voltamp passenger cars. This rolling stock was of elegant quality with etched windows and, following the prototype passenger cars of the period, oval windows where the toilets were located. Voltamp offered its own trolleys as well as an eight-wheel electric-outline locomotive patterned after New York Central's new electric locomotives that were hauling trains in and out of the then-under-construction new Grand Central Terminal. Track for the line was basic coiled steel-strips pressed into slotted wood ties with the rails two inches apart, becoming a member of the "Two-Inch Aristocracy."

Obviously, these Voltamp electric trains were marketed to America's "aristocracy," joining Carlisle & Finch as well as Howard and the Knapp Electric & Novelty Company, which introduced electric train lines in 1904. But why not? Under the leadership of Theodore Roosevelt, America had strode into the twentieth century in seven-league boots. Opportunities seemed endless. America was an international power after winning the Spanish-American War. Steel, banking, railroads, land development, and the new automobile industry were all growing and providing Young Tom's father with motivation to educate his son for a career, for a slice of the world's biggest, fattest pie.

No. 14. Rail Connector.

PRICE, 3c. Each. **By Mail, 4c. Each.**

For Strip Steel Track.

In order to make electrical connection between the ends of the rails when two or more sections of track are used, it is necessary to either solder wires to the rails and twist these wires together or to solder the rails themselves together, or what is probably the best way is to use these rail connectors. They are applied instantly, or removed with equal ease. The two rails are placed with their ends abutting and one of these connectors slipped up from beneath.

The piece of thin brass set into the wood block serves to make electrical connections between the two rails and also to hold them firmly in position. The small screw and washer should be placed on the outer side of the track so as to allow the battery wires to be attached.

———

Tracks and Ties (Strip Steel).

PRICE, 35c. One Set. **By Mail, 50c.**

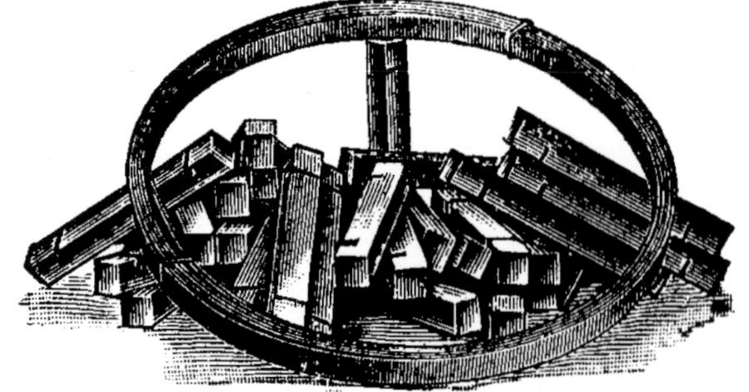

Carlisle & Finch trains ran on two inch-wide steel strip track that was sold in coils and pressed into slits in wood ties. Though the track was of bad design, C&F stuck with it long after everyone else had moved to hollow tubular track in two and three rails for better conductivity. *Train Collectors Association*

A Voltamp electric locomotive made in 1914 on display at the Train Collectors Association Toy Train Museum. It is modeled after a 4-6-2 Pacific-type locomotive used for high-speed passenger runs, weighs 21 pounds, and is 31 inches long including the tender. The locomotive has a working headlight and a powerful reversible motor capable of hauling a dozen 18-inch wood and steel passenger cars. *Train Collectors Association Toy Train Museum, Strasburg, Pennsylvania*

Track Gauges—and Three Rail—Established

Through all this, Joshua Cowen noted that no one was building any trains using the 2 7/8-inch separation between the rails (gauge) he had hit upon for his Lionel Lines track. Since 1904, everyone else was running on either 2-inch gauge, or 1-inch "O gauge," or the No. 1 gauge favored by the Europeans and his main competitor, Ives. In 1906, Cowen changed the gauge of his trains to 2 1/8 inches which he patented as "standard gauge," implying that any other gauge—Ives No. 1 gauge, for instance—was non-standard and presumably therefore somehow inferior.

Besides creating yet another gauge, the Lionel people settled the eventual "look" for all subsequent tinplate toy trains. Two-rail track requires complex wiring anytime track loops around and reconnects to itself, introducing the positive-negative problem of electricity flow and causing a short circuit. Carlisle & Finch's first trolley had run on three-rail track, but the company had abandoned the idea for more-realistic two-rail track. Cowen, ever seeking simplicity and better-running qualities, announced in his 1906 catalog, "Watch out for the Third Rail!" His standard gauge track, with its power always consistently coming down the center third rail, became the standard of the electric tinplate toy-train industry as Ives and American Flyer eventually followed Lionel's lead.

Enter the Transformer

As Lionel was figuring out the best way to get the power to the train from the track, its designers also came up with a better way to get power to the track. Another great leap forward in electric toy traindom was about to happen. Lionel conceived of the electric "transformer" to replace the trembling-hand business of dangling stripped electric lamp cords into jars of sulfuric acid and water to create a wet battery. Dry-cell batteries were expensive and had to be stockpiled if you wanted to keep running trains, as the dry cells died due to the ever-increasing size of the new locomotives and huge illuminated passenger cars.

With the transformer, direct 110-volt house current—the use of which was spreading across America—could power the train. Soft wire wound around a core took the voltage from a wall plug socket or screw-in lamp socket and reduced its potency to a range that safely operated the train. Lionel's 1906 design provided our young engineer friend, Tommy, with eight brass studs—called "taps"—arranged in an arc, over which passed an insulated lever. Each tap, from left to right, allowed more voltage to the track, increasing or decreasing the locomotive's speed. Now, instead of reaching into an acid bath and withdrawing a lead plate to stop the train, Tom had a real throttle.

Curiously, the transformer box had a marble finish and could be mounted on the wall like a decorative fixture. During a long operating session, the wire-wrapped core inside the box that reduced the voltage also radiated considerable heat. Young Tom quickly learned to keep sessions short or adopt gauntlet gloves worn by the real engineers to keep from searing his fingers. Also, as the lever was moved from tap to tap, the speed adjustment was jerky and tough on tiny passengers enjoying breakfast in the tin dining car. If the engineer wanted to reverse his train's direction, a manual lever was provided either on top of the locomotive or protruding from the back of the cab.

Lionel's steel strip track originally offered in 1900 was later formed into pre-assembled switches and bumper ends for stub sidings to allow for more-complex layouts. *Train Collectors Association*

By 1912, Lionel added a separate rheostat, a sliding bar that traversed two steel rods in a simple frame. This device allowed the speed to be increased or decreased gradually as the bar was moved up and down the pair of rods. By now they called their system "Multi-Volt" transformers.

The heat, the jerky performance, the lack of a remote-control reverse would all be solved eventually, but even these early transformers became a critical stride forward in popularizing the electric toy train.

American Flyer Is Born—and Hafner Reborn

But for all this feverish growth in the American toy train marketplace, they were still operating in the shadow of European competition. German toy sales increased from just over $4 million in 1901 to $7.6 million in 1910 according to the 1911 edition of *Playthings*, the trade magazine of the industry. And not without good reason. The European products had a much longer heritage and—in the upscale marketplace—looked more "finished" than even the best American offerings. European accessories—signals, stations, houses,

Lionel abandoned its original two-rail track with this announcement in its 1906 catalog for easier-to-set-up three-rail track. Some prototype electric railways also used power coming from a center rail, so Joshua Lionel felt justified. *Train Collectors Association*

freight depots, bridges, tunnels, and lighting—were dazzling in their variety and colorful appeal.

Even though Americans who bought the German trains did not seem to mind their European styling, Maerklin and Bing—the largest foreign manufacturers—began sending over American-style trains with American road names on the passenger cars and cow-catchers bolted on the front. By 1910, Bing had announced an office to be opened in New York for direct sales. "Over there" was coming over here, and American toy train manufacturers could feel the heat.

Of all the manufacturers, Ives seemed the most beleaguered. Since 1901, it had been producing low-price wind-up trains running on two-rail O gauge track. This track was only 1¼ inches wide, keeping the size and production cost of the trains low. In 1907, William Hafner—also producing wind-up O gauge trains in a considerably smaller volume—met with William Ogden Coleman who owned a piece of Edmunds-Metzel, a farmers' hardware company. Hafner wanted Coleman's financial backing for mass production. Coleman was skeptical about the investment, so Hafner took a sample of his train line and track to a New York toy distributor, the respected firm of Steinfeld Brothers. Steinfeld loved his trains and wrote up an order worth $15,000—and these are 1907 dollars.

Coleman was suitably impressed and not only offered to back Hafner financially but eventually turned the entire production capability of Chicago-based Edmunds-Metzel from farm products to wind-up trains. By 1910, William Hafner was running the toy train side of the business, and the name was changed to American Flyer. These cast-iron wind-up trains were strong competitors, and the low-end line continued into 1935, though the final steamers showed their Depression-era cheapness in cheesy stamped steel with few realistic frills. But, in 1914, William Hafner had split from Coleman's American Flyer and was once again running his own shop, the Hafner Manufacturing Company, producing wind-up trains with the Overland Flyer name emblazoned on the lithographed coal tenders and passenger cars. This line would continue into the 1950s.

The Competition Heats Up

The year 1910 saw the J. K. Osborne Manufacturing Company roll out its Elektoy line of electric trains running on No. 1 gauge—rails 1¾ inches apart—in direct competition with the German No. 1 gauge models. Now, Ives found themselves facing heavy competition in all price ranges. In 1904, to combat European imports, Ives had introduced

Georges Carette & Company of Nuremburg, Germany, produced a beautiful finished line of O gauge electric trains. This train would have competed directly with Lionel and Ives for American dollars had it been let into the country during World War I. Its 1915 steeple-cab, electric-outline locomotive tows a European "goods wagons" and "guard's van" all of colorful lithographed steel. The obvious European styling did not deter pre-war American buyers who considered German toys superior to those of American manufacture. *Train Collectors Association Toy Train Museum, Strasburg, Pennsylvania*

An *Overland Flyer* train from William Hafner poses with one Chicago & North Western passenger car, correctly displaying the prototype's yellow and green livery. In "real life," C&NW and the Union Pacific railroads together operated passenger service between Chicago and the West Coast via Omaha, Nebraska, and Ogden, Utah—the Overland Route. Hafner locomotives were always key-winders and had good, strong motors that lasted for decades. *Don Roth collection*

large and expensive No. 1-gauge locomotives and cars. Typically for Ives, the first of these was a wind-up-run steam engine, an 11-inch-long 4-4-0 brute cast in two pieces—the largest wind-up track train ever built, trumpeted Ives. Now, with only a wind-up "large" scale train, it faced the Europeans from without and Elektoy from within.

The Elektoy electric "tank" locomotive—no coal tender; the coal and water on the prototype were carried on the engine—featured polished nickel-plating and was lithographed in bright colors. Osborne offered two types of four-color lithographed trolleys, four freight cars, and both Pullman and combination passenger cars. Distribution was primarily through hardware and small electrical supply stores—a drawback as department stores became rich outlets for the toy trade.

The April 1907 edition of *Playthings* announced that the American Miniature Railway Company—founded by two former Ives employees—was opening a manufacturing plant in Ives' home town of Bridgeport to produce an electric O gauge line. That particularly sharp spur of competition finally moved the conservative Ives into action. Ives sent its designers to the drawing boards and, in 1910, the company offered its first O gauge line of electric trains: a steam locomotive, an electric-outline locomotive based on New York Central S-class electric locomotives, and, as was the trend, a trolley. Ives' very low-key announcement read:

> The Ives Mfg. Corp. are now showing for the first time their new Ives miniature electric railway system. A great deal of time and money has been spent perfecting this line, and the manufacturer is justly enthusiastic over the results obtained.

Lionel offered no O gauge trains in 1910, and now the toy giant, Ives, was committing its resources to this smaller, low-cost, high-profit line. Cowen was too good a businessman to let this go unnoticed. He looked at his growing and profitable toy train company and wondered if this would be a good time to bail for a good price. Cowen was a young man of 29 with years of new ventures in front of him should he choose to unload Lionel. He decided to visit the 71-year-old patriarch, Edward Ives, and propose a deal.

The elder Ives, who rode to work in a horse and buggy, still questioned the decision of his son, Harry, to get into electric trains in the first place. Now, here was this upstart, Cowen, wanting to sell Ives the keys to Lionel. Edward Ives wanted none of it. Cowen walked out the door with his deal still in his pocket. He would stay in the game. Almost 20 years later, he would sit down opposite Ives bankruptcy receivers with a different proposal altogether.

Feeling the heat on its neck from the large-scale electric train manufacturers, Ives finally offered its first No. 1 gauge electric locomotive—the No. 3240—in 1912. This was an electric-outline locomotive similar to the NYC S-class electrics used to haul trains into New York City. The first train sets offered were made up of passenger cars followed by the 7000 line of freight cars. In 1915 Lionel finally launched a line of O gauge trains that competed directly with Ives. Cowen could step into this low end of the market with confidence because the German imports had been taken out of the race by that great slaughter across the Atlantic, World War 1.

Train Wars in the Trenches

The period between 1914 and 1921 was a watershed for the American toy train industry.

A. C. Gilbert conceived the idea for the Erector construction set after observing the New Haven Railroad erecting new steel catenary (overhead wire) support towers for its New York City–New Haven (Connecticut) electrification project in 1913. American Flyer trains would join Erector in the 1930s when Gilbert acquired the O gauge American Flyer train line from William Coleman. After World War II, Gilbert and his son would briefly propel American Flyer trains to stardom by creating a unique niche for S gauge–a size embraced by those who felt O gauge was too large and cumbersome. *Don Heimberger*

The 1917 Lionel Military Train sweeps its twin cannons across the tracks to slay the dastardly Hun. This train was offered for one year and was very popular. It was a novelty act capitalizing on patriotic fervor as the United States entered World War I. *Train Collectors Association Toy Train Museum, Strasburg, Pennsylvania*

When the New York Central began electrifying its lines into New York City in 1903 to reduce pollution and be able to use extensive tunnelwork for its new Grand Central Terminal, it relied on a fleet of 47 electric locomotives that became known as "S-motors." NYC 100, shown in Grand Central in 1985, was the original, and the S-motors in general were widely replicated by toy-train manufacturers. *Jim Boyd*

Ives Model 3250 electric locomotive was modeled—as were most of the "electric outline" locomotives of the period by several manufactures—after the New York Central S-Class electrics that hauled cars in and around "smoke-free" Manhattan. This locomotive was offered in O gauge from 1918 to 1925. *Train Collectors Association Toy Train Museum, Strasburg, Pennsylvania*

German toy train imports to America were cut off as the Kaiser's troops cut a swath across France and Belgium. Though the United States was neutral in policy, the majority of citizens and their government were allied with Britain and France in spirit and with funds. As the war bogged down in the trenches, America's role as eventual stalemate breaker became clear to both sides.

By 1916, the British and Germans had fed a whole generation of their young men into the battlefield grinders. President Wilson's resolve to keep the U.S. out of war was weakening, and America's industries were making plans for war against Germany. The toy train industry was also caught up in the changes that were taking place.

With the import weight off their backs, 68 toy manufacturers joined to become the Toy Manufacturers of the U.S.A. Alfred Carlton Gilbert, who manufactured the very popular Erector construction sets, became president. Gilbert, a fast-on-his-feet dynamic entrepreneur, would eventually buy up American Flyer and revitalize the name. William Hafner and Flyer's William Coleman were also members. Harry Ives served as Gilbert's successor for three years.

Sitting on the outside looking in was the man whose company would eventually buy up both Ives and American Flyer, Joshua Lionel Cowen. Never a member of the old boys' club of toy makers, he also never forgot the slight. Cowen embraced the war with relish and turned its martial spirit to his marketing advantage.

"Play War!" Cowen trumpeted to his youthful marketplace in the 1917 catalog. "Bring Up the Siege Guns on Tracks! Best fun yet, boys! Now, there's bushels of fun ahead! You can be a general just like the soldiers in Europe. . ."

Unfortunately, the generals in Europe were still fighting with nineteenth century textbooks. But as our troops were drawing their rifles and helmets for the long boat ride to the trenches, Cowen sent forth his own version of "new, terrifying siege guns" in the form of a military train proclaiming that the "bodies of these monsters are made of heavy sheet steel." The olive-drab O gauge train was headed by a locomotive that resembled a battleship turret mounted on a tank body riding on four flanged wheels. Two guns poked forward as it towed two supply cars behind it—"an exact replica of the real thing." In fact, there was nothing like it over there. But with this armored aberration, young soldiers could

Elektoy introduced its line of No.1 gauge trains in 1910. The company lasted until 1917. Limited distribution outlets and wartime raw materials sealed the company's doom. This polished and plated 0-4-0 locomotive competed directly with the European imports and Ives. Its passenger cars are lithographed steel, and the *Richmond* car in the center is particularly rare today. *Train Collectors Association Toy Train Museum, Strasburg, Pennsylvania*

clear the tracks of the dreaded Hun.

Not content with devastating the Germans with artillery fire, Cowen once again opened up on his competitors with broadsides in that same 1917 edition. He took young readers on a "trip through my factory." In the process of showing how Lionel trains were superior in workmanship, and without naming names, he ripped Ives' lithographed details. "This is a very cheap process. The color chips off in flakes . . . There is no joy in getting a cast iron electric locomotive," he went on, "You are always expecting it to fall to pieces." Regarding car manufacturing processes using two or more matching pieces, he assessed the construction method as "extremely shaky, flimsy and rickety and will easily fall apart . . . and the car will soon be a wreck in the ash box." He warned buyers that shady store owners would use Lionel boxes to lure unsuspecting types into their stores then perform the old bait-and-switch to peddle a cheaper train set. "Ask if it is Lionel and look at the label 'sharp.' Get what you ask for!" In every comparison case, Cowen showed Ives lowest cost line next to Lionel's finest. Ives' cars were mangled wrecks while Lionel was pristine.

When Ives used the word "standard" in small type in its price list, Cowen shot off a written rocket admonishing poor Harry Ives to observe some "fair treatment" in using Lionel's patented word. Exasperated, Ives responded, citing Lionel's unfair depiction of competing trains—notably those built by Ives.

With charming chutzpah, Cowen in effect told Ives to stop whining. . . There were no logos on any of the trains shown. Many makers use two-

Lionel "evidence" that "inferior" die-cast locomotives shatter when dropped compared to Lionel's stamped steel. Also, the die-cast locomotive is heavier though smaller than a Lionel—although Dorfan used this point in reverse, hailing better traction and pulling power. Finally, Lionel's motor is heavier than a rival which proves . . . ? *Train Collectors Association Toy Train Museum, Strasburg, Pennsylvania*

motors at high motors are his man.

is strongly , and you

Jumpers

of gravity" This means ose to the his weight l the body ng—makes

d With

ıfacture of has weight;

tive grip the track without loss of power."

But think a minute! It isn't the weight of the body of the locomotive, but the size and weight of the motor, its wheels and its low center of gravity which makes the wheels take hold. Consequently we show this picture (figure 30) of a cast iron locomotive and a Lionel locomotive to illustrate the difference in total weight. Remember, too,

Fig. 29—Smash! There goes the cast iron locomotive—broken into fifteen pieces. The Lionel is only dented.

that bearings wear out very rapidly when the axles are compelled to carry a heavy cast iron body.

Figure 31.—This photograph illustrates how much heavier our motor is in comparison

Fig. 30—Proof that cast iron locomotive (on right) is heavier than the Lionel (on left) although the latter is larger in every way.

with the cast iron locomotive motor. Thus the tractive power of any locomotive depends upon the weight of the wheels, truck and mechanism, and not in the superstructure. In this respect Lionel locomotives are faithful models of the great electric locomotives of the prominent electrified railroads of America. The newest types have still smaller superstructures than any previously built by these big

Fig. 31—Proof that Lionel motor on left, heavier than the other (see text).

9

A collection of Carlisle & Finch trains and trolleys including the Model 45, left foreground, and an ore train, right foreground. They are running on the original coiled steel track. By 1916, the Model 45 had been made cheaper and profits from trains were lagging. C&F was making money with searchlight contracts for the government, so the train line was shut down for good. *Carlisle & Finch collection, Cincinnati, Ohio*

and three-piece construction as opposed to Lionel's one-piece designs. And as for the whimpering finger pointing at Lionel's demonstration of their own three-rail track supporting 110 pounds while the 'un-named' three-rail junk came apart under the stress of only 20 pounds, demos such as that, if you will permit us to say so, has done a great deal to raise the quality demanded by the public for better constructed toy roadbed. So there.

Looking closely at the "demo" photo, the 110-pound weight is supported from a wide leather strap across a standard-gauge rail while the offending destroyed track is smaller, less robust O gauge, and the 20 pounds is suspended by a thin wire. Cowen went on to further beat up on Ives over the use of "standard" in any literature since Lionel had become linked with the word as in "standard gauge" and "standard of the world." Ives capitulated and promised to exorcise the word from its price lists. Cowen accepted the acquiescence and removed the offending product comparisons from future catalogs.

As war production geared up, Cowen's quality production processes so impressed the government that Lionel was awarded several defense contracts and switched over to building compass binnacles and navigational equipment for ships. Lionel would be in an excellent cash position when the war ended.

Its competitor, Carlisle & Finch, developed the first horizontal arc searchlight along with its other electric motor dynamo products. In 1916, while working with government contracts for warships, C&F realized the opportunities that the

The Burlington *Zephyr* would be big news in 1934, and most of the train makers were offering a model. Though Carlisle & Finch had departed the toy-train market in 1910, the advent of streamliners in 1934 inspired the company to assemble this production prototype with an eye to stepping back into the electric train market. The plans were scrapped, however, and the firm stayed on course with its growing line of naval and marine navigation lights and aids for which they are know worldwide today. *Carlisle & Finch collection, Cincinnati, Ohio*

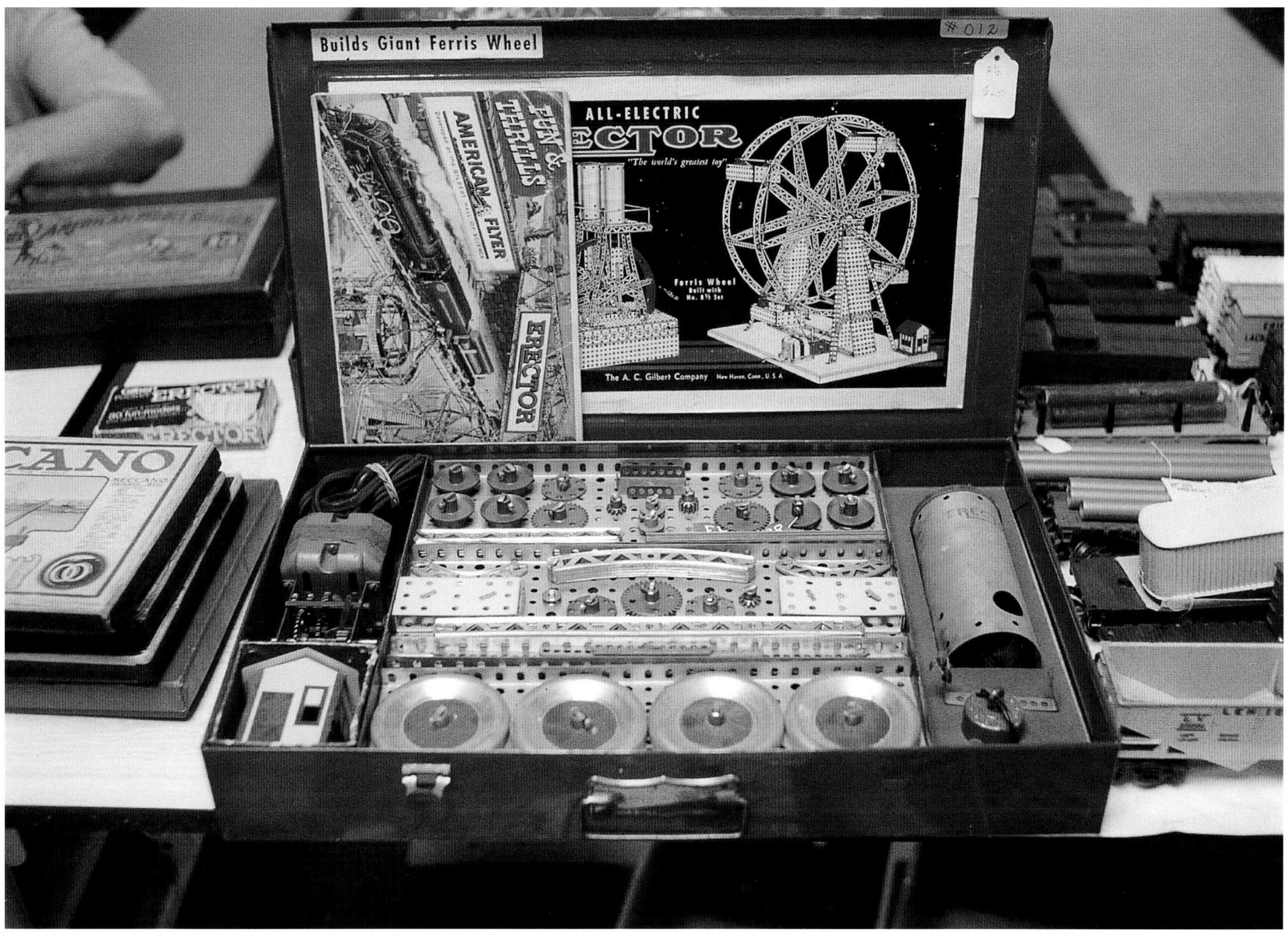

marine lighting market would offer following the war. Since 1909, C&F had been downsizing the number of toy train products in their line. The magnificent Model 45 steam engine had been cheapened, and competition was forcing price cuts. That same year C&F shut down its toy train line for good. Carlisle & Finch turned away from electric train production and never went back except for a mild flirtation with some elegant electric streamliners and steam locomotive prototypes built in 1934 but never put into production. Today, C&F furnishes the lights for Coast Guard lighthouses as well as a full line of marine searchlights and illumination products instead of the finest electric trains money—lots of it—could buy.

Elektoy folded its cards in 1917. Wartime restrictions on manufacturing materials and Elektoy's limited distribution channels doomed the company.

Harry Ives was badgered by Edward Hurley, chairman of the U.S. Shipping Board, to build a line of toy boats powered by the durable wind-up motor. With Hurley's patriotic admonitions in their ears—". . . every play ship we put in the hands of an American boy helps us put real ships in the ocean . . ."—Ives plodded off into what would become a dead-end business that helped drain the company coffers.

Although the A. C. Gilbert Company is often more closely associated with American Flyer trains than anything else, the Erector Set was for many years the foundation of the New Haven-based company. A complete A. C. Gilbert No. 8½ Erector Set in its metal case is a collector's item at a Train Collectors Association meeting in Addison, Illinois. *Train Collectors Association*

A lineup reflecting the "Big Four" O gauge electric-train manufacturers of the of the Roaring Twenties. Top row: A nifty little freight set from Dorfan, a newcomer to the American scene early in the 1920s . Second row: An Ives set with an electric-outline locomotive inspired by prototype New York Central S-class electric locomotives serving New York's Grand Central Terminal. Third row: A Lionel passenger set with a steam-outline locomotive featuring the new Lionel logo that was destined to become a long-lived classic. Fourth row: The American Flyer No. 3116 center-cab Bipolar-type locomotive made of stamped sheet steel and with track-activated reverse. This locomotive was available between 1928 and 1930. *Train Collectors Association Toy Train Museum, Strasburg, Pennsylvania*

Chapter 4

Toy Trains Roll Into the Roaring Twenties

The national roller coaster ride that took place during the 1920s and 1930s was equally chaotic for the toy train industry. When our Tommy came marching home from the bloody trenches of 1918, he was now Tom in search of work. Thousands of Tommys and Johnnys and Amelios and Gustavs came home in 1919 to find war industries winding down—and labor unions protesting salary cuts after the prosperity of overtime cash during the war years. Women had won the right to vote, and the country was officially "dry" by decree of the Volstead Act. The settled life of pre-World War I America was over, and the Jazz Age was approaching. Wages were rising, and credit-purchasing plans were putting luxuries like radios, gramophones, and sewing machines into once-austere homes. It was a time for innovation and invention, and toy train manufacturers were busy making considerable adjustments of their own.

American Flyer in Chicago joined the O gauge competition by introducing its first electric-powered steam locomotives in 1919. The company had modified its best cast-iron wind-up engine—the one having the largest boiler—with an electric motor.

The Twenties Start Roaring

Joshua Cowen had to put his postwar sales campaign on hold because the printers' strike of 1919 shut down his big new catalog. In a letter of apology to his young "boy friends," he vowed, "Next season I will have that catalog printed if I have to buy a printing plant and print it myself." That "next season" saw explosive sales gains for Lionel as its premium standard-gauge train sets captured the market through quality manufacture and never-ending hype.

Despite the progress women were making toward equal rights, it must be noted that toy trains had solidified into strictly a "guy thing." Fathers and sons, "toys for the boy," and other such phraseology were tie-ins deliberately aimed at the traditional family breadwinner who earned the money that could make "...a boy's wish come true." "Which Lionel do you want, son?" signified a bond that excluded daughters. In toy train ads beginning at the turn-of-the-century and passing down to contemporary times, daughters are considered an admiring audience, applauding their brother's skill at handling railroad operations, ". . . just like a real engineer." In catalogs, Sis actually got less photo space than the family dog. If

A big, green "wide (standard) gauge" Dorfan electric-outline locomotive based on the Milwaukee Road's round-hood Bipolar electrics that hauled the *Olympian* and *Columbian* passenger trains over Western mountains. This Model 3930 was made between 1928 and 1930 as a "Loco-Builder," or take-apart engine, that featured ball-bearing axles. *Train Collectors Association Toy Train Museum, Strasburg, Pennsylvania*

RIGHT: "Real Enough for a Man to Enjoy—Simple Enough for a Boy to operate" was the Lionel message for 1927 in this magazine ad. *Train Collectors Association Toy Train Museum, Strasburg, Pennsylvania*

BELOW: Lionel's "kneeling boy" was none other than Joshua Lionel Cowen's son, Lawrence, as interpolated by an artist. Dating from circa 1930, the ad features standard-gauge trains and shows Cowen's name as president. Note that the "dandy transformer" for only $3.40 is "cheaper than batteries." You would have to buy batteries by the crate to run those huge locomotives. Besides, if Dad could afford a standard-gauge train, it can be assumed the house was wired for electricity. *Train Collectors Association Toy Train Museum, Strasburg, Pennsylvania*

Mom managed to squeeze into a shot, it was as a doting parent who was fulfilled by the wisdom of her husband's buying decision and the obvious pleasure of the young male heir.

Cowen had a daughter, Isabel, and as tradition demanded, had pegged her older brother, Lawrence, as heir apparent to the Lionel business. The young man had already posed for the "kneeling boy" illustrations used as a basis for an early catalog illustration. By the time the Roaring Twenties unfolded, Lawrence was enamored with the stock market and spending bags of Dad's money. In their youth, Isabel was not allowed to touch Lawrence's electric trains, but, according to Ron Hollander in his book about Cowen and Lionel entitled *All Aboard*, she seemed to have the mechanical knack her brother lacked. Says Hollander, ". . . as in so many families, Isabel was probably would have done as well, or better than Lawrence at the throttle of the Lionel Express."

The 1930 Lionel catalog, showing 47 pages of electric trains and accessories, featured an electric stove for little homemakers on its back page. This porcelain-clad lure to the opposite sex featured an oven and two working burners. Its price was almost $30—the cost of some full-size appliances as the Depression began to squeeze the economy. To many people, that was a week's wages when a doll could be bought for $2. Cowen's granddaughter, Cynthia, got a stove, but his sortie into the female market fell flat. This lapse would repeat itself decades later in the form of Lionel's famous pink locomotive.

Lionel and Ives Duke It Out

Another effect of the war's end was the return of European products to the marketplace. Actually, it was the absence of these products that spooked American toy manufacturers as Germany's postwar inflation started in 1921 and began to crush the Deutschemark. The Germans refused to make production commitments because the estimated cost of making the trains would be inflated by the time they were ready to be delivered, wiping out any profit. By this time, American manufacturers had increased their prices to match the escalating estimates from across the Atlantic. Department store buyers and jobbers were caught in the middle. Huge inventories sat in warehouses awaiting nervous buyers' orders.

Ives chose this moment to introduce its new line of "wide gauge" locomotives. Wide gauge was Ives' version of the 2⅛-inch gauge Lionel called "standard." This time, Ives fired off a stirring announcement to appear in the January 1921 issue of *Playthings*, the flack magazine of the toy industry that was, as usual, printed without comment.

"The Ives Manufacturing Corporation have brought out their new line of 2⅛-inch Gauge electric trains." Ives used 2½ inches, No. 2 gauge, and wide gauge interchangeably though the track measurement between the rails was 2⅛ inches, the same as Lionel's standard gauge. The article went on: "These trains are a marvelously correct reproduction of original motors. A photograph of one of their large electric locomotives placed alongside a photograph of a New York Central electric locomotive of the same type looks as if they have been made from the same object."

Cowen looked over his shoulder at his rival who was tooting an uneasy horn at indifferent buyers and then watched Lionel designers find room in their No. 42 electric-outline locomotive for another motor. Lionel's 1921 ads hyped the innovation as ". . . being sold at the price of single motor locomotives."

Following a brief recession that started in 1921 resulting in slashed orders and overstocked inventories, the 1920s began racing past, stoked by soaring stocks, bathtub gin, hot jazz, and credit buying. The toy train manufacturers had solved most of their technical problems. Three-rail track was universal for electric trains. Getting electrical power to the track was made easier using transformers, and new, powerful locomotives could haul strings of heavyweight steel passenger and freight cars. By 1924, the market had sorted out into: Lionel leading the electric train pack, with Ives lurching along in second place with new wide-gauge and O gauge electric models as well as its wind-up line; Ives being challenged by American Flyer in both O gauge electric and less-expensive wind-up trains; Hafner in its own niche of wind-up trains—colorful, charming and very cheap—that just kept selling.

Lionel was heading profitably toward its silver jubilee year, 25 years since the wood cigar box circled around the show window of Ingersol's Toy Store. Lionel was in peak form with festivities planned. And then, remarkably, Ives spoiled Lionel's party.

Until 1924, if a young engineer wanted to reverse the direction of his electric train, he had to stop it, crawl across the carpet to where it was stopped, and flip a manual reverse lever located on the locomotive. Ives changed all that.

Two gentlemen, H. P. Sparks and B. A. Smith, worked out a way that the engineer could reverse his locomotive from the transformer. Breaking the current to the locomotive released a shaft that, when current was restored, caused a pawl to pull up on a gear and rotate a little drum to a new set of contacts. The new contacts reversed the electricity flow and the direction of the locomotive. If the locomotive was to continue along its original path once brought to a halt, the engineer did a quick start-stop-start with the throttle to resume. Their invention was so well conceived that during the "stop" portion of the sequence, the locomotive's lights remained on. They licensed this technology to Ives.

Customers were astounded. Ives raised the price for locomotives equipped with the remote reversing mechanism and sales soared. Now it was Lionel's turn to stumble around someone else's patents. Two years later, in 1926, Lionel pushed its own reverse mechanism out the door. Unfortunately, Lionel's solution, cobbled together under intense pressure from the executive office, eliminated the "stop" step. Eight feet of standard gauge *Dinner Express* to Chicago could be thundering westward along the main at 90 miles per hour, and if the current was broken for a fraction of a second, for whatever reason, the whole train suddenly slammed into full reverse at 90 miles per hour causing it (if the motor didn't self-destruct first) to become the *Cadaver Express* to New York City.

Joshua Cowen's gift for painting a smiley face

"Ives Trains make Happy Boys" ad in a 1920 *Boy Scout* magazine shows chummy lads working with their wide-gauge Ives train overlooking a real rail yard in the valley. A kid whose parents could afford that train would live in the big house on the hill. *Train Collectors Association Toy Train Museum, Strasburg, Pennsylvania*

Wind-up trains were introduced in the nineteenth century and continued to be popular until the 1960s and 1970s. This collection pulled by cast-iron locomotives represents examples of models from the 1920s. At top is a Dorfan passenger train from 1920. Second from the top is by Hafner, 1928 (Hafner only made wind-up trains). American Flyer made the red locomotive and cars in 1925, and the bottom set is an Ives product from 1920. *Train Collectors Association Toy Train Museum, Strasburg, Pennsylvania*

on a horses *derierre* came to the fore once again as Lionel ad copy expounded, ". . . The mechanism is so perfect, that when the lever of the control rheostat is quickly lowered and raised twice, the train will continue in the direction in which it ran before being stopped." It was under some fatherly scrutiny that our Tom's Tommy Jr. learned how not to turn $50 worth of shiny standard-gauge locomotive into a bad-smelling 12-pound doorstop with a fried motor. Of course, Cowen hated being second best in anything.

If he could have seen Ives' accounting books, even after the reverse mechanism was on the market for a couple of years, the torment would have been bearable. Ives was going broke. Having been slow to recognize electricity as the new motive power, having turned away Joshua Cowen's deal to buy Lionel, having come out of World War 1 without a war contract cash cushion, having been led down the "patriotic" path of producing wind-up tin boats that were unprofitable, and having come up with a killer technology too late to do any good to its hemorrhaging accounts, Harry Ives stepped down from the presidency, and a new administration tried to save the company.

This Fandor 1012 set was built by the German company that eventually became Dorfan in the U.S. The name comes from Milton and Julius Forchhiemer's mother's two sisters, Fanny and Dora. *Train Collectors Association Toy Train Museum, Strasburg, Pennsylvania*

Dorfan: German Technology, American Born

Ives' new leaders might have saved the company had it not been for William Coleman's Chicago-based American Flyer and a new company called Dorfan. Milton and Julius Forchheimer were toymakers from Nuremberg, Germany and were part of the Joseph Kraus & Company firm that began making toys back in 1910. Borrowing the first names of their mother's two sisters, Fanny and Dora, they had created the Fandor line of trains. World War 1 had devastated German industry and paralyzed the economy, so in 1923, Milton and Julius talked their chief engineer, John C. Koerber, into joining them in flight from a collapsing Deutschemark across the Atlantic to America.

Once in this country, they moved into the top two floors of a three-story commercial building in Newark, New Jersey, to build toy trains. To divorce themselves from the Germanic Fandor line, they ingenuously wordsmithed a new company name by swapping the sisters' names. Dorfan began production in 1924.

A glance around the American toy train landscape revealed formidable competition for two guys from Nuremberg, but the economy was taking off, and these German boys knew their business. They began by making better trains for less money. To this feat they added "educational" value to their models in keeping with the new "progressive teaching" then sweeping America. Joshua Cowen, William Coleman, and William Hafner watched intently.

To build better trains for less money than the competition, Dorfan turned to precision die-casting. American manufacturers had used iron casting for years, and most low-end wind-up

A CORNER IN THE ASSEMBLING DEPARTMENT of the Dorfan factory, where capable swift fingered young women are putting Dorfan cars together.

A glimpse of one end of the machine shop at the Dorfan Factory.

A CORNER OF OUR TESTING LABORATORY showing a Dorfan Loco-Builder Engine in the course of one of the electrical tests. The dials register the results of these tests.

Where Loco-Builder Is Built

THE Dorfan Loco-Builder Engine and Dorfan Trains are strictly "Made in America" products. Every part is designed and made in our factory at Newark, New Jersey. Back of the Loco-Builder idea, and back of all Dorfan products, is the experience of many, many years in the making of metal toys. The men who design Dorfan toys and who superintend the making of them have spent a lifetime in the toy business. And they are in that business because of a love for it.

In the designing of the Dorfan toys, engineering skill of the highest type is employed in the endeavor to put into them the same conscientious effort employed in making real, lifesize locomotives.

The Dorfan factory located in a quiet street skirting the manufacturing section of Newark, is thronged with enthusiastic young workers who put heart and soul into the thought of producing something to bring keen pleasure to young America.

Every Dorfan product, whether electrical or otherwise, goes through a series of tests before leaving the factory that makes it proof against defect. And the Dorfan guarantee is a binding one.

The Dorfan factory shown in the 1926 catalog. It actually occupied only the third floor of the building shown. Much hand work kept manufacturing costs high even though die-casting was the company's chief claim to fame. *Train Collectors Association Toy Train Museum, Strasburg, Pennsylvania*

locomotives still came out of two-piece dies. But Dorfan used what they called "Dorfan Alloy" made of copper and zinc to make large locomotive sections that included considerably more sharp detail than possible with the cast-iron process. Dorfan claimed one of its locomotives could be hurled at a concrete floor and it would not break. For its motors, the zinc castings formed their own shaft bearings since the alloy was naturally slick, eliminating the need for added bearing parts. These hefty, die-cast wide-gauge electric locomotives consistently out-performed Lionel equipment.

Dorfan's low-end mechanical wind-up motors used a long-running spring that employed a device which ran at a constant speed regardless of the load behind the locomotive. The more expensive motors offered a brake that held the drive wheels locked while the motor was wound. The cost of a complete Dorfan electric-outline, O gauge wind-up train, including the tinplate locomotive with its little pantograph, a passenger car, and four sections of two-rail track was $1.

Like the other manufacturers, Dorfan offered expensive, mid-range, and low-end electric trains that came in wide (standard) gauge, or narrow (O) gauge sets. To enhance the play value of the so-called narrow-gauge trains, the locomotives could be taken apart and reassembled by a kid with a screwdriver. These "Loco-Builder" engines won great approval from parents in 1925.

Cowen, who always considered competitors as presumptuous when they infringed on his hard-won turf, reintroduced the 1919 "Bild-A-Loco" concept to his 1928 line, featuring one O gauge and two standard-gauge electric-outline locomotives

BELOW: A Dorfan Model 55 "steam outline" electric locomotive that ran on "narrow gauge" track. Dorfan was able to cram an electric motor into its die-cast wind-up locomotives. It used the term "narrow gauge" to describe O gauge and to be consistent with its "wide gauge" label used for standard-gauge track. The Model 55 is often seen with this unique six-wheel tender, and some 55s had built-in circuit-breaker mechanisms. *Train Collectors Association Toy Train Museum, Strasburg, Pennsylvania*

INSET: Original 1927 Dorfan catalog cover. *Courtesy, Train Collectors Association Toy Train Museum, Strasburg, Pennsylvania*

(the No. 9 and the 381U). Lionel even went Dorfan one better by allowing the motors to be used to power its construction set that competed with A. C. Gilbert's Erector Sets.

Dorfan's "Locomotive Builder" locomotives, reduced to only 15 parts, were offered as kits in compartmentalized boxes and touted as true educational toys to thoughtful parents who equated "play" and "education". Another feature of Dorfan's passenger cars were the three-dimensional passengers framed in each window. Each head had a distinctive profile and rarely seemed to repeat in the same car. Couplers between the cars were simple slotted bent metal.

To further confound the competition, Dorfan introduced a "Distance Remote Control" reversing mechanism in 1930 that skirted patents owned by Ives, Lionel, and American Flyer. Design engineers at Dorfan managed this by eliminating the electromagnetic components that were the heart of the other systems. While the others required some kind of start-stop-start reversing sequence with the throttle to mechanically trigger the reverse direction, Dorfan allowed reversing to take place by changing the motor's electrical polarity without any throttle sequencing at all.

RIGHT: In the 1920s, Dorfan produced the Loco-Builder kits as educational toys—keeping in step with the progressive movement for raising kids. Toys were not to be just playthings, but also taught life lessons. *Train Collectors Association*

How to Put Together the Dorfan LOCO-BUILDER ENGINE

WIDE GAUGE MODEL

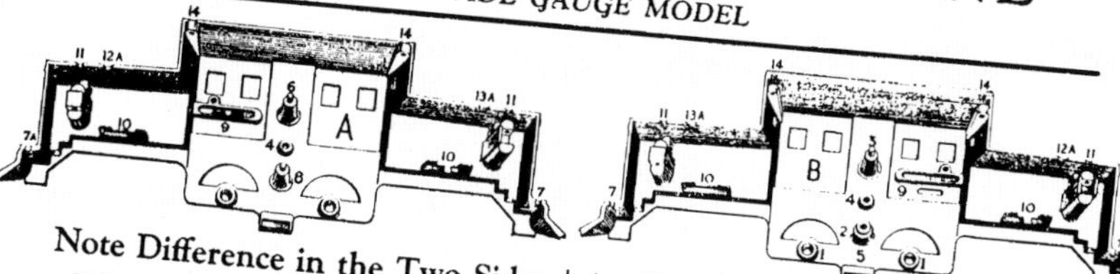

Note Difference in the Two Sides.

Before starting to put your Loco-Builder together, place the two halves of the body side by side on the table. The first one you use is the "Brush-holder Side," marked A.

In following the instructions, remember that all Dorfan parts are built to *fit together evenly*. If you seem to have to force any part into place, stop and read the instructions again, to be sure you are right. A screw driver is the only tool you need to build a Dorfan engine.

1—Where the Brush-Holder Goes

Brush-holder (6)

Place the Brush-holder (part 6) in position, by slipping it over the "stud," or post, 6 on Body. The side of Brush-holder marked 6 should be uppermost. The two hinged arms should rest around Bearing Hole 4.

2—The Collar Comes Next

he Collar) over the ud. You e that the he Collar at one end be- Be sure ar down lder.

:he

rt 8), numbered side uppermost, on body, so that hole 8 on field d 8, and opposite hole on field Insert Screw (part 8A) in hole 8

4—Connect Reverser

Pick up Reverser (part 9) and attach wire now coming from Brush-holder (part 6) to clip marked Y on Reverser. Attach *red* wire from Field to clip U on Reverser. Connect *green* wire from Field to clip O on Reverser. Pick up *long* wire (part 9 A, see picture at bottom of page) and connect one end to clip X on Reverser. Hold Reverser with clip side away from you and black handle pointing up. Slip the end of the flat red part into the Channel 9 in body, having screw rest in slot over figure 9 on body. Fasten by tightening this screw. Bend all wires into the space above Field, under roof of locomotive, and shape long wire 9A around the *wire-wound* end of Field, down to bottom of body. (See diagram at top of next page).

Reverser (9)

5—Insert the Armature

Place Armature (part 4) in center of Field, slipping the shaft, which runs through Armature into the bearing hole in Body, first putting a bit of vaseline into the hole. The gear on Armature should be uppermost. The Brushes—the little black tips on the Brush-holder—must rest against the commutator, which is the round copper surface of Armature.

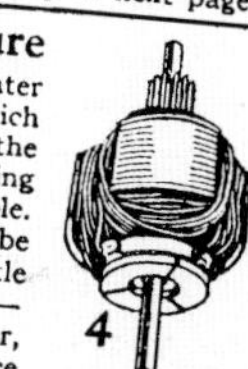
Armature (4)

6—Connect up the Lighting System

12 *Short Lighting Wire (12)*

13 *Long Lighting Wire (13)*

Pick up *short*, thin, black Lighting Wire (part 12) and attach *plain* end to clip F on Reverser, and lay wire in groove 12A on body. Pick up *long* Lighting Wire (part 13) and attach *plain* end to clip B on Reverser. Carry this wire back above field and fit into groove 13A on body.

Assembled Bild-a-Loco Locomotives

TRADE-MARK, PATENTS PENDING

No. 4 "Bild-A-Loco" Locomotive

For "O" Gauge Track

This locomotive is completely assembled and contains the "Bild-a-Loco" Motor described on the previous page. Not only is this locomotive beautiful in appearance and extremely powerful, but the boy will obtain a great amount of education and amusement by being able to remove the motor from the body and take down and assemble all of the motor parts in a jiffy. The body of this locomotive is similar to the No. 254 and No. 254E described on page 8, and is equipped with automatic couplers and 2 electric headlights. All Lionel "Bild-a-Loco" locomotives are in a class by themselves—there is nothing in the world like them. Size—10 inches long—4¼ inches high.

Price $15.00

Code Word "URGE"

NO. 4

BOYS! You'll Double Your Fun By Adding a New "Bild-A-Loco" Model Locomotive To Your Railroad Layout

"BILD-A-LOCO" Locomotives Nos. 9E and 381E for "Lionel Standard" Track have the Lionel "Distant-Control" unit incorporated in them. Not only can you take them apart and assemble them in a few moments, but you can also stop, start, reverse or operate them at any speed at any distance from the track.

No. 9 E "Distant-Control" "Bild-A-Loco" Locomotive

For "Lionel Standard" Track

In addition to the interesting design of the "Bild-a-Loco" Motor, this locomotive also contains our electric controlling unit which makes it possible to start, stop and reverse the locomotive at any distance from the track. The body is beautifully designed and contains many features that are typically Lionel. Locomotive contains two electric headlights so arranged that the front one is always illuminated irrespective of the direction in which the locomotive is traveling. This locomotive is equipped with automatic couplers. It measures 14⅜ inches long, 6¼ inches high. No. 81 controlling rheostat is included. Price $27.50

Code Word "UTTER"

NO. 9E

No. 381E "Distant-Control" "Bild-A-Loco" Locomotive

For "Lionel Standard" Track

This locomotive is the most elaborate in the Lionel Line. The illustration shows the great detail incorporated in it, and special mention is made of the construction of the two 4-wheel pilot trucks which will not derail even when the locomotive is traveling at a high rate of speed. The "Bild-a-Loco" Motor and electric-controlling mechanism can be removed from the body in a jiffy, and the illustration on the previous page shows the accessibility to all parts. The boy can at will take down and rebuild this motor within a few minutes. It is not amiss to repeat that all parts are so accurately made that no difficulty will be experienced in setting it up, and there is not a single wire to be connected, as all electrical contacts are automatically made. It is extremely efficient, and powerful enough to haul a dozen or more of the largest Pullman or Freight Cars with the greatest ease. Nothing in the way of a model electric locomotive has ever been made here or abroad to compare with this supreme model.

Size—18½ inches long, 8½ inches high.

Price, including No. 81 controlling rheostat $42.50

Code Word "ULTI"

NO. 381E

16

LEFT: The Bild-A-Loco versions of the 9E, 381E in standard gauge, and the No. 4 (a version of the 256 in O gauge) were featured in the 1928 catalog. The build-it concept was revived by Cowen from 1919 to counter Dorfan's Loco-Builder kits that were appealing to "educational-minded" parents. *Train Collectors Association Toy Train Museum, Strasburg, Pennsylvania*

Choosing American Flyer wide-gauge trains for Christmas was the thrust of this 1929 ad in the December issue of *Youth's Companion* magazine. Flyer debuted its big trains just before the stockmarket plunge. The expensive sets took the company on a wild ride to the poor house. *Courtesy Train Collectors Association Toy Train Museum, Strasburg, Pennsylvania*

From 1924 to 1925, the Forchheimer brothers had matched and bettered most of the competition's features. Dorfan's locomotives could climb a 20 per cent grade. The new alloy for die casting was non-magnetic, reinforcing its claim that other alloys robbed motors of 15 to 45 per cent of pulling power. Dorfan introduced additional play value by pushing the take-apart "educational" features of its locomotives, and they knew how to take advantage of American advertising techniques. The firm's 1930 catalog offered this familiar refrain with its unique Dorfan twist:

> If you're a thinking boy who isn't satisfied with just 'toys,' then Dorfan is the engine for you. You'll get more fun, more thrills, more real enjoyment out of 'the Engine designed by engineers.' Talk it over with your Dad and tell him you want a real train in miniature, not a toy; explain Dorfan's wonderful features to him—he'll understand.

Flyer Comes of Age

As Dorfan was in ascendancy, Ives and Lionel people woke up one morning to read an ad on page 113 in the November, 1925 issue of *St. Nicholas Magazine*. It read:

> It's Out! The new American Flyer WIDE GAUGE electric train. . . Oh, Boy! . . . but it certainly is a bear!

There had been hints in the trade press all year that American Flyer had something in mind as well as teasers such as an ad in the *Youth's Companion* magazine of June 25, 1925. The ad announced a backyard railroad contest, and down at the bottom the copy asked, "Have you seen the big 'American Flyer' wide gauge electric train? It is already known as a WONDER TRAIN . . . It sure is a BEAR!"

The "Bear" was released among the toy train builders in the form of a series of electric-outline locomotives following New York Central, New Haven, and Milwaukee Road prototypes—a departure from Flyer's introduction of O gauge electric trains back in 1919. Probably because of American Flyer's Midwest roots, its first electrics were modeled after steam engines. Also, Flyer had an inventory of cast-iron wind-up steamer shells into which it could stuff electric motors.

American Flyer's electric-outline locomotives and accompanying cars were stunning in their colorful enameled livery. The names given to the sets of passenger cars stirred patriotic themes: the *President Special*, The *American Legion Limited*, the *Sesquicentennial Special*, or the *Mayflower*. Receiving the $100 *Mayflower* listed in the 1928 catalog would have dropped a kid to his knees. This locomotive was a version of electric-outline *President Special*—the model 4689—that was normally offered in brass-trimmed "Rolls

Royce Blue." The *Mayflower* locomotive and its accompanying 19-inch-long passenger cars were plated to a golden shine using an "electro-cadmium" or "chrome" plating process—depending on which Flyer catalog is consulted.

One of the more reasonable wide-gauge models was Flyer's first Milwaukee Road-influenced electric-outline locomotive, the 4637 *Shasta*, introduced in 1928. This green and "Rookie Tan" engine, which mimicked Milwaukee's famous Bipolar electrics, was encrusted with brass fittings and touted as ". . . a striking example of that consummate mastery of little things by which Scaled Reproduction and brilliance is attained." Of course, it teetered on only four wheels (a real Bipolar had 28) so any reference to "scale reproduction" is pure hype, but when coupled to a set of four matching *Pocahontas* 14-inch-long passenger cars, the effect justifies American Flyer's enthusiasm. The *Shasta* also included remote-control reverse and a ringing bell to add touches of railroad realism.

With the addition of the mid-range-price Shasta to the wide-gauge line, American Flyer offered electric-outline models covering high-, low-, and middle-price trains. Its steam-outline wide-gauge trains followed in 1929 when the Ives model 1134 boiler casting was cannibalized from the bleached bones of that defunct company. The Flyer 4694 steamer clicked out onto the three-rail main line to haul passenger car sets: *Old Ironsides*, *The Warrior*, and *The Minuteman*.

American Flyer's freight cars, introduced in 1926, were equally colorful and robust using unsophisticated slotted metal couplers—each car having a male coupler at one end and a female at the other. It is interesting to note that these cars used bodies made by Lionel.

A 1928 rich kid's stocking stuffer, this American Flyer Model 4689 was the height of pre-Great Depression indulgence when it was introduced. "Electro-cadmium" plated to a brilliant shine, it is the "Mayflower" version of the "President Special" set that was offered in deep royal blue. This wide-gauge train with its 19-inch plated cars is actually a 1990 Lionel re-issue of the original antique brought out for collectors. It poses in front of a Lionel "double" station built to represent a vastly compressed version of New York's Grand Central Terminal. *Robert Lemke collection*

RIGHT: Milwaukee Road's Bipolar electric locomotives, used on the electrified portions of the railroad's Pacific Extension main line to Tacoma, Washington, served as the prototype for Flyer's *Shasta* locomotive. *Milwaukee Road Historical Association Archives*

BELOW: American Flyer No. 4637 wide gauge Bipolar-type electric, the *Shasta,* was unveiled in 1928. It featured automatic reverse and a ringing bell. As with Ives, American Flyer, for its large engine, called $2\frac{1}{8}$-inch-wide track "wide gauge" instead of "standard" because Lionel had patented that name. American Flyer was late entering the expensive large-train market and got caught by the Depression, adding to an already stretched financial condition. *Train Collectors Association Toy Train Museum, Strasburg, Pennsylvania*

Even though competition was fierce among the toy train manufacturers, swapping components between them was a common practice. American Flyer bought the bodies from Lionel—not even changing their colors or stampings; then modified the Lionel hook couplers to match the Flyer model and dropped them on American Flyer four-wheel trucks. William Coleman's people also bought a number of accessories from Cowen's Lionel to fill out the line: stations, crossing gates, street lights, and so forth. At one point, in 1929, the swapping reached its apogee when Ives had been absorbed by both firms and a new tank car for the Ives line was desired by the Lionel and American Flyer management. There were no funds to tool up for this tanker so parts bins were pillaged and the hermaphrodite model 190 tank car ended up with a Lionel 215 body mounted on an American Flyer 4010 frame riding on Ives trucks with Ives couplers.

Ives' Goes Under, and a Dark Horse Emerges

In 1928, Ives slipped below the surface of red ink. Joshua Cowen and William Coleman, with their attendant accountants and lawyers, sat down to carve up Ives between Lionel and American Flyer. The Ives Division would continue to build trains under Lionel's and American Flyer's stewardship, and the inventory lived on under all three liveries in both wide gauge (Lionel's standard) and O gauge. However, economics dictated discarding many Ives designs in 1929 since their cost of production resulted in a loss for every locomotive and car sold.

As the last years off the Roaring Twenties played out, the buyers of electric toy trains had become familiar with Lionel, American Flyer, Ives, and Dorfan with William Hafner happily cranking out his charming wind-up trains in the lowest end niche. Then, as Ives lurched toward bankruptcy and the rest were flying high with wide- and standard-gauge giants and extensive O gauge lines, an unlikely new player bought his way in. He paid for his ticket to the dance with the proceeds made from an Alabama Minstrel Dancer and Zippo the Climbing Monkey. His name was Louis Marx.

For sheer marketing genius and *brio*, Louis Marx had no equal in the toy business. Brooklyn born in 1896, he set a goal for success early in life and, after graduating high school at the age of 15, joined the toy manufacturing company of Ferdinand Strauss in 1912. By 1916, he was managing a Strauss plant. His obsession—one that got him canned from Strauss—was building cheap toys even more cheaply and selling huge volumes. On leaving the Army in 1917, where he had earned sergeant stripes, Marx went to work selling wood toys. The company's sales shot up $135,000 in two years after Louis redesigned the line.

In 1919, he became Louis Marx & Co., Inc. and set out with his brother, David, to achieve his obsession. They had no factory, so they sold toys on a commission basis. Using his contacts with Ferdinand Strauss, Louis rented a factory in Pennsylvania and bought some dies at a very cheap price from his cash-strapped former employer. These were the dies used to manufacture the Alabama Minstrel Dancer, a crazy-legged tin wind-up toy, and Zippo the Climbing Monkey who shinnied up a string. Using the old dies, he managed to make and sell over eight million of each.

By 1925, Marx was a millionaire, and by 1928 his toys were being sold in Sears & Roebuck's catalog. That same year, while searching for new ideas, Louis hit on two. He invented the yo-yo (eventually selling 100 million of them), and he discovered toy trains.

So, while Lionel and American Flyer were carving up the hapless Ives, Louis Marx was purchasing the dies for the tin wind-up "Joy Line" trains manufactured by Girard Model Works. He had sold the trains as a commissioned agent for Girard beginning in 1927 and, apparently, saw the ideal product for his cheap, cheaper, cheapest philosophy rolling down the rails. As the Depression began to bite hard, Girard fired Marx because they could no longer afford his 10 per cent commission. Marx, suitably miffed, bought a plant in Morgantown, Pennsylvania, to make toy lines he lost from Girard. With

Young "future masters of industry" wear their neckties and best clothes to operate a complex wide-gauge Ives rug railroad in this advertisement circa late 1920s—not long before the end of the classic toy-train manufacturer. *Train Collectors Association Toy Train Museum, Strasburg, Pennsylvania*

A Lionel-Ives stamped-steel 257 locomotive from 1931. Lionel had absorbed Ives in 1929. The locomotive came out in 1930; then, in 1931, the "Ives No. 257" was added to the cab side. It was featured in both the Lionel and Ives catalogs. The four-wheel tender has LIONEL LINES curiously inverted on one side and IVES LINES on the other. The coupler is a standard Lionel latch design. *Both, Train Collectors Association Toy Train Museum, Strasburg, Pennsylvania*

time on his hands while the plant was coming up to speed, he made some calls to Girard customers who knew him better than they knew Girard. They said, "Sure, Louis, we'll buy from you." The Girard management stumbled into bankruptcy and had to sell their company. They paid off the debt they owed Louis for back commission money with shares of common stock—a controlling interest as it turned out. Louis went to the employees who held preferred shares and threatened to dump his common stock if they did not release their preferred shares to him at a cost of 50 cents on the dollar. In the middle of the Depression, this was a generous deal. He bought the company and designated it his "train factory" that he ran from his office in New York City. No prospective model went into production before it journeyed those 200 miles for the master's imprimatur. Girard stayed in business making toys and Marx trains until its last products rolled off the assembly line in 1975.

A chill must have touched William Hafner's spine as Louis Marx sent forth his equally charming wind-up train sets. In 1930, the Joy Line upped the ante by producing a cast-iron wind-up locomotive and stamped steel car set as direct competition to Hafner. But then, probably much to Hafner's relief, Marx stuffed an electric motor into the shell in 1931 and brought out a stamped-steel electric locomotive train set in 1932 that returned encouraging sales numbers. Louis Marx and Hafner continued to sell wind-up trains for decades thereafter, but Louis had also planted his own flag alongside electric train builders, Lionel and American Flyer, battling for the minds and dollars of doting moms and dads.

True to form, Joshua Cowen considered Marx an interloper and threatened numerous times to produce a really cheap train set. Marx counter-rumored that he would build an expensive train set—more cars and more track and still undersell Lionel. An "expensive" set by Marx included a steam loco, four cars, track, and a transformer for $3.50. They both blustered and prospered, each on their own side of the fence, occasionally peering through knotholes to check up on each other.

The Great Depression began to squeeze the last gasp from the lively "Roaring Twenties" and that decade-long economic nightmare would take its toll among the toy train-makers.

First-year Joy Line freight set with wind-up locomotive No. 350. This set—though associated with Louis Marx—was built by the Girard Model Works in the 1920s before Louis bought the company. After this first release, an enameled shell or cast-iron locomotive was substituted. *Courtesy, Jim Flynn Collection*

Lionel's M-10000 streamliner, portraying real-life Union Pacific's new "articulated" (sectionalized) streamliner was a financial winner following its debut in the 1934 catalog. Lionel engineers had to design a new way to connect the cars to preserve the articulated look of the prototype. Wheeled vestibules were doubled hooked to each section Still, the M-10000 could only run on wide-radius O-72 track. *Don Roth collection*

Chapter 5

Casualties and Survivors of the "Classic Age"

The Lionel Model 763E locomotive of 1937, a slightly stripped-down version of Lionel's famous scale-model 700E Hudson-type (4-6-4) locomotive. *Train Collectors Association Toy Train Museum, Strasburg, Pennsylvania*

The Wall Street sell-off began on October 24 and by October 29, 1929, Black Tuesday, the bottom had dropped out of the stock market. Americans had reached a height of prosperity previously unknown. Houses had a refrigerator in the kitchen, a console radio in the parlor, and an automobile parked out front—or on the new paved driveway alongside the house that led to the personal garage. The Sunday papers were fat with advertising and orders for silk shirts, fur coats, and pinch-back suits, and other worldly goods were flying thick and fast. True, after 1928 there had been a slow-down in buying, warehouses were crowded with new oak-boxed radios, and luxury items like fast autos built on custom chassis were not briskly rolling out of the showrooms. But middle-class Americans had discovered credit buying, and, by 1929, 10 million purchasers were paying their debts by the month.

In the world of toy trains, Ives continued to build trains in both wide gauge and O gauge as part of Lionel. The tin boat line was scuttled for the time being. Ives' low-end products were parceled out between Lionel and American Flyer in the form of parts and cheap goods. Locomotives were sometimes curious mixed breeds like the Model 257 Lionel/Ives steamer with the Ives name appearing on one side of the tender and Lionel on the other. Many Ives cars were built as transition cars with a Lionel coupler at one end and an Ives coupler at the other. There was also a transition Lionel latch coupler that had a slot added to admit the male hook of an Ives car.

These manufacturers, and Dorfan as well, were building and selling the most expensive train sets they had ever offered in 2 1/8 inch-gauge (wide and standard)—and these huge sets had been moving briskly. Lionel's profits in 1929 stood at nearly $2.3 million in the days before income tax. American Flyer had bet the farm on wide gauge in 1925 and had no intentions of slowing down. Relative Newcomer Dorfan was winning market share with its colorful die-cast wide-gauge models and aggressive salesmanship.

The Great Depression did not leap up and flatten everyone at once. A month after the crash in New York, the *Kansas City Star* business section still predicted a correction and inevitable rally. John Kenneth Galbraith, the economist, flatly stated, "The cliche that in 1929 everyone was 'in the market' is far from the literal truth. . . to the great majority of all Americans, the stock market was a remote and vaguely ominous thing."

It was January 1930 before the creeping tide of failure made its way as far as the Midwestern United States when sources of money began drying up, and banks began to fail. Debts were called in, mortgages came due, and property taxes based on the last prosperous year, 1928, were levied against 1930 earnings—or lack thereof.

Early in 1929, Lawrence Cowen, son of Joshua Lionel Cowen, started a New York brokerage firm, Cowen, Stark & Company. The young scion had begun his career as a runner on the stockmarket floor, graduated to clerk, married Clarice Bernard (on a salary of $18 a week), and settled comfortably into a suite of rooms at Park Avenue's posh Hotel Marguery. Since Joshua could no longer bond with his son across a loop of three-rail track, he paid the highest price for a seat on the Stock Exchange up to that time—$585,000—and gave it to the lad. Lawrence became the youngest member of the Stock Exchange.

Joshua Cowen was heavily involved in the market, and when the crash came, Cowen also lost heavily. During 1930, Lionel's sales dropped $346,000 and profits skidded by $282,000. That same year, Lionel bought out American Flyer's share of what remained of the Ives carcass.

American Flyer's wide-gauge sets, introduced with the 4000-series electric-outline locomotives and car sets in 1925 and fortified with the introduction of electric-powered steamers in 1929 (from cannibalized Ives parts), boasted of "over five million happy owners." Then, 1932 sales were off. In 1933, William Coleman officially killed wide gauge as sales continued to plummet. By 1936 only two sets were offered, using up inventories of the big trains.

Watching sales of the big standard-gauge beauties slide, Cowen turned to part of the Ives Division that still carried the defunct name lithographed on cheap wind-up sets. He also created a new company called Winner, packaging Ives low-end electric train sets. Abstracted from and completely outside the Lionel umbrella, these sets offered, "A Real Electric Train for Little Brother." The orange-trimmed Winner train, including a steam-outline locomotive and three passenger cars, a circle of O gauge three-rail track, and a transformer hidden in a lithographed tin train station with a removable roof, sold for $3.25.

In 1932, as Franklin Delano Roosevelt was busy running for office and outlining his New Deal, Lionel lost another $209,000. The Winner Company was scrapped. Also scrapped was the Ives Division. In 1933, the Lionel board of directors pulled the plug on the losing line. The dies were sold for scrap, and Cowen could relish his ultimate victory over his old rival—or would have had his own fortunes been brighter. Lionel had lost yet another $200,000.

Lionel's train for "Little Brother"—the Winner Line. These inexpensive electric train sets were built around former Ives clockwork locomotives, and the most expensive cost about $5.50 with three lithographed freight cars and a transformer. In 1933, the Winner Line was dropped and the sets were added to the Lionel-Ives Line. Finally, in 1934, they became Lionel Junior sets until low-priced O-27 trains came to the market in 1937. The little lithographed train station houses a transformer that is reached when the roof is slid to one side. *Train Collectors Association Toy Train Museum, Strasburg, Pennsylvania*

A *Blue Comet* 400E locomotive with a "Vanderbilt"-style tender (following a prototype design established by the New York Central System, cornerstone of the once-invincible Vanderbilt empire) sits in front of two of the 400-series Pullman and observation passenger cars that followed it down standard-gauge tracks. The complete train is called *The Blue Comet* by collectors, and the cars are named after actual comets, Westphal and Temple. *Train Collectors Association Toy Train Museum, Strasburg, Pennsylvania*

Doomsday at Dorfan

Over at the Dorfan factory on 137 Jackson Street in Newark, New Jersey, everyone was working hard to keep improving Dorfan trains. In their cluttered offices on the second floor, the Forchheimer brothers, Milton and Julius, and their chief engineer, John Koerber, constantly tinkered with their designs, often spending thousands to retool a die again and again. They experimented with adding ball bearings to drive wheels, detailed valve gear on their steam engines, and constant adjustments to their patented Dorfan Alloy used by the Mount Vernon Die Casting Company in New York to make their castings. Trouble had already occurred with the early alloy. Under certain conditions, the two halves of the die-cast locomotive would bend out of alignment, and since the axle shafts passed through the castings and the armature bearings were set in the castings, the locomotive could not run.

Dorfan's 150 workers labored to hand assemble the cars, connecting brass railings with two cotter pins and tabbing brass name plaques to rolling stock and locomotives that were painted many different colors. While the lowest-end cars were punched out of a single lithographed sheet of steel and folded into shape, the mid-range and expensive sets required much hand labor. One car could have as many as 117 separate parts and sell for $3.75. The resulting end products—even the cheapest lines—were sturdy and pioneered many innovations.

But, out on the streets and in the homes of Depression-squeezed Americans, buying toy trains was not high on a priority list that included financial survival. Dorfan sales began to slip. The heavily capital-intensive startup was easy when loan money was cheap and plentiful in 1924. But constant re-tooling, adding employees to manufacturing, innovating new designs, and offering a wide range of prices for their sets had left the two guys from Nuremberg in a vulnerable financial position. Roosevelt's New Deal was coming too late to save Julius and Milton.

In their experimental room sat a beautiful, handmade 4-6-0 Ten-Wheeler electric-powered steam engine modeled in wide gauge that had been built in 1931 for $2,000 as a demonstrator. Lionel's magnificent Model 400E 4-4-4 steamer had been introduced that same year and was the showboat of the company's line. The Dorfan Ten-Wheeler was a match for it in every detail, and while the 400E was supposed to be a model of the New York Central Hudson-type (4-6-2) locomotive, the Dorfan locomotive was the more accurate model. But the Dorfan model sat in the experimental room while the 400E looked out at buyers from the pages of Lionel's catalog.

It is not recorded when the real disaster was discovered, whether it was reported by telephone ("Guy on the phone for you, Julius. . ."), or from a supervisor walking down from the third floor. The early Dorfan locomotives were literally crumbling. German toy manufacturers called the condition "zinc pest." The specially compounded copper-zinc Dorfan Alloy was unstable. A casting could be bounced off a brick wall and not break, but inside its molecular structure, activity was taking place. For no apparent reason, customers were reporting cracks in their locomotives. Samples in salesmen's cases were becoming fissured with spider webs of fine fractures. Money had to be spent to improve the compound. Damage control had to be applied to sales pitches. Dorfan's unassailable position as a high-quality manufacturer was under attack from a pest within.

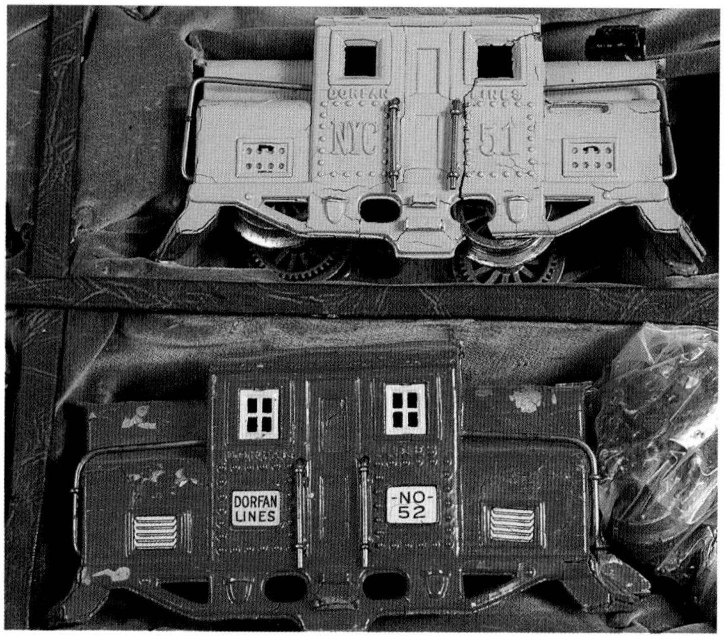

A close-up of two locomotive shells made of "Dorfan Alloy" composed of copper and zinc shows the "zinc pest" that dogged Dorfan. Although an early success because of its durability and "slickness" that eliminated some bearings, the alloy turned out to be unstable and began to crack as it aged. Here, the yellow shell has begun to fissure. Today, finding Dorfan electric locomotives that are not veined with cracks is unusual. *Train Collectors Association Toy Train Museum, Strasburg, Pennsylvania*

It was all over by 1934. Like the Depression, the brothers didn't go broke all at once. In 1936, the last of the inventory was sold. The Unique Manufacturing Company of Newark, New Jersey, bought the dies, but they gathered dust for years. The third-floor factory was abandoned, and everyone who was left moved into the second-floor offices. There, the Forchheimers dreamed dreams of restarting the line with even better trains than before. In 1938, at the New York Toy Fair, the brothers discovered and became enamored with HO model railroading.

Back at the Jackson Street offices, Milton and Julius, along with John Koerber, began plans for a line of low-cost tinplate HO trains. The locomotives would be a kit and the cars stamped out of sheet metal; the cost of a train set would be $6. Nothing came of it, however. Had they gone ahead and applied the same savvy and energy they had mustered for their debut in the tinplate big leagues in 1924, today's HO model railroad scene might be quite different. Hobbyists would find Forchheimer kits on the shelves alongside Athearn, Mantua, Bowser, and Walthers. Instead, the two guys from Nuremberg and their chief engineer faded away from the toy train scene. Today, collectors are fortunate to find a Dorfan locomotive or car die cast from Dorfan Alloy that hasn't crumbled or is not veined with cracks.

New Life for Flyer

And now there were two. Lionel and American Flyer were surviving—barely—still building electric trains, though under the scrutiny of flinty-eyed bankers, for people who had a lot more on their minds than toys. Of the pair, Flyer was the worse off. With its premier wide-gauge line chopped in 1932, the Chicago company limped along with its line of O gauge trains. It continued to build cast-iron wind-up-powered steam-type locomotives and stamped, lithographed cars until 1933, then switched to sad-looking stamped steel locomotives until 1935 when the line was dropped. Electric-outline locomotives only lasted until 1934.

American Flyer O gauge steam engines, manufactured from cast-iron halves riveted together, clunked along until 1936 when a makeover took place. Cast iron gave way to a stamped steel, torpedo-style locomotive that, in turn, gave way to a die-cast Hudson-style locomotive with the trailer truck made to look like it had four wheels instead of the actual two. The same fake trailer truck was riveted to the back end of a Milwaukee Road *Hiawatha*-style streamlined steamer making a 4-4-2 (Atlantic type) into an apparent 4-4-4. Scale-looking die castings followed, and the sick company started to show signs of health.

Unfortunately, Flyer's William Coleman wasn't so lucky. In 1939 his chronic ailments followed him on vacation down to Guatemala, and there he dropped dead. As it turned out, though, in 1938 he had sold the American Flyer Manufacturing Company of Chicago to a tinplate toy maker, A. C. Gilbert. Production was moved to New Haven, Connecticut, and the plan was for Coleman to remain as president while Gilbert did the manufacturing and selling. When Coleman died, A. C. Gilbert became president of American Flyer. This was the same Gilbert who, along with Harry Ives, had helped found the Toy Manufacturers of the U.S.A. back in 1916. And, that was the same organization which had snubbed Joshua Lionel Cowen. Now, Lionel would face American Flyer with a fast-handed, agile-minded entrepreneur at the

helm who was a match for Cowen. But this face-off would have to wait until after World War II.

The Classic Period

Ironically the most beautiful and expensive toy trains were produced during the Great Depression. According to today's train collectors, these were the standard- and wide-gauge sets and locomotives created during the "Classic Period," which lasted from 1923 to 1942. During this time, Ives had created some excellent designs, such as the No. 3243 short cab electric 4-4-4 (1921 to 1928) or the 3245 top-of-the-line version that was repeated in 1930 under Lionel's management. American Flyer came up with beauties like the No. 4689 *President Special* outlined in the previous chapter and brass-trimmed steamers equal to anything on the market.

But it is to Lionel that the laurels must be given for making the Classic Period of American toy trains so memorable. While the 400E and its eventual *Blue Comet* version is Lionel's most famous standard-gauge locomotive of this period, it was preceded by a series of electric-outline locomotives, steamers, and car sets that were absolute classics. There was the 1928 No. 9 boxcab electric, the 9E (the "E" indicating the locomotive was equipped with automatic rather than manual reverse), and the 9U which came as a kit. While the 9 series was not a big seller, its prototype lines and exceptional brass trim for a low cost made it a classic. An electric that preceded it by five years was the 402E. This was a model of a New York Central S-class electric locomotive that, when issued, had a hole in one end that accepted a tap for illuminating a string of trailing passenger cars. A separate kit allowed the 402 to provide the electrical power for its passenger consist by stringing the wire and lights from car to car. What made the 402E such a stand-out was its dual-motor design—one motor for each set of two wheels. It could really pull. But its progeny, the 408E, is what eclipsed the 402's fame.

The large 408E was virtually the same locomotive but sported a pair of pantographs (on the prototype used for collecting current off overhead catenary) that raised and lowered, additional brass handrails on the roof, and a set of four working red and green lights. When it was offered in 1927, it was relegated to pulling medium-weight passenger-car sets—just an upgrade of the old 402. In 1928, however, Lionel introduced the largest standard-gauge locomotive it had ever built, the mammoth 381 and 381E.

TOP: American Flyer's sheet-metal *Hiawatha* train set circa 1935 was a low-end O gauge streamliner based on the prototype Milwaukee Road *Hiawatha,* a steam-powered streamliner inaugurated that same year. Curiously, Flyer designed its model as an articulated train like the *Zephyr* and M-10000; the real *Hiawatha* always utilized regular individual cars. On the model, there were no trucks—just one pair of wheels per car. The hole in the side allows access to the motor's brushes. *Dave Guerriges collection*

ABOVE: The real *Hiawatha* storming through Wauwatosa, Wisconsin, in 1937 en route from Chicago to the Twin Cities. *Milwaukee Road Historical Association Archives*

Relegated as an upgrade for the model 402 and left to mid-range passenger duty when introduced in 1927, the dual-motored 408E became a star when the model 381 faltered. It was the 408E that was tapped to haul the four-car *State* passenger set at center stage in the catalogs. A disappointed owner of a 381 could swap his wheezing behemoth for the 408E in dark green 381 colors. *Train Collectors Association Toy Train Museum, Strasburg, Pennsylvania*

The size difference between standard gauge and O gauge can easily be seen in this side-by-side comparison of the standard gauge 381 electric offered from 1928 to 1936 next to an O gauge 252 from the same era. *Train Collectors Association Toy Train Museum, Strasburg, Pennsylvania*

The 381E was based on the Milwaukee Road's Bipolar electric locomotives (Flyer and Dorfan also offered models of these) that hauled trains over and through the mountainous portions of the railroad's Pacific Extension to Tacoma and Seattle, Washington.

Curiously, considering its size, weight, and flashy good looks, the 381 was not the most expensive Lionel locomotive—nor was it the most powerful. In fact, its power caused Lionel some embarrassment when the flashy flagship could not haul the new *State* passenger car set designed for it without considerable lubrication and preparation. The big beauty had only a single motor. Enter the 408E. When calls came in that the 381E, when coupled to the 24 pounds of *State* cars, just struggled forward, hummed and spun its wheels, the dual-motor 408E was snatched from its medium-weight duty and coupled to the new cars. The 408E became the new darling of Lionel's passenger line as it whisked the massive passenger cars down the main line.

Steam engines were another breed of cat altogether. The early Lionel steamers descended from the original No. 5, brought out in 1906 and continued until 1926 and were models of a different era. They had the look of either "yard goats"—the 0-4-0 and 0-6-0 switchers—or the high-stepper Ten-Wheelers and slim-boilered Atlantics that were the greyhounds of the wood-sided passenger train days. Railroads had changed by the turn of the century. The air brake, Janney knuckle coupler, and larger capacity fireboxes allowed longer freight trains to be pulled. As President Coolidge had said, "The business of America is business." We were truly a two-coast nation, and passenger travel had entered the "heavyweight" period when trains had names and steamed on through the night with ten to fifteen all-steel cars hanging on the engine's drawbar. Pullmans, dining cars, parlor cars, observation cars, baggage cars, mail cars, all linked together formed a small town hurtling across the landscape at 80 miles an hour. The new locomotives had muscle—a big-shouldered look—and the engineer had been elevated to god-like status by American boys. To stand on the platform of a rural flagstop station and watch the *Fast Mail* hammer through on the high iron, whistle wailing and firebox glowing, made the heart beat faster in time with the trembling bricks beneath the kid's feet. Lionel wanted to capture that look.

Between 1929 and 1933, Lionel's designers pushed out the door a series of standard-gauge steam engines that realized the dream of every youngster whose family could put enough dollars together to buy one. They began with the 390E in 1929 and reached the apogee of the design with the 400E in 1931. They all bore the basic stamp.

Steam locomotives have many more parts than electric locomotives, with drive wheels and drive rods, pony and trailing trucks, piping, pilots ("cow catchers"), sand domes, whistles, and bells. They also come in two sections with the tender carrying water and either coal or oil. Rather than model their locomotives after specific prototype Consolidations, Berkshires, Pacifics, and Hudsons of various railroads, Lionel left that degree of reality to the young engineer's imagination. These were big toy steam engines—looking more European than American with their brass piping, color trim, red cowcatchers, shiny stamped steel boilers and large nickel drive wheels with red spokes.

There was good reason for this look. In 1922, Cowen had explored the concept of producing Lionel tooling overseas to save costs. In Naples, Italy, he and Mario Caruso, his chief engineer, established the the Societa Meccanica la Precisa. The designers could not avoid the colorful European trains that dashed across Italian landscape and could not resist adding metal bands around boilers and touches of brass to American-style (read, drab) locomotives. This pioneering overseas venture would prove cost-effective and would help lift Lionel—and tinplate railroading overall—to a new level as the 1930s ground to a close.

One design from la Precisa, the model 392E—a 4-4-2 steamer—featured a glowing red light under the firebox to simulate burning and had a chugger unit housed in the 12-wheel tender. The chugger was a series of rotating gears that created a chug sound as the locomotive moved. Regardless, the 392E remained in the shadow of the 400E.

This largest locomotive ever built by Lionel was the culmination of Lionel's gaudy, flashy toy locomotives—especially as the *Blue Comet*. The real *Blue Comet* was a short-haul passenger train operated by the Central Railroad of New Jersey—the Jersey Central. Cowen often rode the train on its four-hour run down the Jersey coast and decided to immortalize it in standard-gauge tinplate. Although the original was painted dark blue with a black roof, the Lionel version was a glowing royal blue with cream trim.

In his book, *All Aboard!*, the primary resource volume on the history of Joshua Lionel Cowen and his company, author Ron Hollander offers an insight into Cowen's philosophy of color. In a quoted conversation with future HO model railroad magnate, William K. Walthers, Cowen expounded:

"Young man," he said, "do you know who actually buys toy trains and accessories? It's the women—mothers, sisters, and aunts of the kids who play with them. Don't forget, women buy on color and don't give a damn what the thing is just as long as it is bright."

Considering Cowen's constant drumbeat advertising message that buying and operating a toy train set is the bond between Dad and Son, this is an interesting quote.

The 400E met those women's criteria, especially when it was coupled to a matching set of royal blue, 400-series Pullmans with an open-platform observation car bringing up the nickel-plated rear. The original Jersey Central train was a coach-only train.

The flash and thunder of massive standard-gauge trains was also transferred to the increasingly popular O gauge line. The 260E—a 2-4-2 downsized version of its standard-gauge cousins—came out in 1930. This locomotive was the premier O gauge steamer at the top of a line of six locomotives released between 1929 and 1931. The 260E was, in effect, the counterpart to the 400E and was reaching a larger consumer buying base as the economy tightened. Standard gauge was becoming known as "the rich boy's gauge," an epithet at a time when some out-of-work fathers were reduced to selling apples on street corners.

This was also the time of the classic Lionel accessories. As with the locomotives, realistic designs were eschewed for glitzy, compressed, and colorful tributes to the originals. Everything was made of painted steel. Nickel and brass trim glittered. Street lamps as tall as a scale three-story building glowed. Shiny aluminum caught the

Comparing a Hornby locomotive and a Lionel 260E from the early 1930s. America had caught up with European quality and even copied the "brass-bound" look of European motive power. Lionel claims its locomotives had foreign touches because the designs came from their Italian operation in Naples. *Don Roth collection*

headlight's sweep off locomotives chugging around tight curves. The Power Station with its Lionel sign attached to three smoke stacks actually had enough interior room to conceal *two* transformers. Tan electric locomotives clicked across Hell Gate Bridge, based on the New Haven and Pennsylvania Railroads' 135-foot-high span crossing the turbulent waters of New York's East River—the longest railroad bridge in the world when it was opened in 1917. The Lionel version is a squeezed confection that could be doubled by removing one pier and connecting two together.

There was a train station called Lionel City based on New York's Grand Central Terminal, but a standard-gauge steamer waiting for passengers to board its cars dwarfed the structure. The Round House, offered in 1932, had storage sections too small for any Lionel standard-gauge steamer and was served by the Model 200 turntable that was too short for any locomotive other than a stubby electric.

And, frankly, nobody cared.

Light towers, illuminated bungalows, signal bridges with glowing target lamps . . . all reflected off the cream-colored steel sides of red-roofed buildings and sparkled off the strings of multi-hued freight cars. A complete layout was a cacophony of visual activity—a blaze of color and

Standard-gauge layout at the Train Collectors Association Toy train Museum in Strasburg, Pennsylvania. This layout was created by Joe "Bud" Parrott in 1990 and features an orange Model 9U—a "Bild-A-Loco"—in the foreground passing a black 400E steamer passenger train with a Model 318 electric hauling a coal drag approaching the curve on the top level. *Train Collectors Association Toy Train Museum, Strasburg, Pennsylvania*

a rush of motion. This was—and is—the joy of tinplate railroading. Only kids from the most well-to-do families of the 1930s could afford these standard-gauge sound and light shows. Thanks to collectors and groups like the Train Collectors Association in Strasburg, Pennsylvania, we can enjoy them today in public spaces.

Shrewdly, the same accessories were marketed —and looked closer to scale—for use with O gauge sets. Standard-gauge sales were steadily declining despite the glitzy new models.

On May 7, 1934, Cowen placed Lionel into receivership. This was a pivotal year for Lionel. The Great Depression was at its lowest ebb. Roosevelt was struggling to get his New Deal into operation with an alphabet soup of government agencies (WPA, PWA, CCC, etc.) striving to put the country back on sound economic footing and shore up its dispirited morale. Cowen was looking anywhere and everywhere for a magic shot in the arm to boost sales. In 1933, the defunct Winner line of cheap trains had come back under the Lionel Junior banner. Anything was worth a try.

Louis Marx was at the top of his game. His wide range of tin toys sold well in dime stores, chain stores, and large department stores across the country. His low-cost train sets that every kid could own were moving briskly off the shelves.

American Flyer produced its last electric-outline locomotives in 1934 and turned its attention to a project influenced by a new trend sweeping America—a development from the new International and Art Deco commercial and industrial design houses called "streamlining."

Both Cowen and Coleman saw the future and moved to grab a piece of it. When they moved, ever-alert Louis Marx also perked up his ears. Joshua Cowen's grab caused the most splash and received the most press. In 1934, facing Lionel's worst financial crisis, he cast his lot with a yellow train and a mouse named Mickey.

The Union Pacific Railroad, under the leadership of Averill Harriman, was searching for a way to reclaim passenger revenues lost to the Depression—to make a train trip an event as well as necessary transportation. Carbuilder Pullman-Standard, motorcar builder Electro-Motive Corporation and its associate, the Winton Engine Company, proposed a radical new design that result in an entire passenger train that weighed not much more than one all-steel "heavyweight" passenger car, or about 124 tons. Dubbed the M-10000, the train was made almost entirely of aluminum and built low to the tracks. The power car and the passenger cars were fastened together as one unit—articulated—to reduce overall tare and air drag coefficient and to increase speed. At each articulation, one truck supported the ends of two cars, and from railhead to rooftop the little Armour Yellow and golden brown speedster was only 12 feet high—at least three feet lower than most passenger rolling stock of the time. The reduction of the number of required truck assemblies and the elimination of heavy cast journal boxes reduced the train's overall weight while the low center of gravity let her hug the rails around curves at greater speeds. The M-10000 was 204 feet long and powered by a tried-and-proven Winton spark-ignition distillate engine—a compromise to ensure UP would be first out with its streamliner. (Rival Burlington Route was racing to complete its own new streamliner, which was to be powered by a yet-to-be-proven diesel engine.) The power car shared space with a baggage section and Railway Post Office; the second car could seat 60 passengers while the third held 56 and a buffet-kitchen. Best of all, she was fast. That 600-horsepower engine could cruise her along at 110 mph.

All Union Pacific railcars that were used for short-haul passenger service in the boondocks and were powered by internal combustion engines had an "M" designation for "motorcar." Since this super train was to be the mother of all M-series trains, it was bestowed with the high-ranking M-10000 designation.

Passenger trains roar across and beneath Lionel's rendition of Hell Gate Bridge. Modeled after an actual New York span anchored in the Queens and Wards Island and prominently visible from much of Manhattan's east side, the bridge typifies Lionel's credo of color and action over accuracy that marked its period of ascendancy just before and after World War II. The bridge could be used with standard-gauge trains, but looked better on O gauge layouts. *Train Collectors Association Toy Train Museum, Strasburg, Pennsylvania*

RIGHT: Union Pacific's M-10000 may have been considered homely by some, but as the world's first lightweight, internal-combustion-powered streamliner, it was a milestone in railroad history. Streamliners would soon propagate throughout America and boost passenger revenues; they would also influence a similar resurgence in the world of toy trains. *EMD*

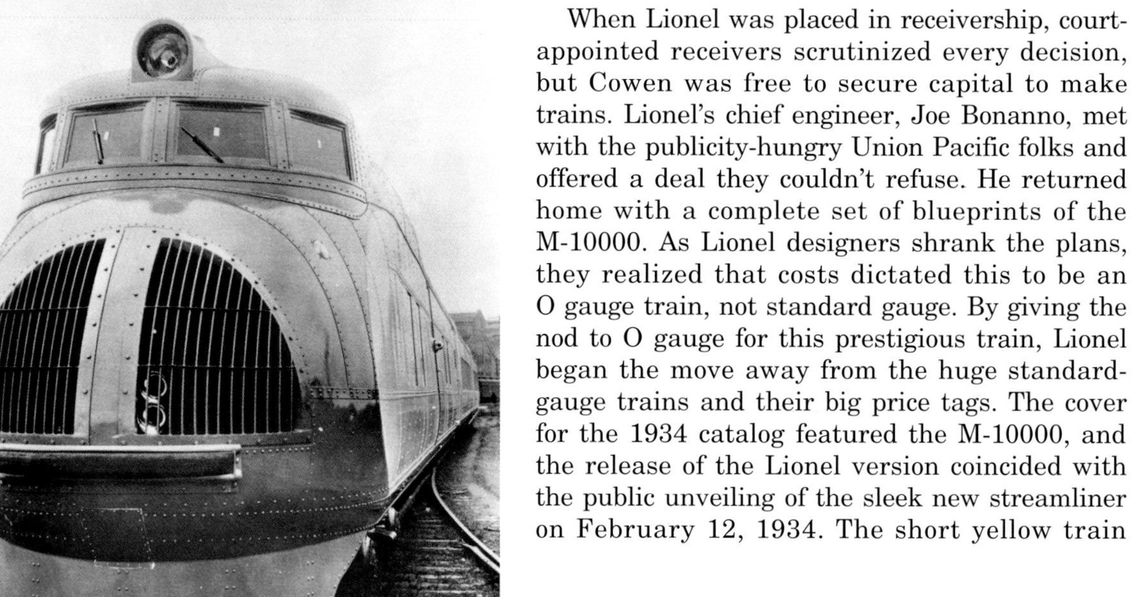

BELOW: Ready for the kids on a chilly Christmas morning in 1935, Bud Garber of Dayton, Ohio, regards his handiwork as a Lionel O gauge M-10000 rounds a curve set on cotton snow. *David P. Oroszi collection*

When Lionel was placed in receivership, court-appointed receivers scrutinized every decision, but Cowen was free to secure capital to make trains. Lionel's chief engineer, Joe Bonanno, met with the publicity-hungry Union Pacific folks and offered a deal they couldn't refuse. He returned home with a complete set of blueprints of the M-10000. As Lionel designers shrank the plans, they realized that costs dictated this to be an O gauge train, not standard gauge. By giving the nod to O gauge for this prestigious train, Lionel began the move away from the huge standard-gauge trains and their big price tags. The cover for the 1934 catalog featured the M-10000, and the release of the Lionel version coincided with the public unveiling of the sleek new streamliner on February 12, 1934. The short yellow train began at once to break speed records, and Lionel's fortunes rode on every one of those runs. The caterpillarlike M-10000 became a symbol of progress as it crossed the country on publicity tours and would continue to cause heads to turn until it was scrapped for the war effort in 1941.

In nearby Burlington territory, another streamliner was unveiled on April 18: *Zephyr* 9900. Since 1932, Chicago, Burlington & Quincy president Ralph Budd had envisioned a high-speed passenger train powered by a diesel engine. Construction of such a train for the Burlington began in 1933 at the Edward G. Budd (no relation) Manufacturing Company near Philadelphia, though it was not certain a diesel power plant would be ready in time for the train's completion. At the eleventh hour, General Motors' Winton Engine Company put the finishing touches on a compact diesel engine that would fit into a railcar (until this time, diesel engines were too large to fit inside a rail carbody).

The Budd Company had been experimenting with stainless steel for carbuilding and developed a method—shotwelding—for joining stainless panels. Stainless steel was virtually indestructible and especially strong in fluted form, but it was not easily fabricated. Shotwelding, in which stainless-steel panels were joined using a jolt of high amperage electricity to create a bond that was stronger than the steel itself, solved the problem.

The *Zephyr* had been in the works since 1932, and American Flyer had been dogging the project's progress. As a result, when the *Zephyr* was introduced, American Flyer licensed use of the name and brought out its own O gauge model of the stainless-steel train.

When the *Zephyr* made its famous 1,000-plus-mile nonstop dawn-to-dusk publicity run from Denver direct to the Century of Progress exhibition grounds at Chicago on May 26, 1934, more than two million people lined the tracks as the three-section speedster barreled through their towns on specially cleared tracks. At some places, the *Zephyr* hit speeds of 112 miles per hour. When the little silver train was placed in revenue service in November 1934, seats on the *Zephyr* were sold out weeks in advance. Later dubbed the *Pioneer Zephyr* as other *Zephyrs* were added to the fleet, the 9900 continued to pay its way hauling passengers on local Midwestern routes until 1960 when it was retired from service and donated to the Chicago Museum of Science and Industry. Today, the *Pioneer Zephyr* is a featured exhibit at the museum's main underground entrance. The American Flyer version of the *Zephyr* remained in its catalog until 1938.

Not be outdone, Lionel chose to model Boston & Maine's new 1935 streamliner, the *Flying Yankee*, in 1936. Also built by Budd and powered by a Winton diesel engine, the *Yankee* was a near twin to the *Zephyr*. The *Yankee*'s first runs cut the travel time between Boston and Bangor, Maine, by 65 minutes and won a 50 per cent increase in passenger revenue.

The legendary Burlington *Zephyr* of 1934, also known as *Zephyr* 9900 and later as the *Pioneer Zephyr*. Though UP's M-10000 was the first streamliner per se, the *Zephyr* was the first successful application of diesel-electric technology to over-the-road mainline service. Virtually all previous diesel-electric rail applications had been for switching. American Flyer dogged the *Zephyr*'s carbody builder, Edward G. Budd Manufacturing, for a set of plans so Flyer was able to release a tinplate version of the *Zephyr* in O gauge simultaneous with the prototype's debut. *Chicago Museum of Science and Industry*

Keeping up with American Flyer and Lionel, both Louis Marx and William Hafner brought out their own M-10000 trains modeled in buttercup yellow tin with wind-up keys sticking out of the power car. The otherworldly look of the articulated one-of-a-kind trains lent themselves nicely to colorful fantasies on lithographed tin. Marx also produced the M-10005 *City of Denver* with a Joy Line motor under the tin shell. As a marketing touch, a medallion was included with the set that was struck using the same type of metal (aluminum) used in the actual streamliner. Model railroads were pacing the real railroads as the streamliner era brought new revenues to large and small alike.

Joshua Cowen needed all the revenues he could handle and his second little money-maker for 1934 was the Mickey and Minnie Mouse handcar.

TOP: A 1936 Lionel *Flying Yankee* leans into a curve with all lights on. This articulated streamliner was based on another Budd-built, Electro-Motive/Winton-engined articulated train that was a virtual twin to Burlington's *Zephyr*. The real *Flying Yankee* was jointly owned by Boston & Maine and Maine Central and revolutionized rail travel between Boston, Massachusetts, and Portland, Maine. *Don Roth collection*

ABOVE: A rare Hafner copper and green wind-up streamliner. This model, loosely based on Union Pacific's yellow-and-brown M-10000 articulated streamliner, was produced in 1938 only. *Chris Rohlfing collection*

The Disney cartoon "Mickey's Choo-choo" ended with Mickey and Minnie pumping a handcar off into the sunset; such must have been the inspiration for the Lionel wind-up model. It was a novelty—maybe even a gimmick—but at the time, celebrity toys were all the vogue, just as they are today. Radio, comic page, and film celebrities were in high demand to add their names to products, and these tie-ins were becoming big business.

Walt Disney was no rube when it came to licensing his little critters, and in 1934 his merchandising program was providing almost a third of Disney's total net profit. For the Disney touch, licensees paid out from $2^1/_2$ to five per cent of their product's income. Ingersol Watch Company was drowning in debt when it put Mickey Mouse on one of its watches. The finger-pointing mouse turned around Ingersol's bottom line.

With receivers peering at his books through icy peepers, Cowen put his pen to paper with the Disney organization and came out with the little wind-up handcar. It sold for a dollar—and sell it did. Over 253,000 whisked into the sales pipeline to be gobbled up.

Between revenues from the M-10000—expensive at $20, not including the special track it needed to form a 72-inch-radius loop instead of the traditional O gauge 31-inch loop—and the sheer sales volume of the cheap Mickey Mouse handcar, Lionel avoided going broke and by 1935 was about $400,000 in the black. Lionel paid off its debts, and the court returned $1.9 million in assets back to Lionel control. The receivers were discharged, and Cowen was even able to anticipate new designs and profits for the promising O gauge line.

The 1935 catalog reflected the rush to streamlining. On the cover is a lad holding a model of the Milwaukee Road *Hiawatha*, a beautiful streamlined steam locomotive, sleek and flashy in orange, gray, and maroon livery. The new *"Hi"* was a sensation on the Chicago–Milwaukee–St. Paul/Minneapolis run in the Midwest. Lionel had broken its Eastern snobbery and had become the only maker of this most desirable model. Also in that catalog was a model of the first steam locomotive to be streamlined, a New York Central Hudson that had been shrouded and subsequently christened *Commodore Vanderbilt*. Longtime president of the New York Central, Cornelius "Commodore" Vanderbilt was of the richest tycoons in American industry; he had died in 1877. The real locomotive was a regular 4-6-4 Hudson to which sheet steel cowling had been applied to cut wind resistance while making it look racy. It was often assigned to pulling the train of the same name between New York and Chicago. Lionel's version was not a Hudson, but a 2-4-2; however the general feel was the same.

Not to be outdone by NYC, the Pennsylvania Railroad hired famed designer Raymond Loewy to design a streamlined shrouding for one of the its K-4s Pacific locomotives, a project completed in 1936. His design featured a rounded nose and sweeping fender skirts; Lionel's version also came out in 1936 along with an O gauge copy of the *Blue Comet*, formerly the sole preserve of the huge 400E standard-gauge locomotive.

Out in the real world, President Roosevelt's battle with the Depression was showing progress.

The economy was looking up, and as the calendar clicked over into 1937, the toy train suddenly made a quantum leap forward—and Lionel was at the leading edge of model train design, absolutely unassailable with a new locomotive designated the 700E.

The brass model of the 700E, made by a Swedish firm in New York, was shown at the 1937 New York Toy Fair. Alongside it was a slightly stripped-down version, the 763E, made of plaster. Prototypes shown to dealers at this fair were often come-ons that would be adjusted for production costs before the actual models were produced. Dealers looked at these two locomotives and shook their heads. Nice looking . . . but Lionel?

The brass 700E was a stunning scale model, not the free-hand caricature that usually came off the Lionel boards. It was a 4-6-4 with narrow flanges on all the drive wheels. Every detail of the original locomotive seemed to be in place: piping, domes, pop valves, drive rods, pumps, reverse gear, steps, wire handrails, firebox—and even the rivet detail. Scale knuckle couplers extended from the pilot and the tender. What did Cowen have in mind?

Joshua Cowen had decided to take Lionel into the scale hobbyists market with these locomotives and the scale freight cars he had on the drawing

A look at "the mouse that saved Lionel" and other variations of the famous wind-up Mickey and Minnie Mouse handcar. In 1934, Lionel licensed the mouse from Disney, and its sales helped lift the train-maker out of financial straits. At bottom is the famous Mickey and Minnie handcar of 1935; second from bottom is the Peter Rabbit or "Chick Mobile" that came out in 1936. To its right is Santa Claus, offered in 1935 and 1936 but not as popular as Mickey. At top is Donald Duck with Pluto in the doghouse, appearing in Lionel catalogs from 1936 to 1937. *Train Collectors Association Toy Train Museum, Strasburg, Pennsylvania*

The cover of the 1935 Lionel catalog drew on the smiling old train engineer with a young lad and the famous Milwaukee Road streamlined steamer featured that year. Nothing like a wise old grandpa to touch the hearts of youth and the thin pocketbooks of Dads. *Train Collectors Association Toy Train Museum, Strasburg, Pennsylvania*

Lionel's 238E version of the streamlined Pennsylvania K-4s Pacific is occasionally referred to as the "torpedo," although it is believed this nickname was used more in reference to the model than the prototype. Behind it is the New York Central streamlined steamer *Commodore Vanderbilt*—a shrunken model of the prototype 4-6-4 shrouded Hudson that used to pull the *Commodore Vanderbilt* train between New York and Chicago. *Don Roth collection*

boards. It was a bold move in 1937, but the prestige factor for this limited-production engine seemed worth it. Dies were made in Italy from the brass prototype. These dies withstood the high-pressure injection of zinc alloy into every tiny crevice down to the last rivet head. The drivers had narrow flanges because Cowen planned to run the train only on T-rail track where the edges of the rails were prototypically sharp-edged and shallow compared to the rolled tubular rails of tinplate track. The minimum curve radius allowed was 72 inches—or Lionel's designation, O-72. The price for the locomotive and coal tender alone was $75. In 1937 dollars, this was a huge sum for a toy train, but Cowen considered this a scale model, and hand-finished beauties available from other manufacturers in brass cost several hundred dollars.

The attention to detail did not extend to the engineer's cab interior, but the number of rivets on the tender was only three shy of the prototype. This news devastated Cowen but was a happy discovery for the hobby's rivet-counters who relish pointing out such heresies. Since it was built at a cost of somewhere between $45,000 and $75,000, Lionel's sales force had to sell 1,500 to break even. To help move the locomotive, the 1937 catalog featured it on the cover and even offered a walnut display stand for salivating dads to show it off in the den, on the mantle, or as the crown jewel of the hobby room. How many kids actually got to hold or operate this exquisite model is open to conjecture.

To accommodate buyers who wanted to run a Hudson on their O gauge tracks and not completely empty their wallets of hard-earned and saved wages, Lionel offered the 763E. This locomotive had less boiler detail, and the middle drive wheels were "blind," meaning they had no flanges, allowing the locomotive to negotiate a tighter radius. It could be had with or without scale knuckle couplers for $37.50.

With Lionel rapidly climbing out of the Depression, the company made its first stock offering at $12 a share in the year of the Hudson. Young Lawrence was also lured from his brokerage long enough to attend meetings of the Lionel board of directors. Bit by bit, Joshua was reeling his son into the family business.

With success came Lionel's first employee

strike. Two hundred workers walked out the door demanding a 40-cent-per-hour raise. Mario Caruso stared them down, and in two weeks they accepted a 15 per cent pay increase—below the 40-cent demand—and went back to work. By 1942, however, the United Paper, Novelty, and Toyworker's Union came marching in under the auspices of the War Labor Board, and the Lionel family became unionized.

Over at American Flyer, Lionel's two years of work on the Hudson had not gone unnoticed. In 1936, Flyer designers stole some of Lionel's thunder with a die-cast Hudson of their own—the 1681. Rushed into the catalog, the 1681 was a considerable jump up from the toylike trend that had preceded it. Of course, American Flyer did not have the deep pockets of Lionel. The 1930s had not been kind to the Flyer line. Although stamped-steel locomotives with manual reverse levers resembled the toylike Lionel locomotives, the iffy seamwork and cost-cutting measures showed, and some of this cost-cutting was carried over into the Hudson. Although the valve gear was impressive with its sliding cross-head and crank action, the trailing truck was stamped out of tin. Instead of four wheels in that truck, there were only two, leaving the lead set of journal boxes empty. Inside the locomotive cab and fastened to the locomotive end of the stamped-steel tender were slabs of lead weight for better traction. The two weights in the engine cab laid side by side like two rounded-top coffins for the crew.

An operating Lionel 700E Hudson rounds a curve hauling a short freight of Lionel scale cars. These 1937 locomotives were built not just to look good, but to run forever. Jim Flynn regularly operates his 700E locomotives rather than keep them static under glass. *Jim Flynn collection*

Later, in 1937, Flyer introduced a cast aluminum tender with a molded coal pile and six-wheel cast trucks. One nice touch American Flyer provided for its customers was access to the motor brushes, which were usually the first thing to wear out. Both brushes peeped out beneath the locomotive's catwalk and thus allowed replacement without the entire locomotive having to be dismantled. If nothing else, the production shortcuts allowed Flyer to sell its Hudson for $15 versus $75 for the Lionel rendition. American Flyer followed up with other die-cast locomotives including a nice little 0-6-0 yard switcher, introduced in 1938, that was based on the Pennsylvania Railroad's Class B prototype, complete with slope-back tender and a back-up light.

Despite these highlights, American Flyer by 1938 was floating rudderless and therefore ripe for purchase—and that's just what happened. At the 1937 meeting of the Toy Manufacturers Association, Alfred C. Gilbert ran into his old friend William Coleman and told him he'd have a new competitor in the electric train business because Gilbert was contemplating launching a line of HO gauge trains. According to Maury Romer, a long-time American Flyer veteran interviewed in *A. C. Gilbert's Heritage* (Heimberger House, 1983), Coleman countered Gilbert with a better idea: "Why don't you take over American Flyer?"

The two men worked out a deal whereby the A. C. Gilbert Company would pay for American Flyer over a period of 12 years. No sooner had the ink dried on the papers when Gilbert moved the manufacturing from Chicago to Gilbert's plant in New Haven, Connecticut, together with about 24 stunned employees and enough administrative help to get the plant operating.

Just before everyone was hustled off to the East Coast, according to Maury Romer in the same interview, a Flyer sales manager named Phil Connell happened to visit the Cleveland Model Supply shop and became enamored with S gauge trains. Modeled to 3/16 inch to a foot rather than the 1/4 inch of O gauge, S gauge seemed to have better proportions and looked more real and less stubby than Lionel models. Combining the best of both worlds and saving considerable dollars, perhaps Flyer could build S gauge models to run on O gauge track while everyone else had O-gauge models. Would that idea play in New Haven?

A. C. Gilbert was born in New Haven in 1884. Before he graduated from Yale, he was building and selling magic tricks as the Mysto Manufacturing Company. In 1913 he conceptualized the Erector Set, inspired by construction crews on the New Haven Railroad who were erecting catenary bridges for the railroad's electrification project. This most popular of all boys' toys established his personal fortune and provided a stepping stone toward the day in 1938 when American Flyer came under his stewardship.

With considerable gusto, Gilbert embraced the idea of 3/16-inch-scale trains running on O gauge track. The timing would be just right, for the new

American Flyer's bullet-nose 4-4-2 Atlantic in streamlined shrouding dates from 1940 and was based on a prototype Baltimore & Ohio steam locomotive used to power the road's Washington, D.C.–Jersey City, New Jersey, *Royal Blue* streamliner. This 3/16-inch scale model in gunmetal gray ran on standard O gauge, three-rail track. It was offered in two-rail S gauge following World War II. In its S gauge incarnation, it was painted in a number of different liveries to become the *Royal Blue, Silver Bullet*, or the deep-red Circus Train locomotive. *Dave Guerriges collection*

dies would have to be made in 1938 for the new train line to appear in the 1939 catalog. The transformation was made, and the new S-scale trains looked great—much closer to the real thing than Lionel (save, perhaps, for Lionel's Hudson of 1937) and much better than any Lionel rolling stock except for the four freight cars designed to be pulled by the 700/763E Hudson. Even the lowest-cost die-cast American Flyer locomotives of the eight steam locomotives in the pre-World War II 3/16-inch scale line looked like an expensive scale model.

Meanwhile, over at 200 Fifth Avenue in New York, Louis Marx was busy keeping up with the other guys. The year 1937 found him trying to come up with a decent automatic coupler. Lionel had created a good-looking manual box coupler in 1936, then improved it as an automatic version in 1938. Louis, on the other hand, had kept the old hook-and-slot or hook-and-hole connectors that required Hand of God (i.e., the toy train's owner or operator) coupling and uncoupling. The couplers worked, so Marx initially thought "Why change?" Marx would rather save a few cents buying tinned steel that had been rejected for soup can stock.

When finally moved to challenge the big guys once again, Marx settled on a mechanic's nightmare of a coupler with springs and lots of moving parts. They were called "one-way couplers." Each car had a male coupler on one end and a female coupler on the other, and only heterosexual coupling was permitted. These complex and costly automatic couplers lasted only from 1938 to 1941 when Louis opted for a simpler hermaphrodite coupler that worked on either end of thc car. He fitted it to his version of 3/16-inch-scale cars in 1941.

Noting that the sound of change jingling in pockets had grown louder as the 1940s drew closer, Louis Marx listened with the same tuned ears as Joshua Cowen and A .C. Gilbert as interest in scale model railroading and a desire for more realism in tinplate trains showed an upswing. While Lionel and American Flyer worked with die casting to obtain realistic details, Marx stayed with stamped steel but augmented the look with lithographed details, handrails, working hatches, grab irons, and other nice touches. It wasn't all actual detail; rather, it was a clever illusion of detail. This approach allowed Marx to offer a complete set including locomotive, three freight cars, track, and transformer for $15—a price that

Continued on page 86

The American Flyer "Challenger" was actually a Northern-type locomotive named after Union Pacific's 4-6-6-4 articulateds. This model from about 1940 is in pre-war 3/16-inch scale O gauge and has remote-control reverse. One operating flaw was the cow-catcher occasionally coming into contact with the third rail and causing an electrical short. The Challenger was the top-of-the-line model in American Flyer's steam-locomotive offerings, both before and after World War II. *Dave Guerriges collection*

This picture should be titled "ugly couplers." It shows Louis Marx one-way, post, or pincher couplers of the late 1930s. On the far left is the prototype, showing the earliest concept of the overly complex pincher (female) coupler. To the right are the production model of the one-way pincher (female) and the post (male). Cars could only be coupled one way. The two-way "dagger" coupler eventually replaced these examples. *Jim Flynn collection*

Hooking Them All Together

The American toy train has always been modeled after prototype railroads, but while toy designers tried to follow the evolution of locomotives and rolling stock through decades of change, their methods for hooking the locomotive to the rolling stock was an exercise in whimsy. For the real railroads, although there were numerous patented ideas, there have been, basically, three kinds of couplers: simple chains looped over hooks like their early European counterparts, various versions of the link-and-pin, and the Janney knuckle coupler—a variation of which continues today. Not so with the toy train.

Floor draggers made by Ives, Kenton, Ideal, and others cast the coupler into the frame—a hole at one end of the car and a stud or pin at the other. Earliest toy electric trains, like the Carlisle & Finch models, used simple bent wires looped over spring bumpers at the end of each car. A basic flat metal hook slipped through a slot served for years with Ives, Dorfan, Lionel, American Flyer, Hafner, and Marx. All these required "hand of God" manual coupling and uncoupling. Later, attempts at "automatic" coupling produced unrealistic designers' nightmares such as Lionel's "latch," the Marx "one-way," and American Flyer's simple, efficient, but hardly prototypical "link."

Each maker worked hard to build realistic, colorful motive power and rolling stock, but could not get the coupling straight until Lionel introduced the first automatic knuckle coupler in 1945. Even this design had too many pieces and had to be simplified. In 1952, American Flyer brought out its own knuckle coupler while Louis Marx, with his fanciful lithographed tin and, later, plastic, trains remained out of the "realism" fray.

Today, virtually all electric train manufacturers—except the new Marx Trains—use automatic knuckle couplers for their tinplate models that can be opened over a magnetic track section or by computer-chip control anywhere on the track.

ABOVE: The Lionel "latch" coupler was introduced in 1924 and billed as "automatic." It was hardly a true automatic coupler—which should allow cars to be coupled from afar if not also uncoupled—but it endured until 1942. *Don Roth collection*

BELOW: Lionel's low-cost Winner line, introduced in 1932, was designed "for little brother" and was built around re-cycled Ives inventory. The coupler was a simple hook—the preferred coupler of the Ives line. *Train Collectors Association Toy Train Museum, Strasburg, Pennsylvania*

ABOVE: In 1938, Lionel followed up its manual box coupler with an automatic version that opened when passing over an electromagnet in a special track section. In that same year, different truck designs also dictated high and low coupler heights, adding to coupling problems when cars were intermixed. *Don Roth collection*

ABOVE: In 1945, Lionel scooped American Flyer with the first automatic knuckle coupler. This coupler was activated by a "sliding shoe" that rode along an isolated rail section in a special piece of track. At a push-button command when the car was over the special track, the coupler's electromagnet opened the knuckle. This system lasted until the magnet was put in the track, eliminating occasional derailments on switches and simplifying the coupler's design. *Chris Rohlfing collection*

LEFT: Two American Flyer freight cars showing the difference between the pre-war-to-1952 "link" coupler on the tank car and Flyer's fairly reliable version of an automatic knuckle coupler introduced in 1952. Though Flyer maintained that being stuck with the link coupler was no impediment to its "realism" claim, the link couplers frequently were airbrushed out of catalog art. Lionel's patented knuckle coupler of 1945 was a marketing coup that lasted six years until Flyer could work around it with its own design. *Mike Schafer collection*

Marx locomotive 897 is lithographed tinplate over a reversible wind-up motor. The lever atop the boiler can be flipped to reverse direction. *Jim Flynn collection*

Continued from page 83

wouldn't buy the tender for a Lionel 700E. Marx's 3/16-inch-scale freight cars looked good enough when they appeared in 1942 that when the cars returned after the war, American Flyer S gauge modelers swapped out Marx trucks and couplers for Flyer running gear and ran them with the more expensive Flyer rolling stock. Production of the Marx 3/16-inch freight line continued until 1955; a passenger line began in 1950 and continued until 1972.

At the Hafner Manufacturing Company, time stood still for the little wind-up trains as color dominated the locomotives as well as the lithographed tin cars. Hafner produced its most prolific design—the model 1010a streamlined 0-4-0 steam locomotive that was offered in a number of cheery color combinations. The big features were a track-actuated bell and, on later models, a battery-powered headlamp. These were true toy trains and sold well into the 1950s.

Hafner catalogs are rare. The manufacturer stayed with wind-up trains until production shut down in the mid-1950s. Notice the basic 0-4-0 wheel configuration. Marx followed the same pattern: a basic wheel set and many lithographed tin shells. *Train Collectors Association Toy Train Museum, Strasburg, Pennsylvania*

The State of the (Toy Train) Union as of World War II

The end of the so-called Classic Period of toy train manufacture had come as the nation moved from the Great Depression toward a war economy. Roosevelt's neutral Arsenal of Democracy was feeding new jobs and lethal products for beleaguered England and France into our economic pipeline. New materials, new manufacturing processes such as zinc die casting, and an awareness of a need for greater realism were driving the new designs as the 1940s arrived. Greater play value was being built into cars and accessories. Lionel, for example, introduced a coal loader, log loader, magnetic crane, and a bascule bridge that could be manually raised or lowered. Coal cars and log flats dumped their loads at the touch of a button. More and more operating features were accessible from button pads at the transformer location.

The big, beautiful standard-gauge trains were gone, replaced by smaller and more affordable O-gauge sets. Ives, the leader in toy making for a century, had faded away, ground under by mediocre management and the crush of the Great Depression. Carlisle & Finch was happy and profitable turning out marine illumination and navigation equipment. The beautiful Model 45 locomotive, the electric crane car, and the long suspension bridge gathered dust in a factory storeroom. Dorfan had exploded on the scene with great trains, giving Lionel a brief run for the money—and then Dorfan crumbled as its diecast locomotives and cars did likewise.

The American Flyer name had barely dodged the economic bullets of the Depression, left Chicago for a new start in New Haven, Connecticut, under the steady and innovative hand of entrepreneur A. C. Gilbert, and was making a major comeback. Lionel had finessed and bullied its way through the 1930s, wisely dropping what didn't make money and using a caterpillarlike yellow streamliner and a pair of mice on a wind-up hand-car to keep on track. Joshua Lionel Cowen's company was poised to keep that momentum going, spurred on by the

ABOVE: Scrap metal was moved between gondolas by the prewar Lionel Magnetic Crane. One button activated the magnet, another swiveled the crane, and a third deactivated the magnet, dropping the metal. It was introduced in 1940 and reissued after the war in 1946–47. *Don Roth collection*

LEFT: The Lionel log loader, first offered in 1940, accepted logs into its rear tray from an automated log dump car. A button-push-operated chain linked arms that carried the logs up and dropped them into the front bin. A second button dumped them into a waiting car on the front track. *Don Roth collection*

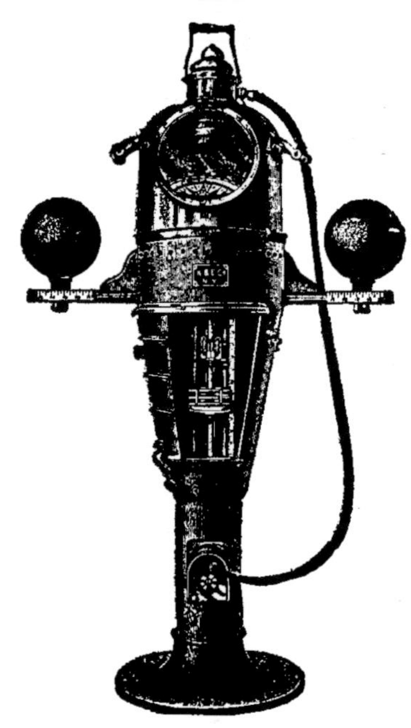

This World War II binnacle housed a compass repeater that gave readings from the main gyro compass to a Navy ship's bridge command. During World War I, they held magnetic compasses. Lionel made these for the Navy during both wars. *Blue Jacket Manual, U. S. Navy, 1939*

new competition from American Flyer.

And then Japanese bombs dropped on Pearl Harbor two weeks and four days before Christmas in 1941. America rolled up its sleeves and toy trains were put on the back burner for the duration. Not that everything just came to a screeching halt. Before strategic materials restrictions shut off the manufacture of toy trains, Louis Marx was pushing his army train featuring a flatcar-mounted gun and a shell gondola. Lionel proposed two snappy war trains for the 1942 Toy Train Fair in New York City. Chosen because it resembled an armored locomotive when daubed with camouflage paint, the old 265E *Commodore Vanderbilt* steam locomotive was now hauling flatcars bristling with cannons, scout cars, tanks, and anti-aircraft guns. Another entry, the *Victoryliner*, was the 1934 *Flying Yankee* streamliner striped along its length in red, white, and blue.

These patriotic trains and concepts for railroad cannons triggered by remote control trundled down tinplate tracks into a dead-end spur as steel, zinc, aluminum, copper, brass, and other materials were diverted to wartime use in the real world. Of course, there are always folks who see opportunities where others see nothing. Louis Hertz, writing in his 1944 book, *Riding the Tinplate Rails*, noted two companies, American Toy Works and the D. A. Pachter Company, that joined in competition with Lionel to provide kids a train made of non-strategic cardboard.

Only Lionel's effort is remembered today. Cowen was desperate to keep Lionel's name in front of American kids until the war was over. Samuel Gold, the premium king who designed prizes for candymakers, brainstormed all over Cowen with the dire warning that a generation of kids would grow up denied the joys of electric trains—the chain from father to son would be broken. Chaos would reign unless Lionel brought out a train made of cardboard. The entire train from locomotive to caboose and track was delivered in a flat pack of cardboard sheets with lithographed pieces—some 250 for a Lionel O gauge train—ready to be punched out and fastened together with slots and tabs. Behind the 1943 tub-thumping slogan, "Lionel Steel Has Gone to War," these cardboard choo-choos were made available to train-starved youth.

Assembling this "paper train" took the patience of a monastery monk, and the end result looked exactly like . . . a train made of paper. Lionel also tried a line of wood pull-toys and railroad accessories—anything to keep the name alive as patriotic kids fed their old trains to the scrap drives. If nothing else, the paper trains and wood pull trains would become eminently collectible a half century after the war.

While Lionel's marketing department was grasping at straws, the back shop was jammed with war contracts. Lionel took up where it left off during the first World War, producing non-magnetic cases called binnacles that contained marine gyro compasses floating in an alcohol solution. Other navigation aids included the pelorus, a special compass located on a ship's bridge wing equipped with precision adjustable vernier scales used to take bearings on near-by shore objects. Lionel also assembled the alidade, a telescopic device used to take bearings off distant objects by means of adjustable scales superimposed over the object appearing on internal front-surface mirrors. Many a merchant and Navy ship owed their successful navigation in pre-radar days to these precision instruments built by Lionel.

Over in New Haven, the Gilbert shops were exercising their patriotic duties turning out piece parts for machine guns and land mines. Gilbert engineers also applied design know-how in creating booby-trap firing devices. Who knows how many enemy soldiers received "Surprise!" gifts from the American toymaker.

Louis Marx, because of his preeminence as a major toy manufacturer, always moved easily within the ranks of business moguls of the prewar years. He tried exploiting these contacts by offering to put real railroad logos on his electric train cars in order to both advertise the railroad and to encourage people served by that road to buy Marx trains. Though Louis was a wealthy man and his corporation was huge, the thrifty Marx went sour on the promotion when railroad officials demanded free train sets. When war came, however, one of his rare free gifts proved to be a profitable windfall.

An obscure major named Arnold stationed at Boling Field in the 1930s prevailed on Marx to get a track switch for an electric train. Grateful, Arnold introduced Louis to other military toy train fans, a Captain Walter Smith and a staff brigadier general over at Fort Myer named Eisenhower. Later, when war was declared, Maj. H. H. "Hap" Arnold moved on to become Chief of the United States Army Air Forces in June 1941. The

This World War II train set was offered by Sears—note the Allstate logo (Allstate Insurance being an associate company of Sears). It is made of rubber and is a floor train. Marketers were doing everything possible to keep some kind of toy trains in the hands of kids during the war. Over the years the rare train has hardened to the consistency of coal. *Jim Flynn collection*

captain became General Walter Bedell Smith, U.S. Secretary of the Combined Chiefs of Staff in 1942 and an acknowledged hatchet man for General Dwight Eisenhower, Supreme Commander of the Allied Forces in Europe. Suddenly, Louis was traveling in heady company.

From 1942 to 1945, Marx plants were awarded numerous war material contracts. After the war, toy train buff Eisenhower asked Louis to travel through Europe and assay those toy-making plants that remained standing for their ability to be converted back to war production. This tour allowed Marx to not only make his report, but to make valuable off-shore contacts. After surveying 171 plants in Germany alone, Louis returned with postwar plans for building toys overseas as well as at home.

During World War II, Hafner made beer bottle caps for the Fox Brewing Company. The lightweight steel Hafner had on hand was too light for any military use, yet all toy train production ended by official decree on June 30, 1942. William Hafner fumed over wartime restrictions and finally passed the company along to his son, John. On December 29, 1944, William Hafner died. Following his death, Robert McCready, publisher of the trade magazine *Playthings*, penned a respectful obituary as quoted in the *Greenberg's Guide to Early American Toy Trains* chapter, "The History of the Hafner Manufacturing Company," by Paul A. Doyle.

McCready held William Hafner in esteem—as a man and a friend as well as for his energy and capacity as a manufacturer. He had a simple code: shoot straight, keep your word, pay your debts, and speak ill of no man.

The war years were bleak for young railroaders as they watched loaded troop and material trains criss-cross the country, and the same prewar toy train appeared during the holidays without any new car, locomotive, or accessory to liven up the play. One artifact discovered during the writing of this book comes from the collection of Jim Flynn, who with his wife Debbie creates today's Marx trains. It is a solid rubber floor train with wooden wheels, and it represents just how desperate the toy train problem became during the war. The steam locomotive is black and the cars are painted red, yellow, and blue. The boxcar is labeled Allstate which suggests Sears, but Jim has been unable to catalog it anywhere. Built of slugs of truck tire rubber, the little locomotive and its cars have now hardened to the density of coal.

When the war ended, both Lionel and American Flyer could proudly wave their war production flags, and John Hafner could stop punching out bottle caps. American servicemen were returning with the GI bill in their pockets and a thirst for the good life after almost five years of war. The baby boom was beginning and a new electric toy train boom was just taking off.

In the post-World War II years of toy trains, catalogs were a critical aspect of marketing. The release of the latest Lionel or American Flyer catalog was in itself an event eagerly anticipated by baby boomers whose Christmas world revolved around their toy train collections. The illustration on this American Flyer catalog cover for 1953 made toy train operation larger than life. *Mike Schafer collection*

Chapter 6

Battle of the Catalogs— Lionel and Flyer Go Head to Head

A quintet of Lionel O gauge F3 diesels. These were the premier road diesel locomotives of the Lionel line since the Santa Fe was introduced in 1948. Shown here are the 2243 Santa Fe, Milwaukee Road, Illinois Central, Wabash, and the Southern. The only one missing from this line-up is the 1956 Baltimore & Ohio. *Chris Rohlfing collection*

By the time the Japanese signed surrender documents on the deck of the U.S.S. *Missouri* in Tokyo Bay, it was September 2, 1945—only four months until Christmas.

America was in shock when the war ended. The country had suffered through four years of roller-coaster emotions as victories were won and defeats suffered, of casualty lists and food rationing, of German submarines raiding East Coast convoys, and Japanese submarines shelling the West Coast. Thanksgiving 1945 was celebrated with real emotion, and Christmas would wring out the last tears of mourning for those who failed to return home and tears of joy for those who did. It was also was the last "rationed" Christmas, the last denial Christmas.

America had survived the war as an industrial giant. A vast retooling process was clanking into place lead by industries that were cash-rich. The Great Depression was long over, and bank savings began to climb in value. War plant workers and returning service men and women became avid consumers once again.

America's railroads played a crucial role in winning the war, but the job had left them decimated. Steam locomotives that had been resurrected for the duration were now clapped-out, leaking tea kettles. Track was badly beat up. Freight rolling stock that had transported over 70 per cent of material between the two coasts, sagged in sidings as the momentum wore down. Passenger cars that had carried 91 per cent of American troops and civilians for four years were gut-sprung and as war weary as the people they had carried. But before the last guns had fired, the railroad industry—in the car shops and locomotive plants—had spun on its heel in preparation to resume its place with new designs in victorious America.

General Motors' new prewar Electro-Motive F- and E-series diesel-electric road locomotives had proven themselves during the war. Steam-locomotive designs had been frozen by the wartime government to allow only the most efficient and capacious solutions to cross-country travel. Multi-wheeled monsters now shouldered their way through the yards to lead mile-long freight trains over the Rockies and through the West Virginia hills.

Toy Train Production Resumes

The day after the atomic bomb turned Hiroshima into radioactive ash-choked ruins, all war contracts at Lionel were terminated. That was August 6, 1945 and, even working as fast as possible with retooling, Lionel could not resume production of electric trains until October. Most frustrating was the huge materials shortage which greatly hampered any introduction of a laundry list of innovations. Such would have to wait until 1946. Lionel faced this challenge under the guiding hand of Lawrence Cowen, Joshua's financier son, who had been elected by the Lionel board of directors in June. Joshua was anointed as chairman.

Cowen had kept the Lionel name in front of kids and parents for four years with slick publications like the *Lionel Railroad Planning Book*. Gazing at track plans and future layouts as the war rumbled overseas had produced the desired effect. As peace returned, dads and sons were chafing to buy new electric trains to put under the Christmas tree in the new house with the new car in the driveway. As the postwar hypereconomy grew, Lionel wanted to be first out of the blocks with exciting new trains and features.

Lionel had to settle for somewhat less. On November 15, 1945, in the redecorated Lionel showroom on New York's East 26th Street, only one little set rushed around the high iron. It was headed by a prewar, die-cast 2-6-2 steam locomotive (an updated Model 224). When it hurried past with its four-car freight, the coal tender emitted a wheezy toot from a remote-control whistle. Just ahead of the caboose was a car that represented a technology breakthrough that would change toy train manufacturing for decades—a black Pennsylvania gondola made of . . . molded plastic.

Under a few Christmas trees in 1945, young railroaders had a chance to be the first to test Lionel's major innovation of the decade, the remote-controlled knuckle coupler. Connecting the cars in train set No. 463W, each coupler had a

A World War II-era cover of the Southern Pacific Railroad's employee magazine, *Southern Pacific Bulletin*, depicting the railroads' part in winning the war by hauling strategic weapons to ports on both of America's coasts to fight a two-front conflict. *Gerry Souter collection*

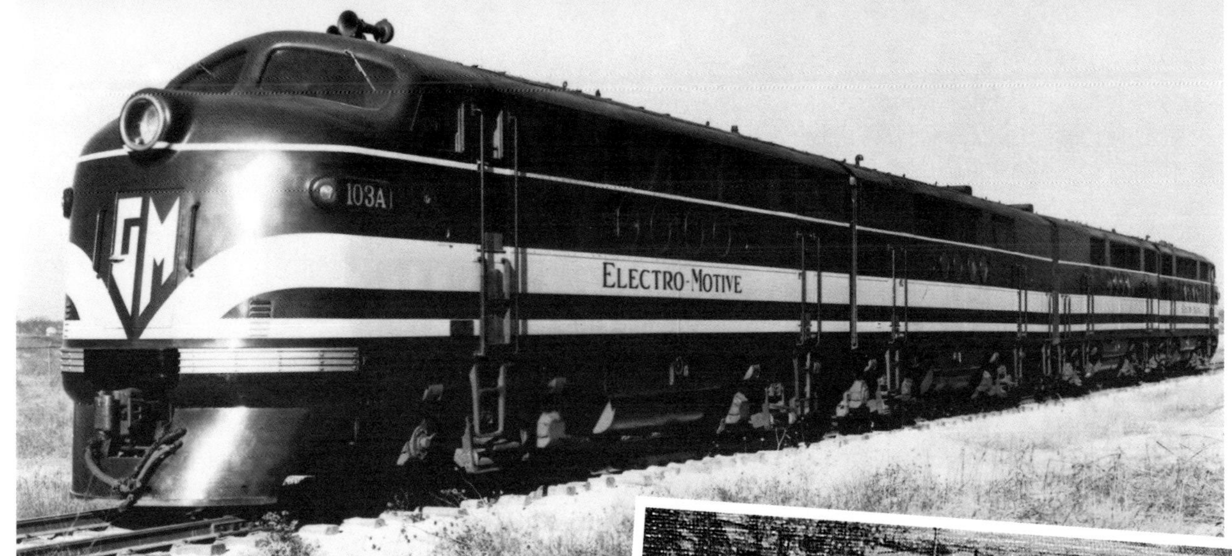

General Motors' Electro-Motive Division built demonstrators of its new FT diesel-electric locomotive and sent them out to the major railroads. This is the original demonstrator FT quartet (actually a pair of A-B sets) of 1939, ready to haul freight or passenger trains. The FT was built through World War II and provided heavy and vital service hauling freight during the war when everything on rails was pressed into service. The FT model was superceded after the war by the F3, which Lionel would hesitantly offer new in 1948. *General Motors Archives*

small electromagnetic coil that opened the coupler's jaw when it passed over a special remote-control track section. This realistic coupler was more of a marketing coup than a practical mass-production unit, for it had too many pieces and was very fragile. In fact, it had been tried in 1939 before being dropped as a repairman's nightmare. Each car featuring the new coupler was equipped with a sliding shoe which made contact with the control rails of the special track section. This shoe was subject to wear and sometimes briefly picked up unwanted electrical currents when passing through switches, causing cars to accidentally uncouple. But it was the first remote-control knuckle coupler in toy traindom, and the mechanism concept was patented.

As Lionel's knuckle coupler was examined at Gilbert's Hall of Science product strategy meeting for 1946, the sound of grinding teeth must have been palpable. A. C. Gilbert's entire premise for his postwar line of American Flyer electric trains was realism. The new 3/16-inch-scale trains running on two-rail track met that requirement admirably, but connecting these beautifully proportioned cars was a "link" coupler that bore no relationship to the knuckle version used by the real railroads. In one stroke, American Flyer had been scooped, out-flanked, and out-patented. This bit of technological upmanship would gall Gilbert, and the visually offending link couplers were often airbrushed out of existence in future catalogs until Flyer came up with a patent-skirting knuckle coupler design of its own in 1952.

Two-rail track and S gauge were American Flyer's tickets to the postwar marketplace. The hiatus in the toy-train field caused by the war provided a clean slate on which to build a new customer base. Prior to the war, a new gauge, Half the size of O—or "HO"—emerged, and after the war began making inroads to the model train market. Though initially HO had little manufacturer support, it did have some notable virtues: one could build larger railroad empires in half the space, and the new gauge featured realistic, scale models running on *two-rail* prototypical track. Gilbert exploited this emerging trend toward realism with its new two-rail S gauge train line, but with ready-built

Electro-Motive's first production E-series passenger diesel was the EA, purchased by the Baltimore & Ohio in 1937. Although they resembled the F-series that would follow in two years, Electro-Motive E-units were longer, rode on six-axle trucks, and contained two prime movers, initially each rated at 900 horsepower. This prewar postcard shows the new EAs powering the *Capitol Limited* along the Potomac River in Maryland. *Andover Junction Publications Archives*

RIGHT: Despite the "Challenger" name it carried, Flyer's largest steam locomotive model replicated a Union Pacific 4-8-4, not a Challenger, which was a 4-6-6-4 on the UP. Nonetheless, UP's Northern's were impressive machines, as illustrated in this view of No. 8444 wheeling along a Colorado highway during an excursion run in 1969. *Mike Schafer*

BELOW: An American Flyer 4-8-4 "Challenger" circa 1947 hauls a freight consist through an Erector Set bridge. This locomotive was Flyer's most impressive steam offering, before and after the war. Both center drivers were blind so that the long locomotive could better negotiate curves. Though it's really a Northern-type locomotive and not a Challenger, one can only surmise that the Flyer folks felt that the Challenger name was more inspiring. *Bill Van Ramshorst*

ABOVE: This is the 1945 Lionel freight set, the only set offered in that year. It is pulled by the Model 224 die-cast locomotive, a tender with a plastic coal pile, the four-door tin automobile car, a 2755 Sunoco tank car, the shape-of-things-to-come plastic cast Pennsylvania gondola, and a tin caboose. The tin cars are carryovers from prewar days, and all cars carry Lionel's big coup—electromagnet knuckle couplers triggered by a sliding shoe under each truck. *Jim Flynn collection*

trains (HO then was almost universally kit-based) that, being larger than HO, were easier for kids to handle.

As Louis Marx had discovered some years earlier, most toy electric trains were bought by moms, grandmas, and aunts for their precious ones. Three-rail or two-rail trains made no difference to them. Nonetheless, Gilbert's realism stance did work to a degree. The problem was that Lionel still had the most recognizable logo in the toy business second only to Marx. American Flyer had to fight for every per cent of market share it could capture. Getting skunked by a knuckle coupler and a whistle-tooting tender while tub-thumping the realism message had to have hurt Gilbert and his people.

But Lionel wasn't finished beating its competition over the head. Realizing that lack of product was bad, but lack of visibility was worse, as 1945 wound down, Joshua Cowen took Lionel $90,000 into the red so he could unleash an advertising blitz that never really ended. Deep pockets and aggressive marketing set a pace that Gilbert—a smaller company than Lionel—could never quite match for its American Flyer line.

LEFT: Lionel's 1945 flyer showing new features for that year with great promises for 1946. Lionel marketing tried everything to get its new postwar trains in front of the buying public. *Jim Flynn collection*

1946: Full Speed Ahead

The year 1946 started out a head-butting contest between the two innovative giants—and Louis Marx as well, to a degree—that would continue for decades. With its super low-cost trains and resultant high sales, Marx was really in a separate league.

Young railroaders anticipated every year's Christmas with goggle-eyed glee waiting for the train catalogs to arrive. Pages of very creative art work depicted each new locomotive, train set and accessory. These full-color dream books were poured over, pages were selectively dog-eared and left in strategic places for parental discovery as the holiday drew near. Despite heroic efforts on the part of all toy train manufacturers reaching back to the turn-of-the-century, toy trains for kids were a December item. If a layout existed on a

ABOVE: A Boston & Albany (New York Central System) Berkshire is in charge of a freight train bullying its way through Newton, Massachusetts, circa 1930. Only a few years earlier, the prototype "Berk" was being tested on the B&A and thus acquired the name "Berkshire" in honor of the mountains through which the B&A passed. *J. R. Quinn, Brian Solomon collection*

A model 726 Berkshire made by Lionel in 1948. Lionel's Berkshire was introduced in 1946 and lasted for over 20 years as the backbone of Lionel's steam fleet. The Berk prototype had a long career as well, hauling both freight and passengers from 1924 to the late 1950s. Lionel's tribute to the design had the right wheel configuration—2-8-4—but squeezed the body to accommodate the O gauge 31-inch-radius curves. *Chris Rohlfing collection*

folding plywood sheet, it was set up in December and put away soon after the New Year. Otherwise, track sections were snapped together around the base or in front of the Christmas tree. In 1952, a Jewish friend of the author's received a Lionel train during Hanukkah. With the innocence of a 12-year-old, the author asked his friend if he set it up around their Menorah.

As usual, it was Lionel who took the lead as 1946 season rolled into high gear. Its new locomotives, the 726 Berkshire and the 671 Pennsylvania steam turbine, led the charge.

The prototype Berkshire was a 2-8-4 that boasted a massive firebox supported by a four-wheel trailing truck, a fat boiler, and steaming capability that was state-of-the-art in 1924. Often, the trailing truck was fitted with a coal-saving "booster" engine to help get the behemoth under way. An Elesco feedwater heater was hung in front of the stack, giving the locomotive a beetle-browed look of concentrated power. Over 600 were built by the Lima Locomotive Works and American Locomotive Company (Alco) in many configurations and weights, from the demonstrator locomotive that successfully tested on New York Central's Boston & Albany route through the Berkshire Mountains (hence the name) in 1925 to

The only S-2 steam turbine built for the Pennsylvania Railroad, No. 6200, blasts through Fort Wayne, Indiana, in 1948. While Lionel's model of this 6-8-6 engine was a huge success on O and O-27 gauge, the real thing was a fuel hog, sucking up huge amounts of fuel at speeds under 40 miles per hour. *R. D. Acton Sr.*

A one-of-a-kind Pennsylvania steam turbine proved to be a big seller for Lionel when introduced in 1946. This 2020 model with double worm gear drive and headlight bulb that also heated a smoke pellet is the O-27 version. It lasted until 1949. The O gauge 671 model endured, changing numbers and features until 1952. *Chris Rohlfing collection*

the last "Berk" built, No. 779 for the Nickel Plate Road, in 1949. The last known Berkshire in regular service hauled freight for the National Railways of Mexico in 1963, but Nickel Plate Berk No. 765 has seen occasional excursion service in recent years while No. 779 stands on display at Lima, Ohio.

Lionel's Berkshire was a die-cast "tribute" to the original, offering the correct wheel configuration of 2-8-4, but little of the muscular brawn. The tight 31-inch-radius curves required for O gauge operation always "squeezed" the Lionel designs, requiring the middle pair of drive wheels to be blind—no flanges—in order to negotiate a half-circle of track without derailing. Lionel's first Berk of 1946 was not a mechanical success. Its worm-drive motor sounded as though it was grinding concrete, and even a moderate load of freight cars made its wheels spin. But she was beautiful and became an instant hit. From her introduction until the last version in 1968, the Berkshire was a constant seller, and while other flashier locomotives came and went, Lionel designers kept her updated and competitive.

The real Lionel mega-hit of 1946 was the turbine—an entirely different breed of cat from the Berkshire. Modeled after the Pennsylvania Railroad S-2-class 6-8-6 locomotive No 6200, a 20-wheel brutish beast of a locomotive but sans traditional cylinders and drive rods (except for those connecting the drive wheels) because it was direct drive, the Lionel version was offered in both O gauge (No. 671) and the lower-end O-27 gauge (No. 2020). A later version offered a 12-wheel tender, putting 32 wheels on the head-end of the train. One of the most successful Lionel designs of all time (far more than its prototype, which was beset by high maintenance and fuel costs), the turbine lasted until 1955 but was reissued in 1985 under the Fundimensions banner in glamorous Brunswick green livery with a silver smokebox. It offered Lionel's "Sound of Steam" and smoke and whistle as its white-striped drive wheels gripped the track with Magne-traction—a use of magnets above or in some proximity to the axles to hold the heavy engines to the rails as they sped around the 31-inch-radius O gauge curves and the even tighter 27-inch radius required of O-27 gauge. The 1946 model also offered smoke that sizzled on a light bulb with a dimple in it.

An interesting train set headed by the 671R steam turbine locomotive was Lionel's O gauge No. 4109WS Electronic Control Freight. This very short freight train comprised a boxcar, an automatic ore dump car, a gondola, and a caboose. What made it unique was its "ECU-1"—the Electronic Control Unit. Two were hidden in the locomotive's tender and one was secreted in each car. The units received discreet radio signals from a remote-control unit. At the push of a button, any of the cars uncoupled anywhere on the layout. The ore dump car tipped out its load, the engine's whistle blew, and the big locomotive started, stopped, and changed direction. For 1946

The unique "Electronic" control 671R steam turbine locomotive and all-operating-car train received its commands via radio from a special push-button command center. Each car had a radio receiver built in. At $75, it was too expensive and required high maintenance. Shown here in the 1946 catalog, the train disappeared after 1947. It was an idea ahead of its time. *Jim Flynn collection*

and 1947, this was pretty amazing toy-train technology. Alas, repair headaches and a high cost of $75 doomed the experiment, but the concept returned decades later when computer chips could do the work.

Thousands of these 671, 681, and 2020 S-2 monsters rolled out of the Lionel plant in direct contrast to the success of the Pennsylvania prototype, of which only one was built. Two steam turbine engines drove the real 6200—a huge one for forward movement and a smaller one for reverse. At any speed above 40 miles per hour, the great hulk could out-pull anything its size and at great speed. Its hauling capacity equaled the muscle of a 6,000-horsepower diesel road-switcher today. But below 40, it ate coal and blew steam like a farmhand at a bean feed. Between loading up at the coal bunker, rolling through the yard, and reaching the head-end of its train, the S-2 almost used more fuel than for its passenger assignments between Chicago and Crestline, Ohio (which occasionally included the famed New York–Chicago *Broadway Limited*). The 1944 Baldwin beast lasted a short time before being scrapped, but during its brief life, in photographs, paintings, and Lionel catalog illustrations, it came to symbolize the power of America's railroads.

The 1946 full color catalog also featured the smoke-belching, whistle-blowing S-2 (Model 2020 LTS) hauling six different lower-cost O-27 train sets with operating coal, lumber, and merchandise cars. The O gauge 1945 Model 224 locomotive hauled three of Lionel's last sheet-metal passenger cars, the 2400 series. New molded and die-cast freight and passenger cars showed exquisite detail. Each "WS" (With Smoke) set promised a "generous supply of smoke pellets" that drove Mom and Dad from the living room to

Green Lionel 2400-series passenger cars. These are postwar sheet-metal cars and were the last of the 2400s issued in prewar days. Die-cast cars eventually replaced all the sheet metal cars. *Jim Flynn collection*

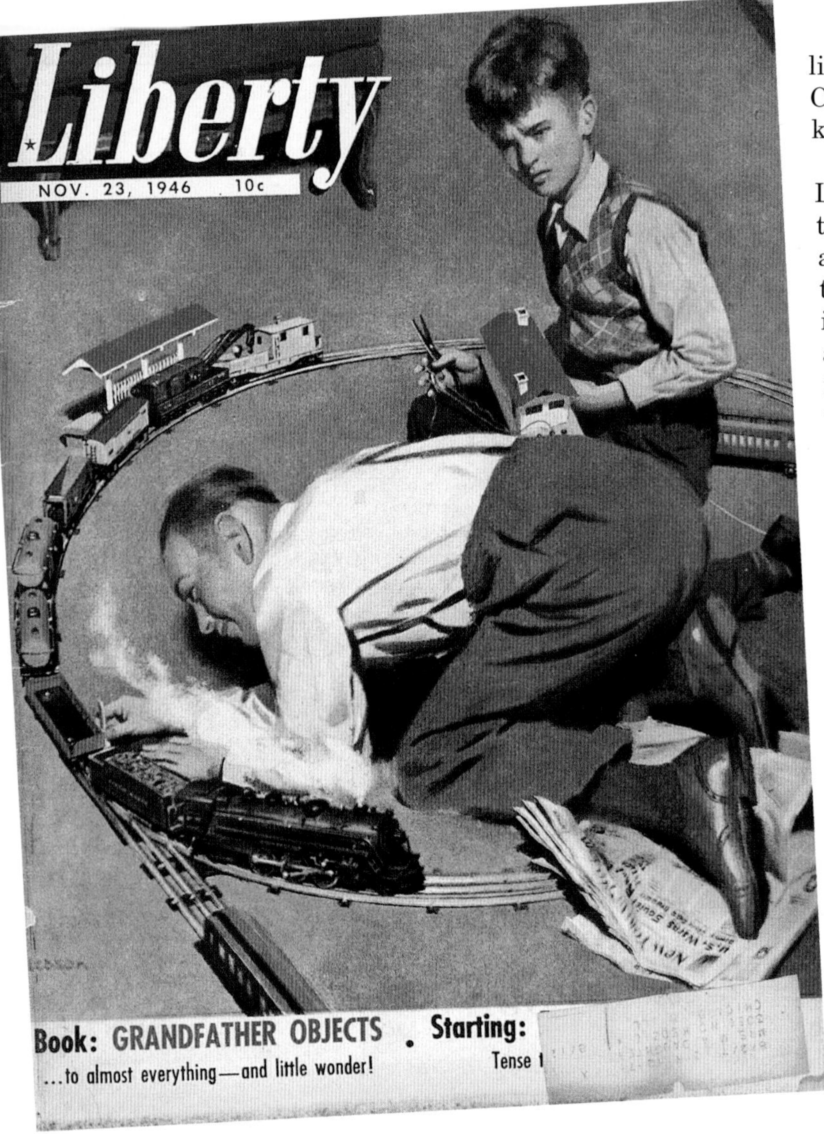

The famous *Liberty* magazine of November 23, 1946, offered Lionel a way to beat a printers' strike and get its catalogs in front of kids. Lionel bought a record 16-page block of advertising space in the magazine and inserted the full-color 1946 catalog. Ten million readers got the word, and the 1946 Lionel line flew off the shelves. The cover features a typical holiday situation. *Jim Flynn collection*

listen to Jack Benny's Christmas show on the kitchen radio.

This line-up of Lionel's most realistic three-rail locomotives and cars available in two price ranges was incredibly impressive as were the electronic innovations. It is easy to imagine, therefore, the bellow of agony that must have exploded from Joshua Cowen's office when he was told that no catalog could be published in 1946 because of a paper shortage.

Casting about for some way to get the word out, Lionel advertising manager Joseph Hanson put in a call to *Liberty* magazine and bought a-16 page, full-color ad in the November 23, 1946, issue. The ad, in fact, was Lionel's entire catalog. One can imagine the whoop that went up at *Liberty*'s editorial offices. No one had ever bought that much ad space for a single issue in any magazine. Percy Leason painted a cover for the issue entitled "Father Takes Over," featuring a happily intrusive dad joining his perplexed son in the running of their Lionel railroad on the living room floor.

Vol. 23, No. 47 of *Liberty* magazine reached two million subscribers and six million readers. This huge advertising coup helped Lionel net a record profit for the year of $10 million and cleared dealers' shelves. The entire production run for 1946 was sold out.

Meanwhile, over in New Haven, the launch of American Flyer's more realistic, beautifully proportioned S gauge trains was not going well. Though A.C. Gilbert managed to beat Lionel to the punch with a giant 32-page, 10 x 29-inch full color catalog on October 11, many of the items graphically illustrated inside were unavailable. Pre-war 3/16-inch-scale cars and locomotives had been adapted to run on the narrower two-rail track. Looking at a prewar American Flyer diecast locomotive head-on compared to a postwar version reveals a production shortcut: Flyer was using the same dies for items in its postwar S gauge line that had been carried over from the prewar line. Although the running gear had been made narrower for the two-rail S gauge track, the carbodies and locomotive shells retained their three-rail widths. The mainstay of Gilbert train sets from 1946 through most of the 1950s was the Atlantic-type 4-4-2 locomotive, a staple for Gilbert's budget train sets. This was one of the locomotives that had been tooled in prewar years, and to the end of its production in 1957 it retained its slightly "fat" look because of the original wider wheel base. The design of this locomotive was based on a prototype owned by the Reading Railroad Company of Parker Brothers Monopoly fame. Interestingly, Flyer's Atlantic modeled a relatively rare prototype of which there were only a handful owned by the railroad, yet the Flyer Atlantic is easily the most common of all Flyer locomotive models.

Flyer offered a handsome S gauge Hudson in New York Central markings to compete with Lionel's magnificent 700 series that was still evolving from its 1937 debut of the 700E. Another new American Flyer entry was an 0-8-0 switch engine based on a Nickel Plate Road version. The catalog featured a huge 4-8-4 Union Pacific Northern-type steamer—the "king" of Flyer locomotives. But while smoke poured from American Flyer stacks and much was promised, very little was new except the track.

Always hedging his bets, Gilbert also featured his established Erector Sets and Chemistry Labs. Lionel also hyped a sinister-looking collection of jars, vials, test tubes, pestles, and scales as their "Chem-Lab!" on the back page of its *Liberty* magazine ad. Lionel promised that young chemists could even turn water into wine.

Unfortunately, 1946 buyers did not greet American Flyer's "authentic two-rail track" with slack-jawed amazement and open wallets, even though Flyer trains cost less than Lionel. The bigger—if clunkier—three-rail Lionel trains offered more play value with a variety of operating cars and accessories. Secondly, Flyer's new track struggled with the same problem that plagued all two-rail systems: track arrangements that featured reverse loops would short out unless equipped with special insulating track joints and specially wired with double-pole, double-throw switches. Devious track layouts were shown that eliminated the problem by designing around it. But with three-rail track, any layout plan would work.

Although American Flyer established its presence as a tough and innovative competitor, the company would always be playing catch-up, a "strong second" to Lionel in a two-horse race.

Meanwhile, Louis Marx came out of World War II with pockets full of profits, overseas contacts, and contracts that helped re-establish his corporation on a huge scale. The postwar economy made hand assembly in America prohibitively expensive, and many Marx toys required that touch. Beginning in the 1930s Marx had established plants in England and Wales, and following the war many complex toys and some trains came from Japan and Hong Kong.

As a merchandiser, Louis Marx stood head and shoulders above Lionel and American Flyer. He

A pair of American Flyer Northerns ("Challengers") On the left is the original 3/16-inch scale casting used on three-rail O gauge track. Next to it is the same locomotive with its running gear reworked to operate on narrow S gauge track. Note the wide look of the S gauge version compared to the original O gauge concept. These and seven other pre-war 3/16 scale steam locomotive types came and went in American Flyer catalogs virtually to the end in the 1950s. *Dave Guerriges collection*

This American Flyer S gauge set from 1952 is a typical starter set of which thousands were sold. The die-cast Atlantic-type locomotive is numbered 302AC indicating the time when Gilbert was still offering both AC- and DC-current trains. Numbering in the millions between 1936 and the 1960s, there were more Atlantics manufactured than any type of AF locomotive. Also shown is a little one-amp transformer to get the smoking choo-choo up and running. *Mike Schafer collection*

This collection of Marx diesels includes a Seaboard Air Line Railroad wind-up set complete with a B-unit (cabless booster) which is one of the scarcest Marx items ever produced. Also shown is a Kansas Southern A-B-B-A diesel set and a twin set of Union Pacific M-10006 *City of Denver* streamliner locomotives toting a caboose. *Jim Flynn collection*

could move product through outlets that were closed to his higher-priced competition, such as five-and-dime stores. While Gilbert and Cowen protected their precious logos and corporate identities, Louis produced train sets in high volumes under a variety of names.

Sears Roebuck & Co. bought Marx trains and sold them first under the "Happi-Time" logo and later as "Allstate." J. C. Penny and Western Auto also bought Marx in boxed sets under their own names. Although the trains themselves often had a Marx logo stamped somewhere, advertising by these department store chains usually did not mention Marx. In the 1940s, Montgomery Ward featured scale metal Marx trains with no mention of the manufacturer, while Sears preferred the plastic sets and let the Marx name creep into some advertising. These mass distribution pipelines would eventually translate into discount outlet channels as department stores and hometown toy and hobby stores succumbed in the 1950s and 1960s, so Marx did not have as much ground to make up as Lionel and American Flyer who sold through authorized dealers.

How Marx managed this market saturation sales plan underscores the gulf between Lionel, American Flyer, and the tin toy maker. Both Lionel and American Flyer produced few additions to each year's catalog and maintained many items for a decade or more. Each product required months and in some cases a year or more in development. New dies and tools were constantly being made and every aspect of production and marketing was fretted over.

Marx would blow over 200 products out the door in a year's time and see what sold. If 20 per cent of these were successful and found instant market acceptance, they would become part of the Marx production line that ran into the millions of units. Those that moved slowly might be re-lithographed or put to use as a different product. One rounded-tin, bread-loaf shape could serve as a boxcar, a passenger car, a coal tender, or part of a caboose. Just change the lithography, add a bit of ladder or hand rail and—*voila!*—you have a new car with a different road name or function. Since individual freight or passenger cars could be bought for 50 cents, or an entire railroad could be set up for less than $5, high volume sales had to be maintained.

Another example was the 0-4-0 locomotive. Marx made more of them than Lionel and American

Size difference between O gauge track and economy O-27-gauge showing the width of the rails is the same, but rail and tie height differs. O-27-gauge trains can run on O gauge track but not vice-versa. *Train Collectors Association*

This pair of cranes shows typical Louis Marx simplicity in providing play value with simple mechanical solutions. As well, Marx used the same parts to create two different toys. *Jim Flynn collection*

Flyer combined. The electric motor that drove the four wheels was a durable die-cast assembly, and the drivers themselves were cast from the same high-grade zamak alloy made of zinc, lead, and tin. Once a kid embraced the fantasy aspect of the train and was fascinated by the movement, color, and noise, the fact that the pilot and engineer cab cantilevered out over nothing made little impression. Adding a pony (leading) truck to the front or a trailing truck under the cab also added a manufacturing step and a few more cents. Virtually all Marx streamliners and steamers were built around a basic wind-up or electric motor that had been exhaustively tested. Even the cheaper two-stage reverse unit developed by Marx was more efficient and durable than the three-stage system used by Lionel and American Flyer.

As far as "action cars" were concerned, a good example was Marx's New York Central Wrecker, based on a prototype used for right-of-way maintenance and restoring derailed cars to the rails. The four-wheel, six-inch Marx version has all the components of the Lionel and Flyer versions: a gear house, a lifting boom, and a flatcar base—even a hook at the end of a string. But that's it. It swiveled and the hook could be made to go up and down with a little wire crank. The Wrecker sold and sold and sold for years while kids' imaginations filled in the details on the little tin car.

Even the remote-control whistle was not lost on Louis Marx. While his rivals honked, wheezed, choo-chooed, warbled, and roared, two of Marx's associates staged a show of their latest train set for a buyer. As described in Eric Matzke's *Greenberg's Guide to Marx Trains*, the buyer was watching the little train hum around a circle when Marx's George Dressler suggested that the buyer wave his hand in front of the locomotive. As the buyer did, ". . . a melodious whistle seemed to issue from the train." What a technological breakthrough! The buyer was busy being very impressed when the other Marx associate, Chippy Martin, stepped from behind the taller Dressler holding the Marx Model 701 whistle in his hand. He put it to his lips, toodled it again, and another Marx accessory was ready for the public.

Although his factories kept popping up like mushrooms on a log, Louis Marx always kept production costs to an absolute minimum but insisted that everything that went out the door was built to last. What is difficult for today's collectors and chroniclers of Marx trains to document is the

ABOVE: The classic Pennsylvania Railroad GG1 as interpreted by Lionel. This is a 1990s Lionel LLC reproduction of its very successful original 1948 locomotive created especially for collectors and operators. *Lionel LLC*

RIGHT: Raymond Loewy did styling work on the Pennsylvania Railroad GG1 electric, one of which is shown at Wilmington, Delaware, in 1979 with an excursion train honoring the locomotive. Even near the end of its useful life, the GG1 looked modern, fast, and brutishly powerful. Capable of a sustained speed of over 100 miles per hour hauling passenger trains but equally at home on freight trains, the GG1 was possibly the most successful locomotive design ever accomplished. *Mike Schafer*

sheer number of products, particularly the variations made for specific sales outlets like Sears or Wards and the recycling of parts among different sets of different eras. Also, there are hardly any catalogs. Marx issued "Timely Timetables" to jobbers and store chains—simple black-and-white lists of products with minimal descriptions. Let the sales channels do the advertising.

So, with the price points set at the end of the war, Lionel's three-rail O gauge trains were the high end and offered the most "automatic" cars. The three-rail O-27 train sets represented Lionel's lower-cost offerings and more closely competed against American Flyer's smaller (and cheaper to produce) two-rail S gauge "scale" models. Further, Lionel customers could upgrade to O gauge track and trains and still use their O-27 locomotives and rolling stock, though not vice versa account of the deeper flanges of O gauge stock and the inability of those items to negotiate 0-27 radii.

Marx and, to a lesser degree, Hafner, represented the low-end, fantasy train market. Hafner had sold out its remaining inventory of wind-up trains by 1942. His son John operated the company after William's death in 1944. The wind-up train market boomed along with the big three, but John decided on early retirement in 1951. On March 8 of that year the Hafner Company ceased production. The tools and dies were bought first by the All Metal Company, maker of Wyandotte Toys, but that company went bankrupt in 1956. They were then sold to Louis Marx who eventually shipped them to his Mexico plant thereby eliminating any further wind-up train competition.

This scene is loaded with American Flyer accessories from the mid-1950s. The focal point is one of many versions of the crossing gate—this one being perhaps the pinnacle model that included a ringing bell triggered by a two track trips. A tiny clear lamp shone up through a tinier hole underneath the roadway to illuminate the red plastic lantern on the gate arm. In front of the crossing is a Highway Flasher and to the left of that is American Flyer's version of the automatic milk car—transporting "Gilbert Grade A Pasteurized Milk"—that had a small man heaving out little base-weighted milk cans. In the background is the bright yellow Branford Diner, modeled after a Connecticut eating place and made from the shell of an AF Pullman. Pulling through the intersection is a No. 343 0-8-0 Nickel Plate switcher dating from the pre-war O gauge era. A fairly rare Central of Georgia box car leads a Western Maryland hopper. Bringing up the rear is an illuminated animated caboose that features a brakeman leaning out the rear platform every time the train stops. *Mike Schafer, Mike McBride, and Jeff Katzner collections*

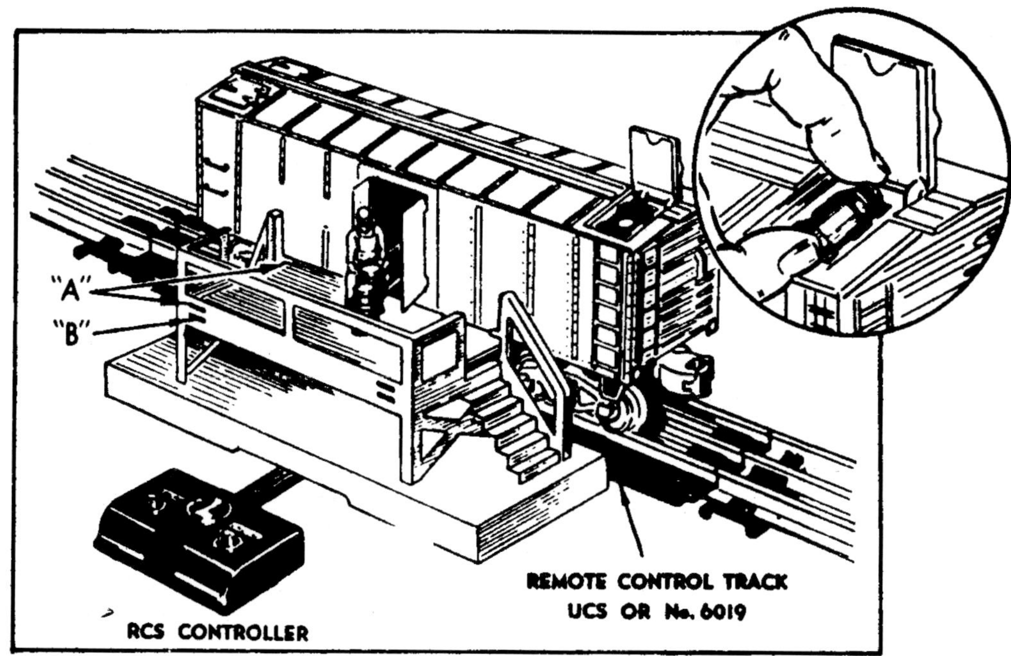

The workings of a Lionel milk car were shown on the instruction sheet. Magnetic base milk cans go in roof hatch and remote-control buttons trigger the action. *Train Collectors Association*

An eclectic mix of accessories are grouped in this corner of Stan Roy's layout. They include a remake of the 352 barrel loader that was first offered in 1952, a drum loader that originally came from American Flyer, the 264 operating fork lift platform of 1957 vintage, an original horse loader, the operating sawmill, the classic milk can unloader platform and a pagoda-roof watch tower. In the background is a stable of MPC-era steamers with the exception of a pre-war scale switcher. *Courtesy, Stan Roy*

Heading for Mid Century

With that first postwar year out of the way, all three manufacturers picked up steam in 1947, roared into 1948, and headed into the 1950s with their throttles tied down and whistles wailing.

Lionel launched two big winners and a big loser in 1947. The latter was an imitation of Gilbert's Erector Set concept, the Lionel Construction Set. Gilbert's variety of toys—Erector, chemistry, and magic sets—allowed year-round sales income. Lionel marketing wanted a similar revenue generator while gearing up for the next holiday train season. It advertised the Chem-Lab in 1946—one of five sizes ranging from how to make ink to how to indelibly stain the bathroom floor, as this author discovered at age seven. Although Erector projects appealed to a sense of engineering and offered a wide variety of girdered, pullied, and wheeled designs, the Lionel version was more limited in its scope and, as dust collected on the boxes, limited sales appeal.

The motive-power hit for 1947 was the Pennsylvania GG1 electric. The prototype had been unveiled in 1934 to run the PRR's electrified corridors between New York and Washington, D.C., and west between Philadelphia and Harrisburg, Pennsylvania. These were heavily used passenger routes that deserved fast, reliable locomotives. After two years of testing different designs, an ugly looking clunk nicknamed "Rivets" (every steel plate in its shrouding was outlined in rivet heads) was chosen as the prototype. What had won the Pennsy's heart—if not its aesthetic senses—was the locomotive's raw speed, power, and apparent durability. Drawing power through two pantographs, twelve electric-powered wheels could wind the "G" up to 100 miles per hour in a impressively short time—and it could run at that speed effortlessly. The GG1 was at home on long heavyweight passenger trains or a long, long line of fast freight.

Designer Raymond Loewy was called in to polish the GG1's "bridge-builder's nightmare" look. Loewy had designed the Coca-Cola bottle, Studebaker automobiles, and now the GG1 locomotive. With welded seams replacing the rivets, rounded-off corners, and inlaid ladders and windows, the redesigned locomotive looked as aerodynamic as her capabilities. The Pennsy had 138 GG1s built between 1935 and 1943. The last of them still hauled trains until the early 1980s, having endured a number of mostly awful post-PRR (PRR and New York Central merged to form Penn Central in 1968) paint jobs following their original PRR liveries of either tuscan red or Brunswick green.

But in 1947, GG1s were still sweeping across the urban landscape of the East Coast and when Lionel's model appeared in the '47 catalog, every kid east of the Mississippi wanted one. The locomotive could run off the power from the track or get its juice from overhead wire just like the real GG1. Besides the preternatural scream of the electric motors at speed, the prototype GG1 had a unique horn. It sounded like a door buzzer, and Lionel techs worked hard to duplicate that ragged sqawk. Of course, Lionel's GG1 followed most of the company's designs in that it was more of a caricature of the real thing than a scale model. It had to be "selectively compressed" to be able to run its twenty wheels around tight O gauge turns. In 1950, a second motor was added as was Magnetraction, and its pulling power tripled. For years, the GG1 was unique to Lionel until scale models from overseas brought the actual dimensions to modelers, but by that time the kids who had lusted after the Lionel catalogs were out of the loop and adults with deeper pockets and memories of their Lionel trains had taken over.

The second winner was a little guy who threw milk cans out of a refrigerator car at the push of a button. Every kid wanted a No. 3462 Automatic Milk Car for his layout, and the white cars and their loading platforms were swept from the store shelves. Its design was the first using a human figure as the moving element. All the pre-war operating accessories—coal station, log loader, magnetic crane, and the bascule bridge—performed a mechanical function, either dumping, loading, or lifting.

The milk-car function involved placing the refrigerated car's doors opposite the loading platform and above a remote-control electromagnet track section. At a push of an UNLOAD button, the doors flew open and a little hunched-over man in cap and overalls whipped out a shiny milk can onto the platform. Push the button again and out came another can until all six cans were accounted for. Inserted into the bottom of each can was a small magnet to keep them upright. The speed with which the little milkman worked could be adjusted by raising or lowering the track voltage. Kids loved cranking the voltage up and watching the cans turn into small missiles, caroming around the platform. Reloading the cans required some "hand of God" work as each can was dropped into one of the roof's open ice hatches.

The product being unloaded was milk, not logs or coal or anonymous barrels. The car, the platform, the little man—everything was milk white and wholesome, and the cans were shiny, sanitary clean. One imagines that moms everywhere led the blitz that kept the Automatic Milk Car Lionel's hottest-selling item to the point where they could not make them fast enough.

Ron Hollander tells the whole story of the Milk Car's creation in his *All Aboard!* book. In this day of corporate toy research and development by computer models in lead-lined secret bunkers, it bears a summary retelling.

The inventor was a carpenter named Richard G. Smith. When he was not hammering and sawing for a living, Smith designed operating cars and accessories for both Lionel and American Flyer. Among his successes since 1938 were the Lionel log loader and log car, the culvert loader and unloader, the barrel-unloading car, and a working ice station. For American Flyer he cobbled together the very popular Railway Post Office car that hooked mail bags "on the fly" as well as flipped sacks out its side door, and a flatcar that unloaded an armored car or snappy roadster from a ramp. It was in 1944 that all the pieces of the milk car came together correctly, but nobody was building trains yet.

Continued on page 110

Blowing Smoke and Whistles—American Flyer and Lionel Clash Along the Main Line

by Mike Schafer and Gerry Souter

Giving kids the thrill of watching smoke billow from a locomotive's stack and hearing the toot of its whistle sparked a fevered competition between the two toy train giants. Lionel and American Flyer launched their solutions for smoke spewing locomotives on the same day in March 1946. Their separate approaches to the feature typified the competition between their respective design teams.

Lionel had already beaten Flyer to the punch with the realistic knuckle coupler in 1945, but it was a terrible design made of 26 separate pieces. The design of a Lionel smoke system was infinitely simpler—once the key was found. The young railroader dropped a pill down the stack onto a specially made General Electric light bulb that had a dimple in it. The bulb eventually heated the pill and smoke came up the stack. A moving baffle pushed air up into the smoke chamber in time with the rods on the rolling wheels and the locomotive puffed. Later on, the expensive bulb was replaced with a tiny hot plate heated with a wire and still later, liquid smoke and a less complex heating system were used. For Lionel in 1946, however, the pill was the key.

Their first experiments produced a toxic killer that would have been at home in a prison's gas chamber. The second idea produced non-toxic smoke, but if swallowed, the little pellet required a speedy ride to the nearest hospital and a date with a stomach pump. The final compound was ammonium nitrate. Burning this pill produced nitrogen oxide—known today as a "greenhouse effect pollutant"—and induced a hacking cough and eye-watering if inhaled in heavy doses. Parents today would be aghast at the idea of giving Little Tommy a pill for his smoking choo-choo that, if swallowed, produced dizziness, diarrhea, and a case of the whooping heaves. Nevertheless, the smoke pill was a huge success for Lionel sales and filled thousands of cheery Christmas living rooms across America with clouds of nitrogen oxide.

A hallmark of Gilbert American Flyer steam locomotives was the smoke and choo-choo feature, the design of which was so clever and convincing that, to this day, people marvel at the added dimension this gives AF toy trains. In 1946, both Lionel and American Flyer were being cagey about their smoke systems in order to maximize impact at the annual Toy Fair in March. Then, due to a press leak, Lionel moved up the introduction of its smoke pellets and American Flyer company modelers worked through the night at Gilbert's New York show room to introduce the Flyer's famous "smoke and choo-choo." Both systems debuted on virtually the same day.

Initially, American Flyer's smoke-and-choo-choo feature was a separate entity housed within the locomotive tender; it was driven by a small electric motor that operated a bellows unit which made both the chugging sound and forced smoke—made by heating pine-scented, paraffin-based oil with a hot wire coil—through a tube leading into the locomotive's cab and from there to its smokestack. The problem of this early engineering was that the unit was essentially independent of the locomotive mechanism itself and as such was costly and did not necessarily synch with the locomotive drivers. Further, the smoke had to be pushed a long distance through a tube, reducing the puffing effect and allowing the smoke to begin dissipating even before it exited the stack. In many cases, the tube worked its way off the nipple in the locomotive's cab and then smoke streamed back through the cab windows as if the engineer and fireman were engulfed in flames.

Another problem was the hurdy-gurdy bellows pumping away in the tender. While it was in good repair, the locomotive could be made to puff smoke while standing still in the yard, or at the passenger station platform—very realistic. Once the bellows became frayed and the gearing worn, the wheezy choo-choo speeded up out of proportion to the locomotive's acceleration and the grinding and churning coming from the tender effectively drowned out the chugging sound.

This flawed system was completely re-engineered in 1948 in a clever yet simple manner that even today is impressive: the bellows was replaced by a piston linked directly to the locomotive drive wheels' worm gear, and the smoke unit was moved to the front of the locomotive boiler. The result? The choo-choo always sounded in direct synch with the drivers, however fast they were turning, while the smoke puffed out copiously, exactly matching the choo-choo sound. Flyer steam locomotives equipped with this popular feature were by far the most realistic of any toy train manufacturer.

The whistle situation was another matter, as Lionel not only beat Flyer to the punch on a realistic, engine-mounted, remote-control steam locomotive whistle, but sued Gilbert for patent infringement. The only appearance of the offending whistle was on Flyer's Pennsylvania K-5 Pacific model 314AW (for Automatic Whistle). In this arrangement, a DC impulse was sent through the tracks by a remote toggle-type controller that activated a DC-powered electric motor, located in the tender, which operated the whistle. The effect was startlingly realistic, and the whistle had a beautiful tone to it. Lionel sued and won

Following this Flyer faux pas, Gilbert was reduced to relying on trackside "whistle billboards" and remote-control air-type horns which Gilbert sometimes referred to as "Air-Chime Whistles," a low-pitched whistle used on some early diesels instead of—or in addition to—air horns so as not to confuse people used to the sound made by steam-locomotive whistles. The billboards incorporated a small motor and impeller mechanism which produced an admirable steam-whistle sound, but the effect worked best only when the locomotive happened to be passing the stationary billboard.

For whatever reason, the air-horn/air chime system did not infringe on Lionel patents. On this arrangement, a push-button activated a resonator in a cardboard "vacuum" tube, and the resulting vibration was sent through the rails via a DC impulse to the locomotive where it was picked up by a speaker mounted in the diesel or in the tender of a steam locomotive. This sound varied according to the type of tube that was used, but a true steam whistle sound was not among them. The system produced a worthy air-horn sound but the questionable air-chime-whistle sounded more like a discontented cat with hiccups. Both were used on Flyer diesels and steam locomotives, since in the idiosyncratic examples of real life that American Flyer often chose to model, you could indeed find air horns on steam locomotives and air-chime whistles on diesels. Nonetheless, air horns weren't what people associated with steam locomotives, so whistles and Lionel's patent of same galled American Flyer to the end.

Billowing smoke streams behind a 1946 American Flyer Hudson on Bill Van Ramhorst's S gauge layout. The tender holds the motor for the smoke unit and a tiny bellows for both smoke-blowing and a chug sound effect; eventually these workings were refined and moved to the locomotive. The 751 log loader was bought by Bill's father back in the late 1940s, and it still works perfectly. Also part of the log operation is the 23796 Saw Mill, a beautiful illusion that seems to turn logs into planks. Lionel jumped on this accessory for its own line. *Bill Van Ramshorst*

Unique to Flyer was the "Diesel Roar" feature, introduced in 1955. The device was simply a vibrator mounted in a dummy diesel (GP7 or Alco PB) and linked to a speaker that amplified the vibrations which, in turn, increased with the voltage. It was an interesting concept which Flyer hyped heavily, although the actual sound required enhancement by one's imagination. Interestingly, the sound also simulated an idling diesel engine when the locomotive was standing. The intensity of the "roar" increased markedly with the voltage, and if the noise eventually got on your—or, more to the point, your parents'—nerves, it could be manually shut off.

Today, sound plays an important part in model railroading. Computer chips and miniature piezo speakers allow startling audio accuracy to accompany locomotives from HO to LGB gauge. The size of O gauge road switchers and steam engines permit complex ProtoSound, and RailSound, and SignalSound, modules to produce actual horns and whistles used by the locomotive's prototype. Idling, brake squeals, dinging bells, yard radio traffic, whistling dynamic brakes, synchronized chugging, air compressors—all of these sounds can be passed along from actual live recordings via EPROMs (Erasable, Programmable, Read Only Memory) plugged into circuit boards. As each new model is planned, a squad of sound engineers takes to the field with wind-dampened boom microphones in hand and Nagra tape recorders stuffed into porta-packs. They haunt modern rail yards and main lines for the annoying squawk and rumble of current motive power as well as restored tourist railroads where old steam and diesel locomotives still clank along the high iron under their own power. Each toot, gong, wheeze, backfire, burp, and grumble is laid down on tape at 15 inches per second. They beg right-of-way permission passes from harried trainmasters and cajole museum curators into staging early morning locomotive runs to get clear sound tracks free of "Look, Mommee! A choo-choo!" in the middle of the beautifully sustained road crossing whistle of a 50-year-old heavy steam locomotive pounding past at speed.

This is the American Flyer K-5 steamer that violated Lionel's whistle patent. The Model 314AW is, therefore, somewhat rare. As usual, American Flyer chose to model an off-beat prototype, because the Pennsylvania K-5 was built in considerably fewer numbers than the ubiquitous K-4. For what it was worth, the AF whistle did sound better than Lionel's. *Jeff Katzner collection*

A pair of classic Pennsylvania Railroad K-4 locomotives. Williams and MTH have reproduced this engine as beautiful scale models in brass and die-cast versions. American Flyer—in its perverse way—chose to model the relatively obscure prototype K-5 for some reason. *Cal's Classics*

Continued from page 107

Smith's first model used a "can pusher" to swing the cans onto a platform, but Cowen and his designers created the little man and the platform design. For his troubles, Smith was offered a 2 per cent royalty instead of his usual flat fee. He had made $2,250 each off the log and the barrel loader. According to Hollander, Smith was accustomed to cash-on-the-barrelhead and was uneasy about betting on royalties, but after some cajoling from Cowen, he went along with the deal. Cagey Cowen figured Smith would earn about $1,200 a year in royalties. Then the car hit the market, and thousands of little men and tens of thousands of shiny milk cans started spewing from Lionel's machines as orders came in. Orders for 1952 alone show sales of 180,000 milk cars and Smith pocketed some $20,000 in royalties. Needless to say, the laconic Smith set aside his carpenter's tools for full-time work in his shop with stovepipe metal, scrap iron, odd springs, and brass bar stock. The tinkerer with no engineering degree, but a keen mechanical sense had come into big bucks.

Nine years would pass before American Flyer came up with a similar car offering "Gilbert's Grade A Pasteurized Milk." From this car, a Black worker wearing a white coat sprang into action, heaving out shiny cans that were bottom-weighted to remain upright. The model lasted from 1956 to 1960.

American Flyer wasn't exactly sitting on its hands when it came to operating cars and accessories, but Flyer was almost always playing catch-up and skirt-the-Lionel-patent. In 1946, Flyer announced the Seaboard coal loader, a log loader and an "Electromatic Crane" that lifted metal scrap from a gondola with a magnet. This was great stuff for the new Flyer fans who now had operating accessories comparable to those offered by Lionel before the war. The designers at Gilbert would finally hit their stride in the 1950s with new trains and ingenious accessories that offered great play value for the two-rail tribe.

The year 1948 was memorable for Flyer fans for the re-introduction of DC power by means of a "new" "Directronic Rectiformer" that produced "Directronic Propulsion," which meant that direction control was handled at the transformer end rather than in the locomotive. Though this shift

The 1948 Lionel catalog featured its ubiquitous PRR steam turbine locomotive passing a streamliner heading in the opposite direction. This locomotive, available in O and O-27 gauge, sold in the thousands and was a consistent performer. *Jim Flynn collection*

had actually occurred in 1947, the result was apparently unsatisfactory, so Flyer hyped their re-do as "new!"

Another Flyer product re-introduced from the prewar O gauge line was the Baltimore & Ohio Royal Blue streamlined steam locomotive. This elegantly shrouded, bargain-priced 4-6-2 steamer had no smoke or choo-choo capabilities. The Royal Blue livery (but not the locomotive itself) was dropped from the Flyer line in 1949 as Gilbert introduced mostly accessories and a curious item called a "track torpedo" based on emergency torpedoes used by train crews to protect a standing (or disabled) train. In actual practice, crews attached torpedoes to the rails at sufficient distances from the standing train to warn oncoming trains. The explosives detonated under the oncoming locomotive's wheels, instantly informing the engine crew to stop. On the Flyer version, a press of a button caused either two "bangs" to sound, causing a train to slow down, or three bangs to stop in completely. Although it was an intriguing idea, the track torpedo was never actually offered.

And, finally, to supplement its "whistling billboards," American Flyer chose 1949 to introduce a very realistic, remote-control whistle on its Pennsylvania K-5 Pacific steam locomotive. Unfortunately, Lionel took note of how the whistle was activated, sued American Flyer for patent infringement, and won, causing the whistle to be absent from the 1950 line.

When 1948 dawned, Lionel was so confident of its new products that it released its new catalog *before* the New York Toy Fair that was the usual kick-off event. At the Toy Fair, manufacturers not only showed their new wares but tested the waters as the trade industry passed judgment on what they guessed would become the winners and the stinkers of the year. Lionel had every right to be self-assured. In that one year, Lionel produced two new products that would forever be linked to the Lionel name. Hobbyists building model railroad layouts in space stations around Saturn will only have to see faded pictures of these two products, and they'll say, "Oh yeah. . . Lionel!"

The first was the ZW Trainmaster transformer.

The beautiful 350 Royal Blue modeled by American Flyer and loosely based on a Baltimore & Ohio prototype. This locomotive was introduced in 1948 and wore many paint jobs, from silver for the *Silver Bullet* freight and passenger sets to bright red for the Circus Train. Production of this streamlined Pacific-type locomotive continued through 1954 with a brief hiatus around 1950. *Mike McBride collection*

This massive controller, sometimes called a "football in a box," had dual levers for running two trains at once plus whistle and directional controls. Later versions put out 275 watts and could control four trains. When released, no one thought twice about its huge output and safety considerations. The only part of the ZW that was UL Approved was the plug-in wall cord. Today, these are most sought after, and a new version has been offered by Lionel that, when combined with four Powerhouse transformer bricks of 135 watts output each, can unleash 760 watts of power.

The big blast from 1948 was a locomotive that almost didn't happen. But when it appeared, shelves cleared across the country and Joshua Cowen was proved wrong. Mainline diesel-electric locomotives had appeared along American tracks back in the mid 1930s when the Electro-Motive Corporation, then a subsidiary of General Motors, brought out its sleek and streamlined power cars and later its E-series passenger diesels, all of which became formidable competition for steam power. E-series diesels had a crew cab set high above and behind a sloping nose. A combination of pulling power, speed, and low maintenance made it attractive for passenger-hauling, and E-units were soon introduced to Santa Fe's *Super Chief*, Baltimore & Ohio's *Royal Blue*, Union Pacific's *City of Los Angeles*, and other trains. The E was followed in 1939 by the F-series, designed primarily for freight duties, but also passenger. It was the F3 model of 1945 that Lionel planned to debut in 1948. But the debut would be a grudging one as far as Joshua Cowen was concerned.

Cowen didn't particularly like diesels, although for some reason he did like the GG1 electric. Regardless, steam locomotives—with their churning drive rods, whistles, and smoke—were Cowen's true love. They looked more alive, more dynamic. As an old adage claims, "diesels go, but steam engines move." Also, there was a matter of what railroad to choose. Lionel, being an Eastern company, had always chosen Eastern roads to model, mainly the Pennsylvania and New York Central. Kids out on the West Coast had no Lionel to call their own. That was about to change.

In 1937, a GM designer had created a brilliantly timeless, colorful paint scheme for the Electro-Motive E1 diesels that Santa Fe had ordered for its *Super Chief* streamliner. From the pen and airbrush of Leland Knickerbocker came the most distinctive paint job in the history of American railroading: the famous Santa Fe "warbonnet" scheme of red and silver with yellow and black trim. It was a design that would become even more famous than Lionel's orange-and-blue boxes. More importantly, the warbonnet scheme and the Lionel locomotive it would rest on would become an icon of Lionel itself.

Cowen gave in to his design and marketing people and okayed doing a Santa Fe diesel as long as an Eastern road (the New York Central) was also offered and if the cost of tooling could be held to a minimum. He expected to sell only a relatively few diesel trains. To make the tools and dies for the F3 diesels, Lionel needed about $30,000 and change. So as not to lose his shirt on what he perceived to be a lukewarm item, Cowen drew up a deal that required that cost be divided equally between Lionel, General Motors' Electro-Motive division, and the two railroads.

The railroads were still recovering from their war wounds and, alarmingly, now were seeing their share of America's transportation market being eroded by newly expanding highway transportation. Auto manufacturers had spit out their last armored cars, tanks, and dive bombers as our troops were taking Okinawa in the Pacific, and had returned to civilian production.

The famous ZW Trainmaster transformer was launched in 1948 as part of a line of "re-designed" transformers. This 250-watt behemoth was the flagship of the line, but the only part safety-approved by Underwriters' Laboratory was the power cord to the wall socket. Junior is shown joyously gripping those two throttle handles—an early example of ergonomics that pre-dates video game controls. *Jim Flynn collection*

Although the 1947 automobiles weren't exactly world beaters, the 1948 models—especially those from the drawing boards of GM's Harley Earl—with their tail fins borrowed from the P-38 Lightning fighter were being swept out of showrooms at list price. And those few who had glimpsed the models of the 1949 Ford could only whistle softly. Cities were already clamoring for government road-building money. Truck-makers were building bigger, long-haul trailers and tractors to take over the portal-to-portal business that was expected to skyrocket. Boeing, Lockheed, and MacDonald-Douglas washed the olive drab paint off DC3 and Sky Train cargo planes that had not been shipped and shoved in comfy seats for growing numbers of passengers. The B-29 bomber was fattened and stretched to become a Stratocruiser for long over-ocean passenger runs, and the four-engine TWA Constellation returned to civilian garb for cross-country hops.

All that the railroads had going for them were their high-profile diesel-electric streamlined passenger trains. Otherwise, U.S. railroads faced volumes of interstate regulations penned decades earlier when they had been greedily gouging shippers. As the 1940s wound down, many railroads—cash-rich from war contracts—were in the throes of dieselization and a number roads and railroad-related industries were involved in public-relations stunts such as Pullman-Standard and GM's *Train of Tomorrow* domeliner at the 1948 Chicago Railroad Fair. Railroads needed all the P.R. they could get to show travelers that they could really compete with buses, trucks, airplanes, and private automobiles—even though reality would eventually prove otherwise.

Lionel's deal was made to order. For about $6,000, each railroad and EMD would be guaranteed a full two-page splash of their livery across one million catalogs a year. Also, Lionel's *Model Builder* magazine, reaching 40,000 readers, featured ads for the new sets. Of course, each Santa Fe or New York Central locomotive sold brought those roads' names into American homes—homes with families who were potential rail travelers when it came time for the family vacation—and that was a good deal even if, as Cowen predicted, only 16,000 or so F3s would be built to test the waters.

Lionel's Santa Fe *Super Chief*, complete with extruded metal streamlined cars, magnetic coil-operated knuckle couplers, and a battery-powered horn that actually sounded like a diesel proved Cowen wrong by *100,000* units in its first year. It was the first locomotive after the war to have dual motors, and though Lionel's version of the F3 was

Classic beauty on the rails, the Electro-Motive's F-series diesel locomotive was a huge success both as a prototype hauling passenger and freight trains on railroads all over America and as a Lionel model brought out in 1948. Although dozens of railroads purchased F-units, those of the Atchison, Topeka & Santa Fe are perhaps best remembered account of their Southwest Indian-inspired red, silver, yellow, and black livery. General Motors' designer Leland Knickerbocker created a curving sweep to the red area of the nose to imply an Indian headdress at speed. Lionel's F3 model of the F-unit series (shown is a later model F7) has become the American icon for the toy electric train in our modern era. *Mike Schafer*

A Santa Fe Alco PA/PB/PA set on exhibit at Chicago's Dearborn Station on October 1, 1946. Although most people associate the Santa Fe paint scheme with Electro-Motive's F-series diesel locomotive, other types of diesels also wore the livery, including the Alco PAs. American Flyer modeled this handsome locomotive in S gauge as its answer to Lionel's wildly successful F3. *Andover Junction Publications Archives*

a bit compressed in scale, it retained the husky look of the real thing. The New York Central livery was offered for eight years while the Santa Fe red-and-silver colors continued for 16 years, with a peak production of 125 units per hour. The Santa Fe F3 became so closely identified with Lionel that it became as much an American icon as the Coke bottle, the Ford Mustang, and the Barbie Doll.

Less identified with Lionel was fishing. Joshua and Lawrence were avid fishermen. While on a fishing expedition with their bait-casting rods, they were treated to an exhibition of spin casting by a member of their party, Bache Brown, who was connected to the Airex Company, the makers of his reel. The 1940s-era model bait-casting reel required the fisherman to "thumb" the reel as the line sped off of it. With heavy line on a reel with a light core, backlashes were common, with ghastly tangled nests of line caused by the line continuing to pay out after the bait had hit the water. Brown's spin-cast reel let the line fall off the face of the reel and could not backlash. The Cowens saw a summer product line that could earn profits between holiday train-selling seasons.

They bought two-thirds of Airex stock in 1948 and began selling the spin-cast reel through their regular retail outlets such as hardware stores. In 1953, however, they plastered a full page Airex ad complete with angling fisherman on the back page of their Lionel train catalog. The culture clash between the realistically illustrated toy trains aimed at fantasy-loving kids and the actual fishing reel from the "real" adult world was too much.

Although viewed by many as a big marketing mistake, Lionel persisted with the ad for a few more years. The Airex reel was very profitable and foretold even more diversification of Lionel non-train products that would eventually bury the company, but that was still a decade away.

Lionel's 1949 sales season dawned with subterfuge, vibrating cattle, and an action car with a rubber guy in it. During the war, a vanguard of small 600- and 800-horsepower diesel switchers began showing up in rail yards across the country. One of these, an EMD NW2, found its way onto Lionel drawing boards as Model 6220 in O-27 and No. 622 in O gauge. Without really big-deal fanfare, the switcher appeared in the 1949 catalog complete with a dinging bell, but it contained an unpublished secret. Hidden among its axles were magnets that helped the switcher's wheels grip the tinplate track, improving traction. In 1950, the feature became the "new" Magne-traction and received full ballyhoo. Now, Lionel locomotives raced at full clip around those 31-inch radius curves—as tinplate railroaders are wont to do—without coming off the track (well, at least not as often). They were also able to haul longer trains with better traction and less wheel slip.

Snookered again, American Flyer finally responded in 1953 with "Pull-Mor" power, improving traction by adding thin rubber tires to some of the locomotive's drive wheels. This practice of adding traction tires continues today on various manufacturers' trains.

To add another action car in 1949, Lionel "headed 'em up and moved 'em out" with the new No. 3656 cattle or stock car and loading pen. Similar to the popular milk-car accessory, this car required careful spotting at the pen so its doors aligned with the platform's ramps. At the push of a button, and for as long as it was held down, the

Comparing the O gauge Lionel F3 diesel in Santa Fe's "Warbonnet" colors with its S gauge American Flyer Alco counterpart in similar livery. This AF 470 model bears the Santa Fe name on its side, but other 470-series releases bore AMERICAN FLYER LINES instead. Flyer was sometimes reticent to use actual road names even though the prototype road's paint scheme could be quite obvious. Flyer's Alco models came in both single and twin-motor varieties; some were equipped with "air-chime" whistles or air horns. *Steve Esposito and Mike Schafer collections*

This O-27 6220 bell-ringing diesel switcher, along with its 622 O gauge counterpart, was the first Lionel locomotive to employ Magne-traction—the placing of magnets near the wheels and axles to better grip the tinplate rails. The introduction was done without fanfare as an experiment in 1949. Great hoopla and drum beating accompanied Magne-traction's official announcement in 1950. *Chris Rohlfing collection*

The Lionel cattle car was introduced in 1949 and was produced until 1955. Its herd filed off the car into pens and would return to stay if the off-track side door was closed. This model was built in 1949-50. *Chris Rohlfing collection*

flooring vibrated, causing the "cattle" (with undersides fitted with special fabric that was reactive to the vibrating flooring) hoofed up the ramps and into the car—or out of the car and down the ramps. To make the cattle stay inside, the door on the opposite side of the car was kept closed. Smooth movement usually required a bit of Vaseline daubed on the cattle bases to allow them to move more easily around corners and against each other. In the catalog, the Milk Car and Stock Car were featured together, but the vibrating bovine shuffle never caught on as well as the Milk Car.

The 3464 Operating Boxcar was offered as a low-cost bit of action. When the car zipped over a UCS track section, Little Tommy Jr. pressed the UNLOAD button. With a zap, the boxcar's door flew open, and there stood a little rubber fellow in overalls. Fingerwork was required to close the door and re-cock the mechanism. Always thinking of improvements, Lionel later had the little guy toss out a mail bag and, later still, boxes of cargo. The snap action fired them out the door like missiles, not exactly adding to railroads' reputation for careful freight handling.

The 1950s: Apex of the Toy Train

Both Lionel and Flyer gave special significance to the year 1950. Lionel trumpeted its "Golden Anniversary" even though Joshua's Lionel Manufacturing Company was incorporated on March 13, 1902. American Flyer beat a drum for "50 Years of Progress" and the catalog carried 50 new toys, 50 lower prices, and 50 exclusive features. Some of the "new" products were recalls of previous offerings while others were merely artist concepts that reached the market in different forms. Despite the smoke-and-mirrors chest thumping, 1950 really was a heady year for both manufacturers.

American Flyer plunged headlong into dieselization with a road-switcher and a streamlined passenger locomotive. The road-switcher was a model of Electro-Motive's GP7 (for General Purpose; it could be used for switching, over-the-road freight hauling, and even local passenger service). The catalog promised a silver, blue, and yellow replica of the original EMD demonstrator GP7 with link couplers and an automatic bell. What came out of the box had no bell and no link couplers, but simple link bars to which link couplers could easily hook; the locomotive would receive knuckle couplers in 1953. Under Gilbert, the Flyer GP7 went on to carry Union Pacific,

Texas & Pacific, and Chesapeake & Ohio liveries, and the promised automatic bell arrived in 1959. Run in pairs—with the powered unit featuring Pull-Mor power and remote-control air horn and the "dummy" unit housing Diesel Roar—the GP7 was a popular American Flyer locomotive, especially in the stunning orange-and-black T&P livery introduced in 1954.

A comparison of two Santa Fe diesel locomotive models. On the bottom is the Lionel 2333 double-motor deluxe F3 locomotive set that swept to incredible popularity in 1948. The die-cast Lionel model cost about $47 back then. Above it is the Marx Model 21 single-motor diesel set using lithographed tinplate and a clever illusion of detail that in the 1952 Sears catalog cost $25—a price that also included five passenger or freight cars, 18 pieces of track, and a 70-watt transformer. Interestingly, Marx's model is a curious mix of a prototype Electro-Motive FT-series four-axle diesel and Electro-Motive's longer E-series six-axle passenger diesel. *Jim Flynn collection*

Flyer's passenger diesel was inspired by American Locomotive Company's 2000-horsepower PA-type passenger diesel unveiled by Alco in 1945. Although the prototype was dogged by engine-design problems and its sales were far outstripped by Electro-Motive passenger diesels, the PA has long been heralded by railroad historians as one of the most handsome diesel locomotives of all time. And, as with the EMD F3, Santa Fe bought a stable of PAs and PBs (cabless boosters), thus allowing Flyer to capitalize on the famous Santa Fe warbonnet paint scheme.

When it came to diesel paint schemes, American Flyer for a time exhibited some curious practices. For example, the Texas & Pacific GP7s originally featured that railroad's name on the flanks as well as the T&P diamond herald on the cab. But on later versions the Texas & Pacific lettering was replaced with "American Flyer Lines," though the T&P herald remained. This constant use of the American Flyer name over specific railroad paint jobs made for some strange flip-flops. The first No. 360 PAs introduced in 1950 featured the Santa Fe livery with SANTA FE lettered on the side. Three years later, the side printing read AMERICAN FLYER LINES.

Interestingly, Flyer PAs began to appear in other railroad schemes (even though some of the railroads never owned Alco PAs) early in the 1950s, but sans the heralds or lettering of the prototype. Rather, they were anonymously named *Comet* (which borrowed the prototype Missouri Pacific paint scheme), *Silver Flash* (prototype scheme: Maine Central), *Rocket* (prototype: Southern Railway [not Rock Island as many collectors incorrectly assume]), and *Silver Streak* (prototype, to a limited degree: Chicago, Burlington & Quincy). After this run of fictitious names, the PAs began to appear again in actual road names and schemes: Northern Pacific and its beautiful two-tone green passenger livery; New Haven and its famous "McGinnis" orange/black/white scheme (conceived by a Swiss designer who was a friend of the wife of New Haven president Patrick McGinnis); Union Pacific yellow and gray; Missouri Pacific and its blue-and-gray colors; and the dark blue and yellow Santa Fe freight diesel colors. Never mind that NP never owned PAs or that Santa Fe's PAs never wore blue and yellow—Flyer's PAs were colorful and eye-catching.

Clearly, Flyer's No. 360/361 Santa Fe Alco PA and PB of 1950 was meant to compete directly with Lionel's hot seller from 1948, the F3. The Alcos illustrated in the 1950 catalog apparently was a pre-production mockup, for it showed virtually no exterior details and rode on trucks appropriated from the coal tender that trailed behind Flyer's Hudson steamer. As it turned out, Flyer's rendition of the PA was possibly the most accurate of any of its model locomotives. By 1953 the PAs were available with twin motors, and the very handsome locomotive was every bit as desirable as Lionel's F3.

One well-received Flyer recall for 1950 was the stunning Royal Blue 4-6-2 Pacific locomotive that had been dropped from the catalog in 1949. Its sheer beauty of proportion and streamlined shrouding easily stacks up against Lionel's 746 model of the Norfolk & Western J-class that would raise eyebrows some years later. The Royal Blue arrived in its original deep cobalt color—and also in deep red heading a circus train. This No. 353 version pulled two flat cars with cage wagons, a depressed-center flat car with a searchlight, a transfer caboose carrying tent poles, and a yellow passenger car for the performers.

Flyer's steamers for 1950 had an electronic "whistle" and the diesels had a horn, and the technology of both sidestepped the Lionel vs. Gilbert whistle lawsuit of a few years earlier. Actually, they both made about the same sound—a kind of tremulous squawk—that was dubbed either a "diesel air horn" or a "chime whistle".

Sad to say that just as the electronically triggered horn/whistles were rolling into dealers, the Korean "police action" came along, and wartime parts restrictions were once again levied. Flyer ended up falling back on its stationary whistling billboards, pleading in a letter accompanying the horn-less or whistle-less locomotives:

> ". . .We hope that you are pleased with this substitution and will derive satisfaction from knowing that you, too, are doing your part in America's Defense Effort."

A flurry of new cars and accessories announced that American Flyer was ready for the long run in the 1950s. Its fans were hardening into a dedicated core. The 1950s would determine if that core was large enough and if American Flyer could continue to meet its fans' high expectations.

The Louis Marx No. 1614 coal dumper accessory shown with the No. 567 automatic coupler version of the New York Central dump car. This charming dumper was Louis' answer to Lionel's automatic accessories. At the push of a button, a pair of arms shoot out of the little house and hammer the dump car, causing it to spew its load into the little trackside tray . . . or at least in its general direction. To reload the car, use the two little shovels provided. *Jim Flynn collection*

Before looking at Lionel's big 1950 push, let's digress a moment to look at what was happening over in the Marx low-rent district. Lionel had brought out its hugely successful Santa Fe F3 and American Flyer its Santa Fe Alco PA. Perversely, in 1952, Louis Marx decided that he would go head to head with Lionel's beautifully die-cast F3 and came out with the Marx (Happi-Time in the Sears Catalog) Model 21—stamped out in lithographed tin. The result was stunning. Place the two locomotives one above the other and step back a pace or two. The illusion of detail on the Marx locomotive is totally convincing. Interestingly, the Lionel dual-motored, knuckle-couplered, diesel-horned F3 cost about $47; the Marx units had one motor and one automatic "dagger" coupler and no horn. But the price also included five passenger or freight cars, 18 sections of track, and a 70-watt transformer—all for $25!

The designers at Marx must have been an interesting group to know. While both Lionel and Flyer were spending big dollars to create realistic die-cast models of accessories and rolling stock, Marx replaced big budgets with penny-pinching ingenuity and a puckish sense of humor.

For example, after the war, Lionel introduced an ore dump car that could be unloaded at any place on the layout using the "electronic" radio system. Later, this car was designed to dump when an electromagnet in a special track section tripped a release mechanism and the car tilted and deposited its "coal" into a trackside bin. Marx, on the other hand, continued to use the same stamped V-shaped bin ore car from prewar days and built an "unloading station." When the car was stopped opposite this little house and a button was pushed, a pair of arms shot out of the house, hammered into the car with a sharp "*whang!*" and tipped over the bin. Coal spewed into a little tray—or halfway across the layout. Lionel and American Flyer provided elaborate operating coal loaders to refill their ore dump cars. Marx included two tiny plastic shovels with the little unloading station.

The boys at Lionel took years to perfect their smoke and whistle systems for high-end electric steam locomotives. Marx, with casual disdain, came up with bell, headlight, and smoke for their wind-up locomotives. These little key-wind cheapies

puttered around their tracks shining forth a battery-powered headlight and whistling a preset signal of two long blasts, a short toot, and another long blast (the standard grade-crossing warning still used by railroads). Sparks spewed from the stack and a bell dinged. As for the "smoke," which actually puffed out in time with the steamer's drive wheels, Marx relied on a rubber bulb that had been filled with baking soda or fine talcum. At every revolution of the wheels, the bulb was thumped to poof out a cloud of the white powder. Now, imagine mom patrolling the right-of-way with a vacuum cleaner after young Casey Jones' operating session.

Lionel's golden anniversary year came in fastened to the track with Magne-traction and pulled by a lemon and an orange. The 1950 catalog was a monument to the illustrative skills of Lionel's house artist, Robert Sherman. His paintings of smoke-belching steamers and gliding streamliners, all hurtling past acres of action accessories, glazed the eyes of young boys from coast to coast. Track after track of O gauge and O-27-gauge rolling stock promised long trains stretching into the distance even though the home track was often limited to a 4 x 8-foot sheet of plywood. The squeezed dimensions of Lionel locomotives—compromised so they could swing around tight three-rail curves—were stretched back to prototype proportions under Sherman's pen and brush. Even the lemon looked great.

The magnificent 700E Hudson of prewar days was a blissful memory. Even the somewhat less-detailed 763 of the same period evoked a sigh. In 1950, Lionel flogged a further scaled-back version of the Hudson, the 773. Not that it was an ugly or a slipshod kin of the original—it even pulled more cars because of its Magne-traction—but costs forced the company to shave here and there. The boiler front came from a Berkshire mounted on a re-designed frame and the smoke unit—which the 700E did not have—was cannibalized from Lionel's steam turbine. The 773 had smaller pilot wheels and a pair of flangeless drivers to negotiate O gauge curves. The drivers themselves had simulated spokes, and the rims were plain, not nickel. Instead of celebrating Lionel's golden anniversary, it served to remind everyone that times they were a changin'. Kids wanted the sleek diesels—not lame shadows of the past.

The 773 was pulled from the catalog in 1951 and did not surface again until 1964 at a time when Lionel was flailing about trying to deal with a new marketplace. The locomotive stayed in the line for two years, but, as in 1950, it was not a

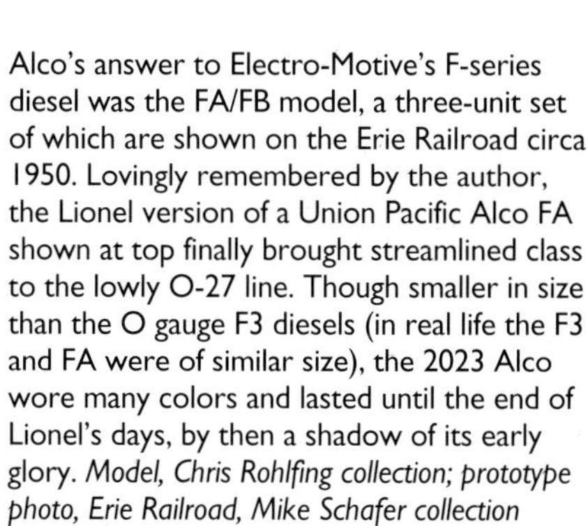

Alco's answer to Electro-Motive's F-series diesel was the FA/FB model, a three-unit set of which are shown on the Erie Railroad circa 1950. Lovingly remembered by the author, the Lionel version of a Union Pacific Alco FA shown at top finally brought streamlined class to the lowly O-27 line. Though smaller in size than the O gauge F3 diesels (in real life the F3 and FA were of similar size), the 2023 Alco wore many colors and lasted until the end of Lionel's days, by then a shadow of its early glory. *Model, Chris Rohlfing collection; prototype photo, Erie Railroad, Mike Schafer collection*

Under the guiding watch of his father, Paul Oroszi, son David explores his new Marx Texas & Pacific train set on Christmas morning early in the 1950s. How often was this scene repeated in the history of toy trains? *David P. Oroszi collection*

success. Today, the 773 Hudson is viewed in a more kindly light by collectors as a sought-after piece of Lionel history. But the Chevrolet Corvair and the Edsel are also sought-after collector items of their time.

A big success in 1950 was the yellow-and-gray Union Pacific Alco FA diesel. It was modeled after the American Locomotive Company's FA1 (cab) and FB1 (booster) introduced in 1946 and was designed mainly to haul freight. The prototype brewed up 1,500 horsepower and was Alco's competition to the EMD F-unit. Though not quite as successful as EMD's long-running line of F-series locomotives, Alco's FA model was heralded for its clean, modern lines—if not so for its exhaust. Alcos were notoriously smokey locomotives and provided what railroad writer Lucius Beebe liked to call "burning of Rome" smoke effects every time they turned a piston. Alco diesels—including the sleek PA modeled by Flyer—were thus called "honorary steam locomotives" by railroaders and railroad historians.

Lionel's Alco diesel had its curious side. To begin with, it was the first two-unit diesel to ride on O-27 track and was offered with freight cars or with matching passenger cars referred to as the "Anniversary Set." Lionel's FA diesel had a reliable, smooth-running motor, Magne-traction, die-cast trucks, the same realistic horn as on the F3, and a slick paint job. This was no hand-me-down sop to the low end of the line.

On the other hand, those touted die-cast trucks were the wrong trucks—they came from the 1949 6220 GM switcher. Also, though the prototype Alco FA was nearly the same size as the EMD F3, Lionel's model FA was significantly smaller than its O gauge F3 cousin. But for O-27 railroaders who had labored in the steam-bound past, that flash of Union Pacific Armour Yellow and Harbor Mist Gray whizzing around those tight 27-inch radius curves was a tonic.

Lionel's Alcos remained part of the line until 1969, sporting various liveries as popular as Santa Fe and New Haven, or as obscure as the U. S. Navy. Eventually, as Lionel's fortunes fluctuated downward, the FA was gradually stripped of its features until all it had left was a headlight and one coupler. Variously tarted up in garish colors or pushed out the door as single units in weary monochrome, it became part of faded plastic sets competing in the bush-league basements of discount outlets. But in 1950, that Union Pacific FA was all splash and dash and a breath of fresh air for kids—like the author—who toiled with the other bottom-feeders in O-27 gauge.

The year 1950 marked the start of almost a decade of great tinplate trains from Lionel, American Flyer, and Marx. But, while there were many innovations and items produced that would go on to become very collectible memories by adults who inherited what the kids had abandoned, this period was also the swan song of the toy train. We will look at some of these landmark trains and accessories, but with the understanding that outside the toy train manufacturers' world, American life was changing drastically.

Low-cost housing was erupting from former farmland, answering the postwar promise of a better life after the deprivation of the Great Depression and war rationing. New cars were churning out of Detroit and forcing the construction of

While Lionel used real road names for their diesels, for a time in the early 1950s American Flyer preferred fictitious tags on its S gauge Alco diesel sets. Despite the "Rocket" name borrowed from the Rock Island Lines, famous for its *Rocket* streamliners, the livery on the Alcos on this Flyer passenger set is based on an early diesel scheme used by the Southern Railway. This 1955 set is unusual in that it offers three dome cars. Although somewhat foreshortened, Flyer's streamlined passenger cars were a surprisingly accurate rendition of postwar cars produced by the Budd Company. *Mike Schafer collection*

multi-lane highways and turnpikes. A war pitting Americans and other United Nations countries against Communism was raging in Korea. The government's Office of Price Stabilization was battling serious inflation as its "OPS– Ceiling Price" stickers were being slapped on all levels of consumer goods, including toy trains. The railroads were beating their drum for a piece of the transportation action, but were losing the battle. Trucks were hauling freight door-to-door over an expanding highway network, and former rail passengers were now flying. Multi-prop DC-7s and Constellations and jet-powered airliners such as the DeHaviland Comet and Boeing 707 were helping build a new transportation network more in tune with the faster pace of postwar life.

Television, with its seductive sound and pictures that no print medium could match, lured kids from their old toys to discover the "Space Cadets," "Captain Video," and intelligent robots. News programs showed films of America's fledgling attempts at launching rockets into outer space. On October 4, 1957, the Soviet Union beat America into earth orbit with *Sputnik*, a melon-sized satellite that beeped and made Americans second-class space explorers. American rockets fizzled and exploded on their launching pads and a call went out to schools: "Science and Math Wizards Wanted." The dweebs, dorks, and geeks who couldn't climb the rope in gym class finally ruled! Science and math were in and suddenly it was unpatriotic to be mystified by slide-rule calculus or stumped by the laws of physics. The pressure was on to "beat the Commies" who were already firing dogs and Yuri Gargarin into space with monotonous regularity on the nightly TV news. Kids' playtime was becoming serious business.

Amidst all this, how relevant was a toy tinplate train circling a track? The Big Three would soon find out.

In 1952, the demands of the Korean War caused a shortage of Alnico magnets that stripped Magne-traction from Lionel locomotives. Although some new sets were produced—running on a dull, gray alloy track instead of steel—a bunker mentality settled over the company. Lionel waited for the United Nations' "police action" in Korea to conclude and the subsequent lifting of restrictions on price and raw materials. One highlight of the year was the *Super Speed Liner*—seven feet of extruded aluminum passenger cars hooked up to a pair of Santa Fe warbonnet diesels. Though it was very expensive at $89.50, the long silver train was the cherished set of the time.

American Flyer chose this inauspicious year to announce its new knuckle coupler. Though A. C. Gilbert had lost the coupler realism race to Lionel back in 1946, official company policy deemed the feature to be ". . . not significant." However, Gilbert's corporate angst was evident in the 1951 catalog as car after car was illustrated with an airbrush smudge where the offending link coupler

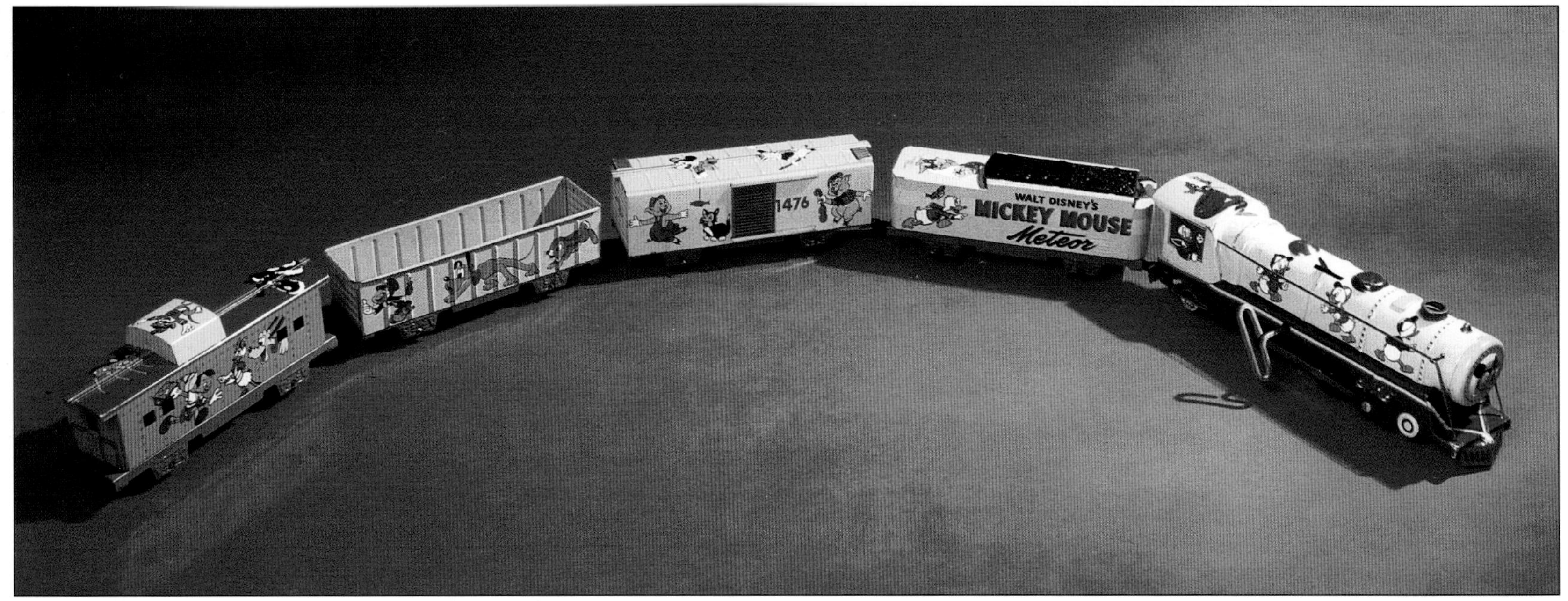

Louis Marx *Mickey Mouse Meteor* train made about 1952. The set was all lithographed on tin and featured characters licensed from Walt Disney. *Jim Flynn Collection*

Marx's low-end diesel line included a locomotive that is best described as a "mimic" of the prototype Electro-Motive F-series. They came painted in several liveries, such as this Baltimore & Ohio set hauling two four-wheel lithographed tin freight cars. The illusion of detail lithographed over the stamped tin shell provided incredible value for train sets that cost a fraction of the prices paid for Lionel and American Flyer. Marx electric and wind-up motors are still running today after decades of use. *Steve Esposito collection*

should have been. Management rationalized that the costs of refitting the entire line with the new coupler were prohibitive. With dollars committed to augmenting its S gauge converted prewar offerings with new locomotives and rolling stock, little was left but for Flyer's R&D group to tip-toe through Lionel's patent minefield that blocked A.C. at every turn. Having been burned by the whistle infringement lawsuit in 1949, Flyer designers blew on their singed fingertips and toiled hard to come up with a reliable knuckle coupler they could safely call their own.

As they had done in 1949—trying out a whistle installation on only one locomotive—Flyer's shops cobbled together handmade sets of knuckles and frugally attached them to expensive 1952 sets, the $52 "Pacemaker," hauled by a 4-6-4 Hudson, and the $57 "Challenger" featuring Flyer's largest steamer, the 4-8-4 Northern. The most noticeable difference between the competing coupler designs? Lionel's electro-magnet opened the coupler by pulling the unlocking pin down while Flyer's pin was pushed up by a track-mounted uncoupling ramp, either manual or electrically remote-controlled. Flyer's coupler was a success; Lionel's camp was silent. American Flyer had achieved parity with its rival (except for that nagging whistle) and now the real competition could begin.

Television became a dueling ground as both manufacturers sought to get as much air time as possible for their trains. American Flyer had its setup on the *Dave Garroway Show*—a popular

morning program that featured the soft-spoken host and a chimpanzee named J. Fred Muggs. Lionel signed New York Yankee star Joe DiMaggio for $125,000 to film 13 programs for NBC called *The Lionel Clubhouse*. Since the rivalry between the Yankees and the Brooklyn Dodgers was at its peak, Roy Campanella, the Dodgers' star catcher and hitter, was snared by Lionel's public relations flacks. Campanella—the third African-American to break the pro-baseball color barrier—was already a Lionel owner and fan. Ron Hollander's book *All Aboard!* parlays a great story about how Roy was about to be featured on Edward R. Murrow's fluff-piece celebrity interview show, *Person to Person*, where the famed broadcaster "visited" guests in their homes on live TV. Lionel's best layout team descended on Campanella's basement to gussy up his already formidable set of tracks. Unfortunately, during the live interview, the baseball star showed his trains but never mentioned Lionel by name. As Hollander put it, "It didn't really matter because Lionel had become synonymous with electric

A Fairbanks-Morse Train Master demonstrator locomotive set testing in Milwaukee, Wisconsin, in 1953. The huge diesel was powered by a single 2,400-horsepower marine engine designed for use on America's largest Gato-class submarines. Many of the 105 units sold went to Eastern railroads such as Reading Lines, Lackawanna, and Virginian for coal-train service. Jersey Central used its Train Masters on high-speed commuter service account of the locomotive's ability to accelerate rapidly. *Andover Junction Publications Archives.*

Lionel's Lackawanna Fairbanks-Morse Train Master diesel road-switcher squats on the three-rail track like a maroon-and-gray brick. This Model 2321 diesel was introduced in 1954 in Lackawanna colors. Later it appeared in other liveries and was a successful design for Lionel, if not for Fairbanks-Morse. *Chris Rohlfing collection*

Here, the Lionel 6464 box car line is represented by the 300 Rutland, the 325 B&O Sentinel and the 650 Rio Grande. As the line progressed, the cars became more colorful and the graphics improved. *Courtesy, Chris Rohlfing Collection*

trains, a proper-noun-turned-generic like Jell-O or Kleenex or Frigidaire."

Combating that American icon status, in the 1954 American Flyer catalog, A. C. Gilbert cautioned, "Buying an electric train is an important step for most people. It frequently represents a sizable investment, not only in dollars, but in hours of future happiness for that boy of yours—and for you." After this paternalistic preamble, A. C. (or perhaps a copywriter with the founder's imprimatur) proceeded to dump all over three-rail, squat, and stumpy trains built like they were ". . . in the early days." He trumpeted American Flyer's modern scale models of real trains and, generously, tossed the poor, deluded three-rail boobs a bone:

> . . . They look sawed-off and out of proportion, instead of long and low like real trains. Naturally, there is a reason for this. These big gauge trains cannot be made to scale because they would be too large for the average home or apartment and would be far to expensive for most people to buy.

Having mercilessly disposed of Lionel as short, fat, and cheap, Gilbert capped his argument by playing the TV card.

> American Flyer trains have been used in miniature movie sets and on TV shows to represent real trains moving across the countryside. No other make of electric trains could have possibly been used in this way.

By 1952, thanks in part to Louis Marx's postwar jaunts, Marx toys were being produced in London, England; Swansea, Wales; Sidney, Australia; Toronto, Canada; Durban, South Africa; Sao Paulo, Brazil; Paris, France; and Mexico—the longest lasting production plant.

His people had done a deal with Walt Disney during the early 1950s and produced one of their most charming sets. The *Mickey Mouse Meteor* was a wind-up lithographed tin train that used the "Hudson" locomotive—actually an 0-4-0 with fake pilot and trailer trucks that were part of the tin stamping. Across the locomotive, tender, boxcar, gondola, and caboose, Disney characters flitted and frolicked in full color. With the train, the buyer also got a dozen pieces of two-rail track—all for $3.98. The 1950s also saw Marx's electric tin streamliners in various liveries including Southern Pacific, Monon, Seaboard Air Line, and Baltimore & Ohio. Louis preferred steam locomotives because of their action, but his colorful diesels were popular sellers complete with track, transformer, and a half-dozen plastic telephone poles thrown in for good measure.

Although 1953 marked Lionel's peak profit year with sales of $32.9 million, two of its most popular products came out the following year: the 2321 Fairbanks-Morse Train Master diesel locomotive and the type 6464 boxcars.

The protype Train Master came out of the Fairbanks-Morse shops at Beloit, Wisconsin, in 1953, pumping 2,400 horsepower generated by a single diesel engine (other locomotives of the period of high horsepower often housed two engines) into two sets of six-wheel trucks. It was a massive hill-hauler of long freights and—although not very streamlined—was also nimble with fast passenger schedules. In seven years, F-M sold 105 Train Masters—not an earth-shattering number. Though successful on many levels, the Train Master was a case of being ahead of its time—it was almost too large a locomotive for railroads of that period—and it employed an unusual opposed-piston power plant that had been developed for marine application, reliable but of technology that was foreign to many railroads already embracing Electro-Motive and Alco diesels.

Like the prototype Train Master, Lionel's version was a brute and—contrary to Gilbert's "sawed-off and squat" zinger—was almost scale in dimensions. The stamped steel hood and cab harkened back to pre-die-cast days and gave a tip of the hat to Louis Marx's cost-cutting ways. The six-wheel trucks had a blind set of center wheels so the beast could swing around tight curves. Originally offered in Delaware, Lackawanna & Western livery, the Train Master would eventually be seen wearing Jersey Central, Wabash, and the particularly memorable Virginian colors.

Also new to the Train Master was a mechanical knuckle coupler. From 1946 to 1954, Lionel's couplers had been activated by an on-board electromagnet receiving its orders from a sliding shoe as the shoe traversed a special track section. The new coupler had a metal disc that was pulled down by an electromagnet in the track, releasing a pin and opening the knuckle. While the system was proven, big locomotives that could haul long trains—e.g., the Train Master, 773 Hudson, the F3 diesels—had a problem with the coupler being pulled open by sheer weight on the locomotive's coupler. Lionel's new and cheaper-to-make coupler

Dating from the mid-1950s, this red "heavyweight" passenger set from American Flyer modeled prototype all-steel cars—baggage car, combine "smoker," Pullman sleeper, and observation lounge—from the 1920s and early 1930s. These die castings date from pre-war O gauge days, but this late offering features sintered-iron trucks and knuckle couplers. *Mike Schafer collection*

From the Lionel 1957 catalog, this unique train set, No. 2297WS, is pulled by the exceptional 746 Norfolk & Western J-class 4-8-4. Two things make the set unique. First, all cars were operating: a culvert unloader car, horse car, fork-lift platform car, milk car, and the bay-window caboose. Second, the J-series N&W steamer was used primarily for passenger service after the war though they had been classed as freight engines during the conflict. *Chris Rohlfing collection*

The same young Dave Orozsi pictured on page 120 has in this photo from the late 1950s graduated to a basement table layout—once a staple of many American homes with boys in the household during the 1950s. Note, too, that David now has American Flyer trains, although at the time he also sometimes set up his earlier Marx set side by side to create a "double-track" railroad. *David P. Orozsi collection*

always worked better with less-powerful locomotives hauling shorter trains.

As diesels began replacing steam on the real railroads, Lionel in 1955 matched the trend by adding its own Electro-Motive GP7 road-switcher to its line (Flyer had already done this in 1950 with its No. 370 GP7 in General Motors demonstrator paint). But while the trend continued unabated with the prototype roads, toy train manufacturers clung to steam trains with smoke, choo-choo, whistles, and a Flyer feature called "Red Glowing Smoke"—a bit of red plastic above the headlight that shone up through the smoke stack. The thrashing, noisy, smokey action of steam power had always been a big selling point in toy trains. After all, steam engines represented the memories of the fathers with the cash, not the streamlined stainless-steel world of the sons.

The other enduring 1954 Lionel entry was the 6464 boxcar. Eventually, there would be 279 variations of 28 different numbers produced. This boxcar looked like the prewar scale model designed to hang behind the 700E Hudson. But the reason for its die-cast existence was to bring colorful railroad and shipper paint schemes to Lionel layouts. Once again, although these schemes were derived from prototype boxcars, they were also "interpreted" by Lionel designers. Nonetheless, the result was quite acceptable, and they are much sought after in today's collector market.

Before the page turned over on 1954, Lionel entered the photography market. The Linex stereo camera and viewer set cost about $50 and was offered as yet another shot toward diversifying Lionel's product line. The stereo camera had two lenses and simultaneously recorded a pair of pictures. When viewed in a special viewer, the photos overlapped and gave the viewer an impression of three-dimensional depth to the subject matter. There was a surge of 3-D photography in the 1950s matching the efforts of Hollywood studios to combat TV with 3-D movies, but the fad petered out well before the 1960s. Together with the Lionel Airex spin-casting reel, the Linex was just another harbinger of horrors to come.

Both the sublime and the ridiculous were offered by Lionel in 1957. The sublime was represented by a very accurate model of the Norfolk & Western J-series steam locomotive, and the ridiculous was offered up as a marketing clunker on par with the Edsel: a steam train designed for girls.

The J-class streamlined steamer, shrouded in black bullet-like contours with a Tuscan red stripe with gold pinstriping, was one of those breathtaking designs that, when seen at speed with drive rods whirring, smoke streaming back, and whistle screaming, brought a lump to the throat of every train lover. N&W's Js were built during the World War II era and were the fastest steam passenger locomotives of her time.

Lionel's model 746 was a faithful reproduction, borrowing the 4-8-4 running gear from the Berkshire and adding the streamlined shroud with the red stripe extending right across the flanks of the tender. In its debut, the 746 presented the prototypically correct "long stripe" tender, but later tenders—using heat-stamped instead of silk screened colors—had a shorter stripe. Except for the proportionally smaller running gear of the Berkshire, the Lionel J-class model stands alongside the 700E Hudson and the Santa Fe F3 as one the company's most beautiful designs.

It is almost beyond reason that the same people who could present a beautifully conceived

LEFT: In 1956 Lionel offered the 6342 culvert unloader car. It worked with the 342 culvert unloader platform, and in 1957 the 345 culvert loader was added. Both platforms butted together made for considerable trackside action. *Chris Rohlfing collection*

BELOW: The 785 coal loader was another favorite American Flyer accessory from the 1950s. Three buttons controlled clamshell movement. The trick was loading the coal from the trackside tray into the bunker, which then emptied via the chute into coal hoppers positioned underneath. Three buttons and a keen eye added up to considerable play value. *Mike Schafer collection*

locomotive like the 746 could also inflict a pink steam engine hauling pastel-colored cars on its buying public. Called the Lady Lionel, this marketing stinker came as follows:

- 2037 steam engine in pink
- 6462-500 gondola in "Pink Frosting"
- 6464-510 boxcar (NYC) in "Robin's Egg Blue" (actually light green)
- 6464-515 boxcar (Katy Railroad) in "Buttercup Yellow"
- 6436-500 coal hopper in lilac
- 6427-500 caboose in sky blue

Everyone hated it, and Lionel couldn't give them away with boxtops. Women thought the Lady Lionel was demeaning. Men and boys laughed at it, and most of the pathetic pastel permutations gathered dust in shop windows until the salesmen took them home to their own kids who didn't want them either. But the boys who laughed so hard would have gasped if they had seen what was supposed to be released simultaneous with Lady Lionel: a "Boy's Train" (Laddy

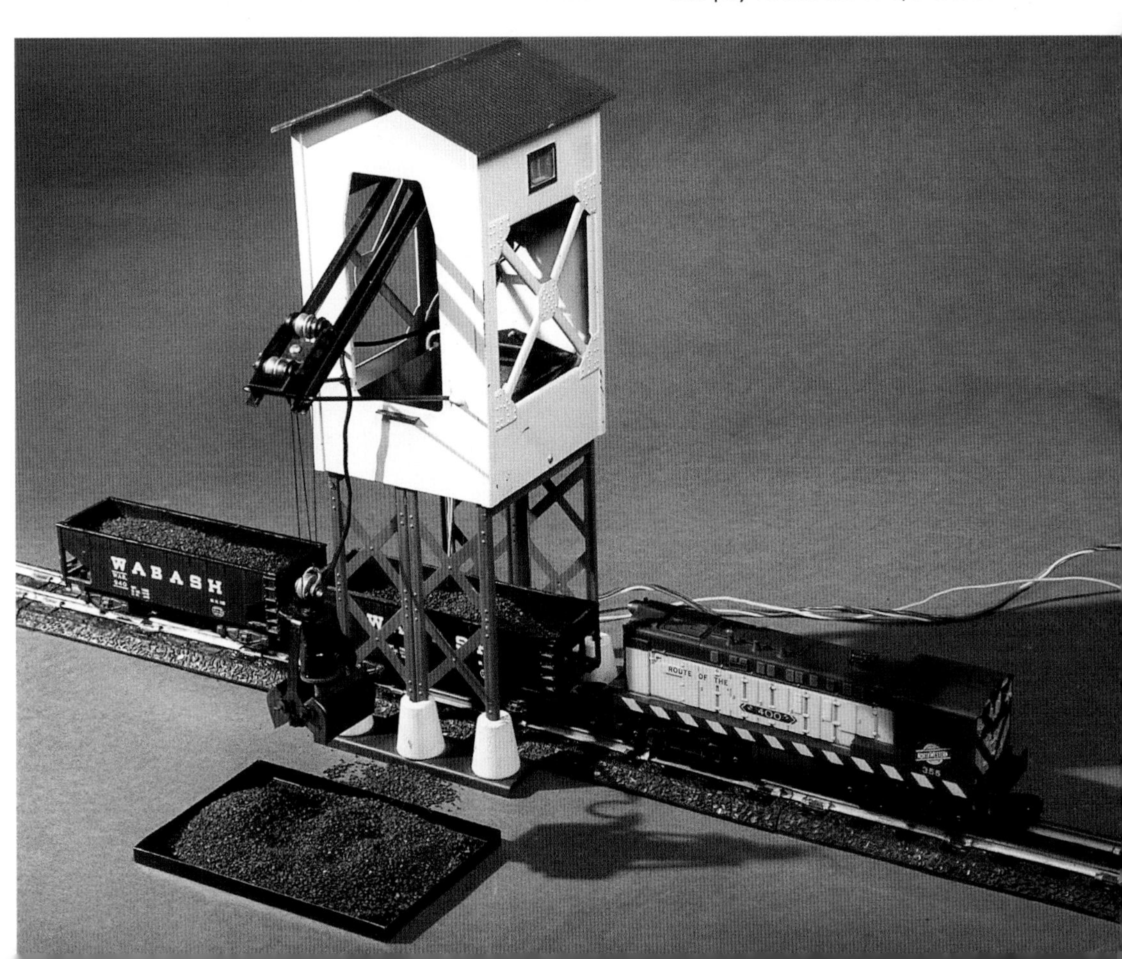

The Stinker-of-All-Time award for tinplate trains goes to the Lionel's "Girls Train" of 1957. Designed to appeal to Tommy's sister, the train set wound up gathering cobwebs in display windows. Somehow, a pastel pink locomotive and sky-blue cars didn't appeal to the female gender, much less the male. However, in an ironic twist, the train's rarity inspired Lionel to reissue it as a collectable in 1991. This model is one of those reproductions. *Chris Rohlfing collection*

Lionel?), which was to be headed up by a manly bilious blue locomotive. Fortunately, Lionel did not officially release this second gaffe, and only a few are in the hands of protective collectors since their value today is in the thousands of dollars.

As the 1960s approached, the Big Two began to thrash about, trying to rev up interest in their respective toy trains. By 1957, Lionel had recognized that a downward skid was beginning. In the real world, commercial airliners had sucked passengers from the railroads. That year marked the first time that more passengers were moved by air than by train. Adding fuel to that fire, former General and now President Dwight D. Eisenhower was fathering interstate highway building programs in the name of national defense.

Between 1953 and 1955, Lionel sales had dropped 38 per cent while American Flyer's numbers plummeted by a third. Lionel hung tough and introduced "Super O" track that used lots of realistic plastic ties and a far more inconspicuous center third rail made of a narrow strip of brass. Super O looked more like real railroad high iron, but it was more difficult to assemble and the narrow third rail quickly wore ruts into pickup shoes. But even as Lionel was trying to go uptown with its new track, plans were afoot to cut production costs. Lionel had already sneaked an "under $20" set into its 1956 catalog to compete with Marx.

Marx eventually adopted all-plastic trains as this Sears set illustrates. The die-cast 666 steam locomotive smokes. *Jim Flynn collection*

For Marx customers, 20 bucks could buy an entire railroad complete with accessories. Furthermore, Marx had upped its own ante by shifting to plastic "scale" train sets that looked better than its steel stampings and was shipping 100,000 sets—about one third of their total production—to Sears & Roebuck alone. These were low cost, but not cheap. Marx preserved a vigilant quality control, and both wind-up and electric trains in collectors' hands today still run as well as they did when new.

Even so, Marx was also feeling the pinch as raw materials and production costs continued to rise. A thriving market for the almost endless variety of Marx military train sets and individual military cars fell off during the early 1950s. Kids no longer equated trains with the travails of World War II much less the Korean War. Saber jet fighters, Thunder Jets, and P-80 Shooting Stars were the toys of choice. As the 1960s drew closer, Marx's off-shore production facilities became more important.

American Flyer's production during the mid-1950s was considerable and, as usual, unique. To counter the Lionel line of electric prototypes, particularly the GG1, Flyer in 1956 introduced its one and only electric, a model of General Electric's new (in 1955) EP-5 ignitron-rectifier passenger locomotives. These flashy locomotives were double-ended (crew cabs at both ends) to eliminate the need to turn them at the end of a run. The EP-5s (sometimes mistakenly referred to by collectors of Flyer and Lionel EP-5 models as "Little Joes") were used in high-speed passenger service between New York City and New Haven, Connecticut.

By 1958 Flyer had introduced a small freight set powered by a "Docksider" steam switcher, a stubby tank locomotive based on a Baltimore & Ohio prototype that worked primarily around wriggling industrial trackage. Also new in 1958 was the Missouri Pacific Alco pulling Flyer's surprisingly accurate rendition of prototype MP's

Two hefty American Flyer transformers—one twin-throttle No. 22080 300-watt (Flyer's answer to the Lionel ZW) and one 110 watt No. 22040—from the 1950s look down on a Flyer streamliner wearing the Northern Pacific *North Coast Limited* livery introduced in 1956. In the background are Flyer's Mystic train station and a rotary beacon that operated off heat convection. *Bill Van Ramshorst*

The 1949 Lionel catalog cover shows Mom, Dad, Sis, and a rapturous Sonny, all peering through a shop window at a glorious collection of motive power, rolling stock, and accessories guaranteed to thin Dad's wallet. Harkening to the catalogs of the 1920s and 1930s, everyone is dressed in their winter holiday best adding a subtle quality cachet to the owner of a Lionel train. *Jim Flynn collection*

AMERICAN FLYER "Sunshine Special" Twin Unit Diesel Freight

- √ BUILT-IN "DIESEL ROAR"
- √ NEW DE LUXE ACTION CABOOSE
- √ REALISTIC ELECTRONIC HORN
- √ REMOTE CONTROL
- √ PULL-MOR POWER

No. 20355 AMERICAN FLYER FREIGHT SET

When these two powerhouse General Motors GP-7 Diesel Locomotives team up to haul your freight drag, you really get results! Plenty of massiveness in the right places plus worm-drive and Pull-Mor Power mean speed on the flats and hauling capacity where it counts on the grades. Both loco units carry authentic Texas & Pacific R.R. color scheme and lettering; rolling stock is highlighted by brand new bay window type Caboose with action trainman. Locomotive also has built-in Diesel "Roar"—duplicates to uncanny degree the big motor sound of idling and running Diesel motors! Track measures 160″. Train is 69″.

Transformer of 100 watt capacity, or greater, should be used to operate train.

FUN WITH THIS ACTION CABOOSE! Every time train stops, this busy brakeman leans out to see what's going on up ahead — and to keep a check on the cars. When train resumes trip he returns to middle of platform. Automatic action!

Sunshine Special Freight includes:

No. 21908 Texas & Pacific two-unit Diesel Locomotive with Diesel Roar, Horn and Pull-Mor Power
No. 24209 Jersey Central Cement Car
No. 24313 Gulf 3-dome Tank Car
No. 24206 C. B. & Q. Coal Car
No. 24416 Northwestern Reefer
No. 24116 Southern Gondola
No. 25036 De Luxe Action Caboose
No. 26708 Diesel Electronic Horn Control
No. 26752 Electric Remote Control Uncoupler
12 sections 26720 Curved Track
4 sections 26700 Straight Track
16 No. 26693 Track Locks
No. 26690 Track Terminal
Illustrated Train Manual

22

One of the more collectible American Flyer sets today is the No. 20355 *Sunshine Special* freight set feature a twin-unit GP7 diesel set painted for Texas & Pacific. The dummy unit contained Flyer's "Diesel Roar" sound effect which was essentially an electronic buzz amplified through a speaker. The intensity of the sound rose with an increase in track voltage. *Mike Schafer collection*

Colorado Eagle domeliner that ran between St. Louis and Denver.

For sheer product availability, 1958 was the watershed year for American Flyer. The catalog was packed with 18 exciting train sets, new accessories, and paragraphs of ringing rhetoric. But a close look revealed the fraying edges of the line precipitating a dizzying spiral downward. The popular twin-unit Texas & Pacific GP7 set was reduced to a single locomotive as was the famed Northern Pacific *North Coast Limited* set. On its stalwart Atlantic steam locomotive, the drivers were given plastic centers while the 0-6-0 Pennsylvania switcher lost its tender back-up light. This same year, some promotional wizard came up with the "Yard King Special" freight set—"The longest train ever made!" This one-trick pony hung 13 freight cars behind the 0-8-0 switcher such that on its figure-8 layout the engine just missed the caboose at the crossing.

In 1959, the number of American Flyer sets was chopped in half to nine. "It's 9 for 59!" trumpeted the catalog. Celebrating its Golden Anniversary, A. C. Gilbert bravely if dubiously announced, "The Most Compact Train Line in American Flyer History." Consumer catalogs were changing over to a two-sided fold-out poster that was much cheaper to produce. The Hudson lost its whistle, and a shift to military missile hardware was announced with the Defender Set that hauled a rocket-launching car and detonating boxcar. Nostalgia was offered alongside the missile destruction cars in the form of The Frontiersman set, a rather well-done old time 4-4-0 locomotive trailing yellow Civil War-era passenger cars. At this time, Westerns were big on TV, and in the movies so any old hook would do to turn a buck.

Turning that buck was desperately needed in 1959 because American Flyer's sales had dropped by 50 per cent.

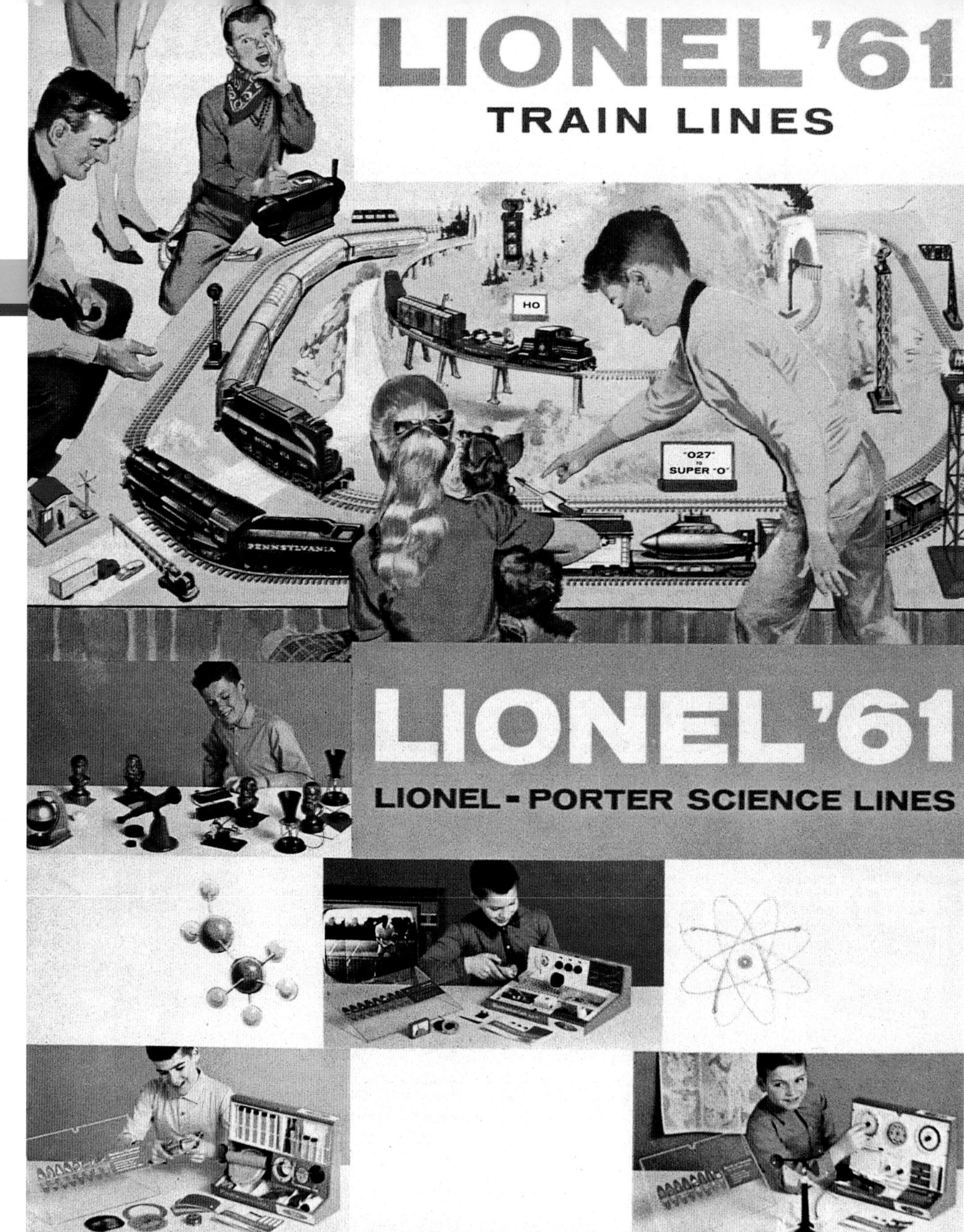

Both Lionel and American Flyer were watering down their train offerings with lines of chemistry and construction sets in the early years of the Space Age—the 1960s. Science was being pushed in the schools, so play and education were fused to create new revenue generators for the profit-desperate train manufacturers. *Jim Flynn collection*

Chapter 7

Toy Trains and Railroads —Bankrupt Dreams

As the 1950s had dawned full of hope and promise, the 1960s arrived beneath storm clouds and a fading market. Toy train manufacturers had in a sense been double-crossed by the real railroads. America's railroads were an institution, a revered industry that had "grown" the country, shepherded it through wars, and moved Americans and their goods from sea to shining sea. Railroads had roots that went all the way back to the *Tom Thumb* and the Golden Spike that joined the continent on a barren, windswept landscape in Utah. What happened to all the great road names that were now referred to as "fallen flags?"

As the 1960s unfurled, rival railroads Pennsylvania and New York Central were in the final stages of their longtime plans to merge—two drowning giants trying to stay above the red ink. Their unfortunate fusion on February 1, 1968, would result in the "new" Penn Central and, subsequently, its bankruptcy in 1971. Passenger service that was once the railroads' polished public face had deteriorated and was skidding further down the priority list as ridership plummeted. A loss leader since World War II, the once-gleaming passenger trains disappeared one by one, worth more as scrap than transportation. Engineers, the heros of young boys since earliest steam days, now went to work like clerks or bus drivers—no less necessary, but anonymous in their sealed diesels that all looked alike except for the paint on their sides. Vast train yards at the nation's rail hubs became more valuable for their "air rights" and commercial real-estate potential. Long ribbons of unused rails followed steam locomotives into the steel mills' melting crucibles.

Another blow to the toy train manufacturers was the suburban explosion fueled by the building boom of the 1950s. Populations streamed into the new developments fringing the big cities—and with the people came a new form of retail outlet, the low-overhead, high-turnover discount store.

Instant destruction with the push of a button is implied for this American Flyer 25059 Rocket Launcher car. As American Flyer and Lionel entered the late 1950s and early 1960s, they offered cars that either fired something or exploded when hit. "Play value" for boys meant combat while electric trains became weapons platforms. These offerings were part of American Flyer's swan song. *Jeff Katzner collection*

In an effort to pump up sales in 1959 with military offerings, Lionel produced this self-propelled No. 44 mobile missile launcher. It could pull a small fleet of weapons cars as well as fire four missiles in sequence by remote control. *Courtesy, Chris Rohlfing collection*

By 1960, Lionel was pushing its line of HO gauge trains hard but was finding few takers. Although the new gauge was becoming popular among scale hobbyists, Lionel's frivolous approach—in keeping with its tinplate roots —of kid-oriented "action" cars and non-scale motive power did not interest the adults who were buying HO gauge for themselves. *Jim Flynn collection*

Acres of farmland now sprouted these concrete-block mega-stores that catered to new homeowners who were starting from scratch and had sunk most of their money into the roof over their head as well as the new car that took Dad to work. These stores were mutant department stores, but paid lower rents, employed fewer people on the shopping floor, and bought everything in bulk from the lowest bidders.

City department stores like Sears and Montgomery Ward built huge facilities in these new malls surrounded with acres of asphalt parking lots, but their buying strategies were still geared to their established vendors. The discount stores owed no such loyalties and put the squeeze on makers of plastic buckets, kitchen chairs, nylon jackets, and toy train makers alike to cut prices if they wanted shelf space. As for kids' toys, weapons of mass destruction, outer space rockets, anything having to do with missiles, jet aircraft, and fast cars got the biggest play.

Lionel and American Flyer had dealt with "mom and pop" toy and hobby shop dealers, hardware stores, and friendly department stores for "price" sets during the year and window display extravaganzas over the winter holidays. Now, price drove everything; service and quality were secondary.

Joshua Cowen had absented himself from the daily operation of Lionel allowing Lawrence to run the company. What had been a family company built on close, working relationships was fractured in 1954 by a strike involving 2,500 Lionel workers—their fourth since World War II—that ran deep in acrimony during negotiations. Stockholders now held management led by Lawrence Cowen accountable for the plunge in profits, and "the old man's boy" felt the pressure.

Even though Lionel had emerged from the Korean Conflict with war contract profits, the fishing reel and the Linex stereo camera had cut a swath through its capital. In 1957, Lionel had even attempted to invade the HO marketplace. It had tried a smaller gauge in 1938, adopting the British OO gauge, but had abandoned it because the market was so small. By 1957, highly detailed HO locomotives and rolling stock were finding space in the smaller tract homes then being built. It was also easier to fold up and store an HO train set during the peripatetic 1950s. Lionel and American Flyer both tackled HO in their declining years, and both missed the market entirely.

Lionel subcontracted its HO line to Rivarossi in Italy, but the designs of locomotives and rolling stock were aimed at kids—not the adults who were buying the small, intricate, and very realistic trains. Lionel HO looked cheap and used rubber-band motors—a strip of thin rubber carried the motor's power to the locomotive wheels. While Varney, Ambroid, and Mantua were striving for prototype realism in their HO rolling stock, Lionel had rockets firing from flatcars and boxcars that "exploded" when hit. Still, Lionel catalogs railed against complicated two-rail track wiring and pooh-poohed "small-is-better."

Understandably, 1957 was the last year the toy trains that had built the company showed a profit. A drastic new direction was needed for the 1960s. Lawrence Cowen was overseas hunting for fielders' gloves and baseball bats to add to Lionel's World Wide Sporting Goods Company, a trademark acquired through Airex, when news reached him that his father, Joshua, had sold out to a group headed by Cowen's great-nephew, Roy Cohn. In effect, Lawrence was out of a job. With Lionel sitting on losses of $583,000 and all of the chart arrows pointing precipitously downward, Joshua and his wife had unloaded $825,000 worth of stock—55,000 shares—to a lawyer who had shot to prominence by whispering in Senator Joseph McCarthy's ear during the Senator's infamous, career-ruining communist witch hunt.

Cohn had emerged from the McCarthy hearings relatively unscathed. He was brilliant, self-possessed, and loved keeping many balls in the air at once. Lionel became one of those balls. With Lawrence back in his brokerage wondering what had happened, the board hired former NASA missile chief and ex-general John Medaris. Cohn,

CANNON BOXCAR

for O27, O and Super O Track
No. 3666

The roof of the car opens and cannon muzzle elevates to firing position–at this point the shell fires automatically–all by remote control.

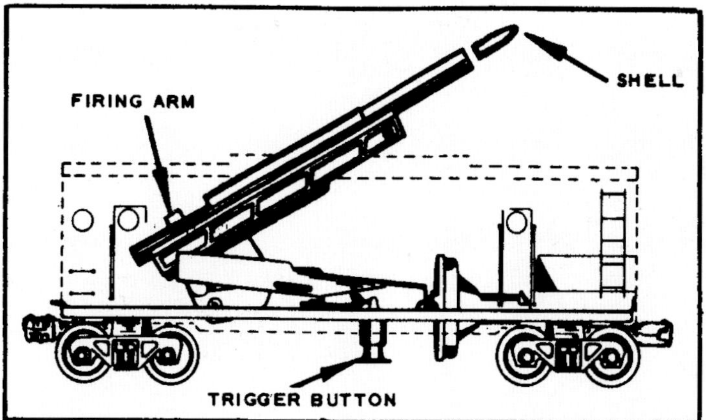

OPERATING PROCEDURE

- Place a shell in the cannon muzzle with cannon in firing position.
- Cock the firing arm by pulling it back against the firing spring and hold in that position.

NOTE: *The arm can be set at several different positions, thereby adjusting for distance.*

The "Cannon Boxcar" allowed young engineers to creep up on unsuspecting enemy tanks and blast them to flinders with this keen elevating and firing artillery piece. Also a great idea for clearing the right-of-way of slow trains. *Train Collectors Association*

By 1959, Lionel was thrashing about, mixing antique concepts like the "General" set, a colorful diamond-stack throwback to Civil War railroading but—in keeping with Cold War headlines—with missile-firing cars, ballistic rockets, and bunkers. Featuring "duck-and-cover" nuclear war fears as nostalgia for a simpler time seemed appropriate to Lionel's fevered marketers. *Jim Flynn collection*

with diversification at the top of his priority list, was after the military contracts that was expected to come flowing Lionel's way through the general's associates. While Medaris cut a dashing figure, he was also preparing a book lambasting the very military he was hired to court, for failing to create a bigger, better missile program.

Cohn did not so much run Lionel into the ground as he did overinflate it with acquisitions until it became an unwieldy assembly of poorly managed divisions. He himself was involved in five travel agencies, a savings and loan company, a New York City bus company, two airline insurance companies, and was promoting the Floyd Patterson-Ingemar Johansson heavyweight champion fight. Medaris was scooted to one side after a $1.8 million loss during his first year. Cohn continued on until Lionel had managed to lose $14

million, then he bailed. He sold his shares, bought from Cowen for $15 each, for little more than $5 apiece. Lionel's stock under Cohn's shaky hand had dropped from from 15 to 6 in four years. By 1963, Roy Cohn was ducking around town avoiding subpoenas and running for his financial life. Lionel had become a shoddy shell of its former glory with locomotives and motors made in Japan.

On September 8, 1965, Joshua Lionel Cowen, who had raised his company from little cigar boxes on wheels to the status of a national icon, died of a heart attack in Palm Beach, Florida. Two years later, at age 63, his son, Lawrence, also died of heart failure. For all practical purposes, Lionel was now only a logo on a letterhead.

American Flyer's champion, Alfred C. Gilbert had died in 1961. The family was forced from control in 1962, and a year later the heir to the company, Alfred Jr., followed him. The company was suddenly rudderless and it showed. The 1962 catalog led off with model airplanes, followed with slot-car race sets, and eventually got to the toy trains, both S and HO sets. A *Pioneer Flyer* set that had ". . . the flavor of the railroading era when Casey Jones made his famous run" was in reality a sad little three-car freight with a mis-proportioned 4-4-0 with painted-on cab windows, no headlight, no smoke, and no choo-choo sound; it sold for $17.98. Touted as more realistic, new Pike Master track had more ties, but the realistic T-rail of yore was gone and the radius was much sharper and therefore less realistic. Sadder still, the kids of 1962 didn't know this Casey Jones guy from deep center field.

Interestingly, Flyer brought back the die-cast Hudson steam locomotive. It came with a five-car freight that also featured an exploding boxcar. A Santa Fe *Chief* set featured the handsome Alco PA towing three passenger cars on Pike Master track, while a Pacific locomotive led the *Champion* freight train around 12 pieces of track, also Pike Master. For a capper, the price-conscious designers fielded Flyer's "F9" diesel. Though based on Electro-Motive's incredibly successful F-series locomotives that had inspired Lionel's classic F3 model of 1948, the Flyer F9 was at best a clumsy, cartoonlike interpretation of the real thing—far worse than any Lionel interpretive model ever made. This year marked the last time Gilbert showed a profit.

American Flyer soldiered on, but by 1965, the entire toy train line featured only 14 items including three steam locomotive-powered sets and no passenger cars at all. In June 1966, Gilbert's name was stricken from the rolls of the New York Stock Exchange following a stock price drop from $42 a share to $20. In January 1967, a $4 million loss forced the company to shut its doors. What remained of value was divided up among creditors, auctioned off, or sold . The New Haven plant buildings went for $444,251. There was only one bidder for the American Flyer name, tools, dies, and rolling stock. For the sum of $150,000 Lionel stepped up and bought its long-time competitor. Lionel's triumph was brief, however. The old rivals ended their battle in a dead heat. On August 7–11, 1967, Lionel Toy Corporation liquidated its own machinery and equipment.

Ron Saypol, Cowen's grandson-in-law, had been jumped up to vice president of Lionel during the Cohn regime, but not long after, he bolted. In 1968, however, after Cohn had nipped off two strides ahead of the sheriff, Saypol returned and led a group that took over the hemorrhaging company, and he became president. He abandoned trains altogether for developing toy stores as a holding company.

The impervious Lionel name was still well known, and in 1969 cereal empires—notably General Mills and Nabisco—were snatching up toy companies. General Mills leased the Lionel name from Saypol's Lionel Corporation for a royalty against annual sales, and the dormant train-manufacturing dies, the remaining tools, and parts were moved to the cereal company's Fundimensions plant in Mt. Clemens, Michigan.

Taking advantage of the original dies, the name's recognition value, and its own deep pockets, Fundimensions managed to revive the line. "Not Just a Toy, a Tradition" was the comeback slogan, and Lionel was added to the stable along with Kenner (of building-set fame) and Parker Brothers (of Monopoly fame).

With leftover inventory, Fundimensions launched the rebirth of Lionel toy trains among the "Me Generation" of the 1970s. Fundimensions people managed to keep the best qualities of the 1950s locomotives and rolling stock, and they flogged the heritage theme in merchandising, resurrecting (figuratively) Joshua Cowen as their inspiration in absentia. His image appeared on special boxcars and ads, giving his vision mythic

ABOVE: The 1962 A. C. Gilbert catalog offered a "World of Transportation" rather than just trains. Fickle kids were becoming jaded with trains running on tracks when airplanes and fast cars were now available. *Mike Schafer collection*

ABOVE RIGHT: Slot cars were all the rage when Gilbert's World of Transportation catalog hit the streets in 1962. Electric trains were shunted back a few pages and cheaper sets were featured to entice parents who thought their jaded little tikes should have an electric train—a cheap one at least. *Mike Schafer collection*

importance, but, as author, Ron Hollander, put it in his 1981 Lionel book, *All Aboard!*:

> . . . Fundimension's trains are excellent. In some ways they are even better than the originals. They carry the Lionel name . . . but something is missing. The new catalogs make them look like pieces of hardware. They are photographed against plain paper backdrops, lifeless lumps of metal and plastic. No longer are they pictured roaring through idealized farmlands and country towns where children wave and look to distant horizons . . . The trains are "product," so many to the shipping carton, so much in freight charges. They are no longer the source of dreams.

Children were indeed slipping out of the loop. Kids need heroes, and there was nothing heroic about the state of railroads in 1970s America. The government had to rescue the remaining passenger trains from extinction by creating, in 1971, a new semi-public corporation—Amtrak—to operate them. Only freight made significant money—but not always. In 1976, the government once again had to step in to ward off financial disaster, merging several bankrupt Eastern freight carriers into the new Conrail Corporation. Further, the U.S. was at war again, bogged down in the political swamps of Vietnam where heroism burned brightly, flared, and died, returning stateside in flag-draped aluminum coffins. With the country ripped apart with protest and political corruption, many turned away from the headlines to the times of their youth when toy trains had provided escape from Cold War fears. The two- and three-rail toys changed from childrens' playthings to adult collectibles, from a circle of track assembled over the holidays to huge permanent layouts with full scenery surrounded with shelves of tinplate memories on display. The toy trains of the post-World War II kids had been transmuted from imagination machines into collectibles and long-term investments.

In 1969, that transformation had begun as Ronald Saypol was busy dumping Lionel's train line in favor of real-estate investment. Two members of the Train Collectors Association (TCA), a data analyst named Jerry Williams and his friend Fred Mill, started making trains for other members. They called their effort the Classic Models Corporation. Although their homemade standard-gauge box-cab electric and 2-4-0 steam locomotives sold well, they were not world beaters. Jerry thought the future of the business lay in reproducing old "classic" designs for new collectors who couldn't afford the actual antiques and others who wanted to run their trains, but not endanger their valuable collectibles. Fred thought otherwise. He and Jerry parted, and while Fred continued with the Classic Models Corporation, Jerry set up Williams Reproductions in December 1971.

As the 1970s wore on, the toy train market resumed an ascendancy that overall would accelerate as the century waned.

The 1960s heralded the precipitous downturn in American Flyer's fortunes. AF introduced the "Pike Master" series running on arguably better-looking track with closer tie spacing that was also cheaper to make. The Great Northern F-type diesel is little more than a cheesy, grossly out-of- scale shell hauling equally sad plastic cars. The plastic steam locomotive has painted-on windows and a one-piece side-rod churning plastic wheels. This GN "Klondike" set No. 20764 typified the steep skid that marked AF's end by 1963. Nonetheless, the Klondike set has become quite collectible. *Jeff Katzner collection*

A Budd RDC (Rail Diesel Car) issued in 1990 by Lionel passes through a Lionel bridge and over a Southern Pacific *Daylight* locomotive in front of Mike Moore's ZW-powered control center. The RDC represents the 1950s and 1960s era while the *Daylight* represents the late 1930s into the early 1950s. Mike's layout mixes eras and adheres to model railroaders' rules: "Rule No.1: It's my layout. Rule number 2: If you don't like what I've done, see Rule No. 1."

Chapter 8

Toy Train as Adult Collectible —the Rebirth

The famous Henry Dreyfuss-designed "Hudson" locomotive built to haul New York Central's *20th Century Limited* as interpreted in lithographed tinplate by the new Marx Train Company in 1998. In keeping with Marx's longtime simplification of detail, a 2-4-2 wheel arrangement is used to represent the prototype's 4-6-4. And, the new model has illuminated markers and Illuminated smokestack just like the Louis Marx trains of the 1930s and 40s. *Marx Trains*

The 1970s, 1980s, and 1990s run together as far as our story of the toy train is concerned. In effect, the toy train ceased to be just that—a toy. Even though new trains were designed, built, and sold, the original motivation—purchasing a toy for Little Tommy to grow up with—gradually faded away. The story of what came next during those three decades rings curiously familiar however.

Lionel managed to hang on, though hammered by the market, abandoned by the family, and sold off to a cereal conglomerate. There was still the name, that persistent logo, that spark of life that drew benefactors to it. As Lionel struggled, new competition emerged that created a new market—a market of memories reborn. Oddly, this new competition would develop along the same vaguely incestuous path that had been taken by the early pioneers of tinplate trains: Lionel, Chicago Flyer, Ives, Dorfan. All except one. Who else but Marx? We lost Louis in 1982 at age 86, but the whimsical spirit of his vision somehow ended up in the hands of a young Illinois couple who have taken on the job where he left off. But their story comes later.

This last part of our history evolves like those Russian matrushka dolls, one inside of another, inside of another, etc., and it began with Jerry Williams in 1971. Jerry, a data analyst, had joined the Train Collectors Association (TCA) in 1968. This group had organized to keep alive the rich history and operating excitement of tinplate railroading. Members spend an inordinate amount of time at flea markets, toy train swap meets, collectors' conventions, and prowling through the estate sales of departed toy train collectors. This is how a collection is amassed. It takes time and, in the case of rare finds, considerable "disposable income."

Jerry Williams followed the collectors' familiar pathways and managed to put together a respectable collection of tinplate trains. There was a kernel of dissatisfaction, however, in this pursuit. Many of the really desirable models had been scooped up or were priced out of the reach of younger collectors or those with a shallow bottom to their pockets. After talking to a number of members about building faithful reproductions of hard-to-get classic toy trains, he decided to test the waters with his new company, Williams Reproductions.

For his test, he chose an Ives No. 1694 electric in O gauge. This rare locomotive appeared in 1932 long after Lionel had absorbed Ives' assets. Very few were made, which added to its value. Williams borrowed a repainted 1694 from a collector friend, disassembled it, and used those parts to have dies made, assembling 300 for his first offering. They sold briskly even though no motor was included. The TCA Committee on Reproductions compared the Williams model with the original and requested he add some distinguishing mark to his copy—a tribute to the quality of his work. In later batches he had an "R" stamped on a pilot truck pivot underneath the locomotive to indicate reproduction.

Naturally there were rumbles of discontent as Williams plowed the money earned from the 1694 into dies for his next venture: copies of the Lionel Model 9 box-cab electric in standard gauge. With barely indistinguishable copies proliferating like mushrooms on a log, what would happen to the value of the actual antiques?

In fact, because the dies were still being made, he had no production model to photograph for his advertisement of the 1694. Williams shot a picture of an antique Ives locomotive as a stand-in. There were several differences between a Williams reproduction—such as the absence of solder to hold sides and roof together and the number of pieces that added up to the final model—but to the untutored, a side-by-side comparison was identical. Williams added another

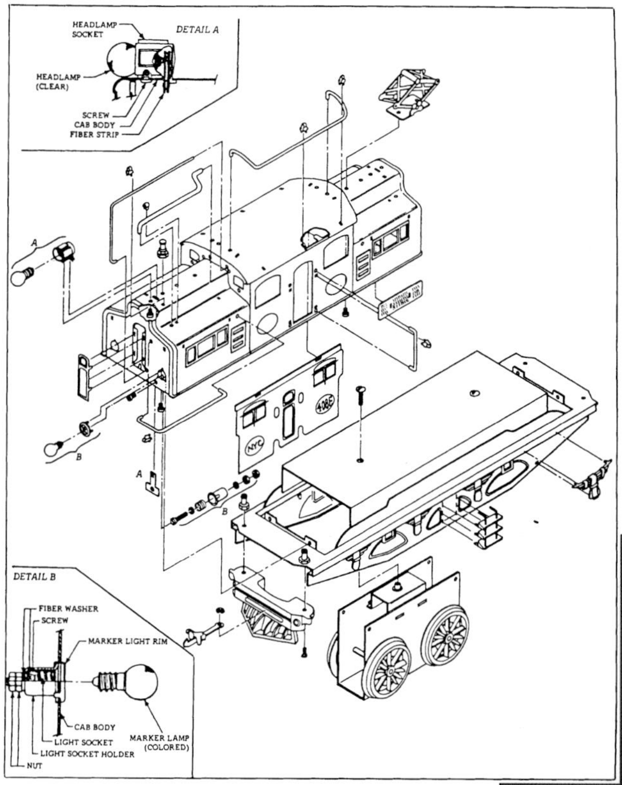

The Lionel 408E was a standard-gauge classic, and Williams' reproduction in kit form allowed toy train operators to run a 408E without taking their pristine collectible down from its showcase. *Williams Electric Trains*

A modern reproduction of the original Lionel 408E by MTH-Rail King. MTH's Mike Wolf took over creating reproductions of famous and sought-after classic locomotives and rolling stock after separating from Jerry Williams. This MTH reproduction testifies to the sheer beauty of the early standard-gauge locomotives built during the Golden Age of toy trains, the 1920s and 1930s. *MTH-Rail King*

wrinkle to the Model 9 and 9E locomotives, a "Repli-Kit" version the collector could build. One hundred of these were offered as part of the 1973–1978 runs. How many of these kits were actually built and how many were used for parts swapping in the antique Lionels is unknown.

These larger standard-gauge locomotives strained the working space of Williams' house-and-garage industry. As orders were going out the door for 1694s, cartons of stampings for the Model 9 were arriving in the driveway by 18-wheel trucks. To help out with assembling and boxing, Williams hired neighborhood kids and housewives. One of them was a 12-year-old boy named Mike Wolf. While other part-time employees came and went, Mike stayed on, becoming a valuable member of the company.

The huge Lionel 381 in standard gauge was next in line for reproduction, followed by the equally formidable 408E. As his manufacturing line grew, Williams moved from his house in Laurel, Maryland, to an industrial park in nearby Columbia in 1979. By this time, in seven years, Jerry Williams had created a considerable catalog of standard- and O gauge trains that represented an eclectic choice, including the Lionel 256 boxcab, a General Electric Amtrak E60 passenger electric locomotive, replicas of Lionel's popular *Madison*-series heavyweight passenger cars, and an excellent Pennsylvania GG1. His other passenger-car offerings included the huge standard gauge *State* cars (originally designed to ride behind the Model 381, but could only be pulled efficiently by the dual-motored 408E), a set of 418/428 cars in O gauge, and extruded aluminum modern Budd-type cars to accompany the E60 Amtrak electric-outline locomotive and GG1.

By this time, the TCA requested a silver version of the GG1 with silver *Madison* cars to be offered to TCA members. The reproduction market was flourishing to the point that Williams had to move again in 1980, to larger quarters across the street. Also by this time, Jerry Williams was no longer an employed data analyst but a full-time electric-train manufacturer who never looked back. His runs were now in the thousands as his visionary senses grew.

Looking to find a broader market, he turned to freight cars. Tooling for this wide variety of rolling stock was cost-prohibitive, but as luck would have it, the Kusan Corporation had been producing freight cars from dies owned by Andrew Kriswalis of Endicott, New York, a fellow TCA member. The line had not been successful, and after a year of negotiations, Williams bought the dies for freight cars, three locomotives, and some track parts. With these Kusan dies, he offered freight cars as kits sans trucks (the truck molds had to be reworked because of their bad condition) in his 1981 flyers.

By 1982, Williams used the dies to expand into low-priced O-gauge kit offerings and developed more attractive store packaging. At the same time, he was contacted by Samhongsa in Korea as a possible American outlet for the intricate brass locomotives made by that firm. The deal they worked out was for scale models that would run on either scale track or tinplate track. These models would have exquisite detail, but not so many small parts that they would be easily damaged by handling.

The reproduction kits, parts, and assembled pieces of the 1970s no longer figured in Williams' product direction, so in 1984 he sold the lot to his former employee, Mike Wolf, who had started his own company back in 1980 while still employed by Williams. The company was called Mike's Train House, and it shared the same building with Williams. By 1985, Wolf severed his ties with Williams, choosing to take MTH in a different direction.

In that same year, Williams moved again to larger quarters and decided to pitch only the middle and high-end market. He sold his Kusan dies to another manufacturer, Maury Kline, who had entered the field selling O-27 track and accessories under the name, K-Line. Together with some Marx plastic-car dies, K-Line used the peripatetic Kusan dies to launch its assortment of O-27 freight cars in the 1986 catalog.

Maury D. Kline grew up in Philadelphia peering longingly at the electric trains running in the window of John Wanamaker's department store back in the 1950s. He never lost that love for model trains, and today, almost 50 years later, that same store carries his MDK and K-line products made in Chapel Hill, North Carolina. From that first catalog to the present, K-Line comes close to renewing that bond with the 1950s when toy trains were truly a kid's world. Although the locomotives are O gauge scale (1:48 proportion) and the cars are excellent die-cast replicas, the value offered for the dollar is striking. While laboring in the shadow of Lionel, K-Line managed—even in its initial offerings of

A tinplate A-A set of Electro-Motive F7s made with a plastic molded shell tows a sleek line of aluminum Union Pacific passenger cars. This 1980s set is an original interpretation by Williams of the prototype. *Williams Electric Trains*

economy O-27 tinplate cars and locomotives—to offer surprising details.

Mike Wolf was nothing if not ambitious. After leaving Williams in 1985, he proceeded to carve a niche in the market for the original standard-gauge golden oldies like the Lionel 381 and 408E. His overhead was low, and he still shared space with Williams. By 1987, he had been approached by Lionel, then under the stewardship of millionaire train collector, Richard Kughn, to develop some highly detailed scale designs conceived in brass that would form a high-end Lionel product line. He did this, creating sophisticated steam locomotives, Alco PAs, and even a lift bridge. When Lionel terminated the relationship—due, according to Wolf in an interview with Bob Keller of Kalmbach Publishing Company's *Classic Toy Trains* Magazine, to ". . . perceived competition between himself and Lionel's in-house staff. . ."—he found himself without a Lionel dealership, with $750,000 worth of unfilled Lionel orders, and a product commitment to his Korean supplier, Samhongsa. A lawsuit eventually settled the situation, and MTH went on to release more new products than any other train manufacturer.

Continued on page 148

Early K-Line boxcars together with the 1987 FA Alco diesel. The 5111 Pennsylvania Railroad car is one of the first boxcars to be produced by K-Line; it was made from a Louis Marx O-27 mold in tuscan plastic and has die-cast wheels, plastic trucks, and operating couplers. Next to it is the first K-Line O gauge boxcar, the 6407, made from a Kusan mold. *K-Line Electric Trains*

A collection of K-Line freight cars. From the top, a Rio Grande die-cast scale hopper produced in 1997 from carbody drawings and photos of a 70-ton quadruple hopper. This car represents current state-of-the-art detailed scale modeling for O gauge scale and "hi-rail" (tinplate) operators. It has fully sprung trucks, die-cast wheels, operating couplers, opening hatches, and small detail parts such as ladders, brake wheels and grab irons. The car is gratifyingly heavy, and a long line of them would require a strong locomotive. Below it is a New York Central wood-sided reefer from a newly-tooled K-Line mold. Coupled to it is a Union Pacific tank car featuring a mix of generations: the tank itself is from a Kusan mold seated on a heavy frame made by K-Line. Bottom left is a K-Line Collector's Club Railway Express car . Built in 1996, it represents K-Line's careful paint applications and new molds that require metal detail parts to be added later in assembly rather than be part of the mold. To its right is the Pennsylvania Merchandise Service boxcar, part of K-Line's Classic Line of rolling stock. *K-Line Electric Trains*

"If it weren't for these toy trains..." The TCA and TTOS Associations

It's no fun collecting toy trains unless one can show his treasures and swap stories. With that in mind, Ed Alexander and Bill Krames organized the first meeting of what was to become the TCA—Train Collectors Association—in June 1954 at their homes in Yardley, Pennsylvania. Alexander and Krames had known several collectors over the years and thought the time was right to form a group of "kindred and congenial souls"—as the invitation stated—to meet and share their experiences. As with most special-interest organizations, the first get-together was a casual affair, but so successful they decided to schedule an organizational meeting for October that same year.

At the second meeting they formally adopted the name Train Collectors Association, and formed a constitution. The founders of the TCA decided the association was not only a socializing and swapping group of toy-train buffs, but a means of grading new and used equipment, restoring old equipment, and trading information on unscrupulous dealers or collectors. In addition, to keep the lines of communication in place between the June and October meetings, plans got underway for publishing a quarterly periodical and a directory of collectors.

Enthusiasm for the organization had far exceeded the expectations of Alexander and Krames. Collectors in California had already formed the Western Chapter by September 14, 1954, one month prior to the first National meeting. By 1961 the association numbered as many as seven chapters across the country. Later, the chapters were known as "divisions," and although the board established boundaries, members chose their own division name; by 1988 there were 19 divisions in the United States.

The *Train Collectors' Quarterly* first appeared in January 1955, devoted to tinplate collecting and operating. The first few issues were mimeographed or multilith printed by TCA members. Eventually they used the services of a commercial printer and by 1968 had developed its present 40-page, full-color format. In addition to the quarterly, the TCA also publishes a newsletter six times a year. Starting in January 1959 as a four-page publication, it has grown to 80 pages of notices, notes, train ads, and museum news. That's right—there is also a museum dedicated to toy train collectors everywhere.

The idea for a national headquarters and museum was born out of necessity. Business office locations—all in Pennsylvania—had moved from a garage to a storefront, and eventually the directors decided it was time the TCA had its own building and museum. The organization was offered property adjacent to the Red Caboose Motel in Strasburg, Pennsylvania. After several board meetings, a marketing survey, and reviewing contractors' and architects' bids, the group held its groundbreaking ceremony in April 1976, and the museum was dedicated one year later. It now houses five operating layouts, donations and loans of trains and equipment from members across the country, and a toy-train library. The volunteer committee

Tables full of tinplate electric trains and accessories for sale or swap fill a high-school social room during a weekend Train Collectors Association meeting in Addison, Illinois, near Chicago. *Train Collectors Association*

works several hours a week repairing and restoring vintage toy trains. The library committee also maintains a collection of books, periodicals, and catalogs, as well as an up-to-date filing system for researchers.

Another organization dedicated to lovers of toy trains is the Toy Train Operating Society. As its name suggests, the purpose of the TTOS is not only collecting and preserving, it also is dedicated to the mechanics of operating the locomotives and rolling stock. These are the late twentieth century's "recycled kids." They not only search for the elusive collectible, they play with it. They truly represent the "railroad engineers" of the hobby.

As its membership application states, the "TTOS was formed in 1966 to further the toy train hobby and to promote fellowship." The organization publishes its bulletin six times a year; members contribute articles on accessories, locomotives, publications, and layout construction. The TTOS recently lost a well-known model railroader when Honorary Lifetime Member Frank Sinatra passed away in 1998.

Although most toy-train aficionados cannot be pigeonholed into "collectors" or "operators," the interest and love of toy trains lives on. These two associations assure that there will always be fellowship keeping their interest alive. As one TCA member stated, "If it weren't for these old toy trains . . . you wouldn't know all these wonderful people."

Continued from page 144

This constant re-tooling—$17 million invested—and announcement of new products—41 diesel and electric locomotives, 30 steam engines, and 36 different freight-car types—has forced other makers to respond, increasing the competition for hobbyist dollars. Wolf's Rail King line of trains includes such disparate offerings as a Lionel 408E standard-gauge replica and an original O gauge Hudson as well as a Pennsylvania Railroad K-4 Pacific in both standard and streamlined versions.

An example of this competition is the Electro-Motive GP38–2 diesel road-switcher introduced in 1998 by K-Line. A 1997 EMD F-unit diesel presaged the GP38–2, raising some eyebrows among hobbyists with its attention to scale and detail, but the GP38–2 is stunning. When the author brought this model to his HO model railroad club and told them it ran on tinplate track—and then told them the suggested retail price, $333—some of our crustiest, prototype, scale-model rivet-counters had to sit down and reconsider many tinplate prejudices.

Weaver, founded in 1965, is another company that imports exquisite brass models that ride on deep-flanged tinplate drivers and trucks. These are models that truly bridge the gap between two-rail scale and three-rail tinplate railroading. Its "Gold Edition" Union Pacific 4-6-2 *Forty-Niner* is a very desirable streamlined steam locomotive with smoke, sound, and an engineer and fireman in the cab. All Weaver "Ultra Line" cars and locomotives are equally well finished and home-built in Northumberland, Pennsylvania.

And during all this time, where was Lionel? Management at General Mills struggled with their Lionel line of electric trains. They even carted the whole manufacturing operation down

This model of a Burlington Northern & Santa Fe GP38–2 road-switcher from K-Line stunned reviewers when it was introduced in 1998. It is a scale model designed for finicky hi-railers to run on standard O gauge tinplate track. Twin vertical motors make it a powerhouse for long trains, and the details are rigorously accurate. Rivet-counters will appreciate the tiny lift rings on the hood (with extras provided in case one breaks) and the rotating fans beneath their grids. Doors open, and railings are meticulously scale-model thin right up to the chain across the nose rails. It put K-Line into the top ranks among current manufacturers. *K-Line Electric Trains*

Weaver Models offers a mix of die-cast and brass scale models that run on two-rail scale track or three-rail tinplate. Today, brass models are built overseas in China, or Korea and are exquisite examples of the modeler's art. Of course, they are priced accordingly. This Union Pacific *Forty-Niner* Pacific-type steamer with streamlined shrouding is a good example of the stunning workmanship that is available today to adult operators and collectors alike priced at over $1,000. *Weaver Models*

to Tijuana, Mexico, in an attempt to cut costs. The intricacies of toy train manufacture suffered drastically, and the experiment only lasted from 1982 to 1984 when everything was trucked back to Mt. Clemens. Bruised and battered by the volatile economies of the toy business, General Mills dissolved Fundimension in 1985, stuffing Lionel into the new Kenner-Parker toy company.

This latest deal soured in a year and train collector Richard Kughn bought the company in 1986, changing its name to Lionel Trains, Inc. Kughn addressed Lionel's sales channels by creating a "Value Added Dealer" program with draconian restrictions that virtually eliminated free-lance dealers who undercut Lionel pricing to dump slow-moving products on the market.

To diversify the product line, beginning in 1987 and lasting through 1993, highly detailed brass locomotives were designed (some by Mike Wolf as discussed earlier) and built by Samhongsa in Korea. Further technical innovations included RailSounds, a digitally recorded sound system perfected in 1994 by railroad buff and rock musician Neil Young. He formed a partnership with Kughn to create a sound and control R&D operation called Lion Tech. Richard Kughn's re-energizing influence literally turned the company around.

Lionel Trains, Inc. became Lionel LLC in 1995 when it was purchased from Kughn by Wellspring Associates, an investment firm headed by Martin Davis of Gulf & Western and Paramount Communications, investment specialist Greg Feldman, and Lion Tech founder Neil Young. Gary Moreau, formerly of Oneida Silver, became president and chief executive officer.

So, the old firm approached the millennium with new sound systems, TV cameras built into computer-chip-laden locomotives (RailVision), Disney and Warner Brothers cartoon characters cavorting on the three-rail tracks, and revivals of classic locomotives from the past like Lionel's signature model, the Pennsylvania GG1. Hand-held, wireless Trainmaster remote-control units can operate trains from anywhere around the layout, and they have re-issued the original "football-in-a-box" transformer, the ZW, with its pair of control handles and up-to-date innards.

Dick Kughn, the last sole owner of the Lionel brand name from 1986 to 1995, was a millionaire toy train collector who turned around Lionel's fade into obscurity. He moved the brand toward high-quality brass models made overseas as well as rejuvenated rolling stock and accessory offerings from Lionel's classic era. Under his stewardship, Lionel also moved into "Lionel Large Scale" models (LGB and G scale) that harkened to the burly, golden days of standard gauge. *Lionel LLC*

A Lionel locomotive even appears on a U.S. postal stamp.

Best of all, to Lionel's everlasting credit, its advertising shows kids playing with the trains. It may be only a mirage, but bringing back the kids—as the luster of the real railroads has been restored since deregulation in 1980—could only be a good thing.

And what of that ghost of competition past, American Flyer? Despite Lionel's numerous changing of hands over the years, Flyer has remained Lionel's stepsister since its acquisition in 1969. However, the train line remained dormant until 1979 when a limited selection of Flyer items (three freight cars) was reintroduced as interest in toy train collecting suddenly vaulted. Three more freight cars followed in 1980, and then in 1981 Lionel (Fundimensions) released two entire sets—the first American Flyer train sets since 1966. These two offerings—a Baltimore & Ohio freight set and a Southern Pacific *Daylight* streamliner passenger set (both powered by Alco

A Lionel LLC model Electro-Motive GP9 diesel road-switcher hauls a string of 6400-series boxcars on a modular tinplate railroad at the "High Wheeler" train show sponsored by the Fox Valley (Illinois) Division of the National Model Railroad Association. Displaying Milwaukee Road colors, the updated model is computer-chip command controlled and has "Crewtalk" and Railsounds; in 1998 dollars it cost about $340. *Mike Reese, His n' Her Hobbies*

ABOVE: The Kleinschmidt family mans the TCA modular railroad at the High Wheeler train show sponsored by the Fox Valley Division of the NMRA as a pair of MTH Northern-type locomotives rush past in a blur. Costs running as high as $1,000 per locomotive have in part made collecting toy trains an adult hobby. *Jim Kleinschmidt*

RIGHT: Bill Van Ramshorst's American Flyer layout was started by his father 40 years ago. Bill remains loyal to AF, but also keeps up to date as this Lionel/American Flyer "GP20" (in reality a low-nosed GP7) in Burlington Northern livery of the early 1990s rolls past a 752 Seaboard Coal Loader first offered in 1946—the dawn of two-rail S gauge. *Bill Van Ramshorst*

On April 29, 1998, the electric toy train was honored by the United States Postal Service with its own commemorative postage stamp. Although the stamp doesn't mention Lionel, the gaudy prewar O gauge locomotive and the unique "latch" coupler of that period establish Lionel as representing the electric toy train. Need more proof? The backside of the stamp (the part you lick) reads: "Children played with remarkably realistic toy trains complete with tracks. Transformers, stations and accessories. The most popular sets were produced by Lionel." *Lionel LLC*

Regressing to the Mickey and Minnie Mouse handcar that helped bail Lionel out of a financial hole during the Depression, licensed Warner Brothers characters Wile E. Coyote and his speedy—if unhelpful—prey, the Roadrunner, board a large-scale powered handcar in 1991. *Lionel LLC*

PAs)—were the first in what would be a long run of Flyer's "Historic American Railroad" series.

In 1983 the Electro-Motive GP7 road-switcher was re-released, and in the mid-1980s a "new" Flyer diesel was introduced, the GP20—in reality the GP7 with a low nose. In the 1990s, the New Haven EP-5 electric was also reissued.

The news hasn't been so good for steam locomotives. The 4-6-4 Hudson was set to be re-released—in Wabash and Santa Fe markings, no less—in 1988, but a hefty price tag caused consumer angst, and the locomotive was never produced.

In the mid-to-late 1980s, two Flyer accessories were re-issued, the popular Drum Loader and the clever Saw Mill. In the 1990s, a new passenger car—a streamlined dining car—was introduced to augment Flyer's handsome and surprisingly accurate line of Budd streamlined passenger cars.

For a time, Flyer production was handled in Mexico, but quality problems, particularly with locomotive motors, dogged Lionel and Flyer production was shifted back to Michigan. On the plus side, the paint jobs on all Lionel-sponsored Flyer items have been stunning. Lionel has wisely been offering historic paint schemes aimed at baby boomers, although a number of more contemporary railroad liveries have also been offered such as Conrail, Chessie System, and Illinois Central Gulf. The Historic American Railroad series has produced a number of sets which have already become rather collectible, including Boston & Maine, New York Central, Wabash, Nickel Plate, and the perennially popular (in all scales) Pennsylvania Railroad.

As the twentieth century approached its end, Lionel's American Flyer product line faced an uncertain future. Sales of new Flyer over the two decades since the first 1979 re-release have met with mixed success, and as of 1998 Lionel was

offering only the Santa Fe Alco PA and PB. There has been talk of Lionel licensing the American Flyer product line to a company better suited to market and distribute to S gaugers, who do seem to be thriving—well enough to support not one but two S-oriented hobby magazines.

Meanwhile, a new company, American Models (featuring packaging reminiscent of Flyer's yellow-and-blue box era of the late 1940s and early 1950s) has began producing exquisite S-scale models that can operate on tinplate American Flyer track. Ron Bashista received his first American Flyer train in 1953, mourned the demise of the A. C. Gilbert Company, and was disappointed with the S gauge offerings of the late 1970s, 1980s, and 1990s. He sold his house and put the cash into tooling an Electro-Motive FP7 (designed for both freight and passenger service) locomotive. With encouragement from S-scale modelers and American Flyer S gauge collectors, he learned the tool-and-die trade, eventually going on to produce a line of locomotives, rolling stock, and accessories. In 1994 AM moved into a new 8,500-square-foot production center. The company motto is "We believe 'S' is the perfect size and will make no other."

And are Marx trains alive and well? Yes, they are in the capable hands of Jim and Debby Flynn. Actual production of the original Marx line ended in 1975. Louis died in 1982 and the Louis Marx & Co. trademark belongs to American Plastics, a Miami-based company owned by Jay Horowitz. Its main toy lines feature big-

Continued on page 156

Lionel Trains, Inc offered this "High Plains Runner" beginner train set in 1992, featuring a plastic locomotive, five cars, a bridge, and a flatbed truck. Of all the current toy train manufacturers, Lionel has continued to consistently feature kids in its ads and promotional pieces. *Lionel LLC*

Giant American Flyer Railroad—A Moveable

By Mike Schafer
Photography by the author

One of the nice things about being an adult no longer trapped in the confining reins of childhood is that you can make childhood dreams come true. One of these just-out-of-reach ideas I had as a kid was to amass enough American Flyer track and equipment to build a railroad that would blanket the floor of a house. Blessed with an understanding spouse, fellow dreamer Mike McBride shared this quest, and one Christmas we began "tinkering" with the circle of Flyer track around the McBride household Christmas tree. By the following Christmas, the normally conservative tree layout had gone berserk. Eventually we figured out that we didn't have to limit our absurdities to the holiday season.

Together Mike and I began pooling our resources to form the McBride & Sons, Barnum & Schafer Traveling American Flyer Show in 1986. Combining locomotives, cars, and an astounding quantity of tracks, crossings, and switches acquired at toy-train flea markets, we began creating incredibly elaborate floor layouts.

To operate these complex rug railroads requires several people, so these "Flyer Fests," as they have come to be known, have become giant parties complete with refreshments, video taping, and lots of two-rail track action. (Of course, the concept is in no way limited to American Flyer; any toy train system will work, particularly three-rail with its easy wiring.) Best of all, the whole family gets involved—and sometimes so do the neighbors. We send out invitations and, supplemented by word-of-mouth along the grapevine of fellow toy-train buffs, we draw adults and kids from all over to see the M&SB&STAFS trains race raucously 'round the carpeted countryside.

Our format generally remains constant. We build one long mainline loop equipped with passing sidings at regular intervals into which a train heading in one direction can park while an opposing train on the same track goes rushing on by.

What makes this all pretty tricky is that the main line re-crosses itself many times with plenty of opportunity for wrecks. While our inner child loves a good wreck, we try to avoid them since much of our equipment is fairly collectible—although we go out of our way to *not* use equipment of very high value. With that in mind, most of our trains are powered by Flyer 300-series Atlantics (4-4-2s). Our record thus far is a 1,000-foot main line with eleven passing sidings and 12 trains running simultaneously, six in each direction.

All the trains are operated by a single No. 22090 350-watt Flyer transformer whose double throttle system is wired in *parallel* (not series, or you'll send your locomotives to Mars and fry them in the process) and the two throttle handles operated simultaneously. This maximizes the amperage necessary to pump those 18 volts though the rails. Nonetheless, a network of feeder lines are required to track sections farthest from the transformer since the resistance caused by loose track pins and such quickly reduces the voltage. Since one main transformer is used to control all trains, all of them start or stop at the same time when the transformer is turned on and off.

To keep opposing trains from hitting each other head on (a "cornfield meet" in railroad jargon), "meets" are staged at passing-track sections. American Flyer switches are "power routed" such that when the first train along reaches the passing section, the switches are turned against it and the train halts. When the opposing train zooms by, one of the passing-track switches is reopened and the parked train is re-nergized, resuming its journey to the next passing-track section where it meets the next opposing train—and so on.

Wherever the main line crosses itself on crossing tracks, we set up a Sam the Semaphore Man to stop trains to let another pass in front of it. We don't always have enough semaphore signals to do this, so at some crossings we have to rely on the "Hand of God" to reach down and hold one train back to prevent a "T-bone" collision.

To show how serious this can get, both Mike McBride and I have even built *permanent* tunnels through the walls of our homes for our Flyer Fests (and the McBride cats love to use them as shortcuts). When Mike and I built our respective new houses, the floor plans had locations for future tunneling projects.

The appeal of toy trains remains with us and many other baby boomers, and we keep that interest alive with our American Flyer traveling "road show." The event appeals not only to toy-train fans, but to folks of all ages, male and female. I think Alfred C. Gilbert would be proud to know that more than a half century after the introduction of American Flyer S gauge trains, they are still entertaining generations of Americans.

LEFT: What started as literally a circle of track around the Christmas tree early in the 1980s grew into a holiday happening that drew visitors (and local newspapers) from all over within a 100-mile radius of their northern Illinois home. With the help of friend Mike Schafer, also a Flyer collector, Mike and Judy McBride and their two sons concocted elaborate S-gauge railroads by pooling equipment and track. Here, Mike McBride is at the "command station" (in reality a double-wired No. 22090 350-watt Flyer transformer) of one of the sprawling layouts.

RIGHT: Passing-track operator Otto P. Dobnick carefully controls a "meet" between two opposing trains, a freight powered by a Flyer GP7 (custom-painted in New Haven colors) and a Union Pacific 4-8-4 Northern pulling the *Overland Limited.* The track behind Otto's left hand dives into a tunnel underneath the bottom step of the stairway to the upstairs. The track re-emerges in the kitchen. Although the complexity of the track arrangements seen in these photos may suggest that the layout is comprised of several smaller, independent loops, in all cases it is but a single main line contorted to intersect itself numerous times.

Continued from page 153

wheel-type tricycles and little girls' vanities and playsets, all made from large plastic moldings—a far cry from tin toy trains.

Jim Flynn's first toy train was a Marx set. Later, he replaced it with a Lionel, but the little lithographed tin train had made its mark. Debby played with her friends' trains as a kid, but when she met Jim and they began collecting, she realized trains were going to be a part of her life. Collecting is one thing, and manufacturing is something completely different, however. After meeting Horowitz by way of the TCA and mutual friends, they failed to motivate the president of American Plastics to revive Marx trains. Then, for a year, they agonized over the decision to license the Marx name themselves. In 1993, they made the big step.

Today, they are Marx Trains, based out of their home in Addison, Illinois. Their line of locomotives, cars, train sets, and accessories do credit to the old man's name and philosophy.

"Louis Marx . . . was a very wise man," says Debby, "always trying to get the most bang for his buck. And that's what we're doing today, trying to be very creative and manufacturing here while everyone else is doing it in China."

It helps that, coincidentally, Debby works for a metal-stamping plant, and the owner was itching to get into toy manufacturing. "I had worked for the company for a number of years," Debby says, "and gave them our business. They pay me as an employee, but I take care of our account. So it's a fine line I walk between being a customer and an employee."

Jim's background is in graphic arts, and he designs shopping malls. They work out of their home amidst graphic-design computers and numerous antique collections, including a prewar Lionel layout. In their basement is an impressive and well-preserved collection of Louis Marx trains, Marx toys, and vintage Lionel pieces. When they are not home or working at their day jobs, they are lugging their Marx Trains product line to various train shows including TCA's twice-yearly big shows at York, Pennsylvania. They have to love what they are doing to keep up with that schedule.

Their first effort, in 1993, was a set of four Canadian Pacific passenger cars in a dark maroon color scheme. They do not make replicas of previous Marx products. For instance, the CP cars use

New Marx Trains come full circle. Maroon Canadian Pacific passenger cars are Marx Trains' first offering from 1991, and on the top track is the latest—and extremely popular—Chicago Transit Authority elevated train, which was a hit with Chicagoans in general, not just toy-train collectors. The trains pass a Tin Town high-rise made of Marx Trains tin cubes. On a siding to the left, a *20th Century Limited* steamer is parked. These excellent examples from new Marx Trains' first eight years would make Louis very happy. *Jim Flynn collection*

CANADIAN PACIFIC
CANADIAN PACIFIC
VICTORIA
40

A trio of Lionel O gauge F3 diesels and an Alco PA are poised to start up from their ladder track positions. These date from Lionel's MPC era that began in 1969 when General Mills took over operations. The flagman in the foreground is genuine post-war Lionel dating from 1947. *Stan Roy*

the lithography of the 6-inch cars, the body style of the 7-inch Milwaukee Road cars, and trucks that are based on Marx scale rolling stock.

"We don't copy anything that's been done," Debby adds. "We may use the same body styles, but all our graphics are original. We don't anticipate doing any replicating because there's no need to."

Like Louis, they re-use stamped shapes with new lithography. A shape may be a caboose cupola on one car, a bay window on another, and then show up as a dump base on an ore car. The basic "loaf-of-bread" car shape has appeared in many different guises. It will even be the basis for a "dinor" (that is, an eating establishment—and that's the correct spelling in the Erie, Pennsylvania, area) that original Marx tried as a test model, but never built.

The Flynns added a beautiful 1938 Henry Dreyfuss-designed New York Central streamlined "Hudson" (in reality a 2-4-2)—the famous locomotive assigned to the *20th Century Limited* and *Commodore Vanderbilt*—to their line of locomotives and in the late 1990s released a unique and charming set of 1950-era Chicago 'L' (elevated) electric cars that run on raised O-27 track. The cars not only go, but have lights at both ends and full Lectra-Sounds sound effects with familiar Chicago 'L' station stops called out as well as chimes and bells. Boxcars, tank cars, hopper cars, and gondolas—shiny new Marx rolling stock in dazzling colors rolls past a modular hi-rise building made of individual interlocking tin cubes.

Louis' penchant for military trains is also reflected in a train set featuring "dangerous-looking" ordinance in Army olive drab. To complete their homage, Louis Marx's likeness is featured on the "Toy King" boxcar of the 1996 Louis Marx 100th birthday set. But these tributes to the colorful days of lithographed tin are very much the creations of Jim and Debby Flynn.

It is appropriate that we end our story of the American toy train with the Flynn's nostalgic recreations. Though they sell primarily through hobby and specialty stores as well as filling direct factory orders from their dedicated collector-operator fans, these jewel-like little trains are, in every sense, toy trains. They recall the days when toys represented more than hardware, a time when young imaginations rode the rails and inhabited miniature worlds. They are the stuff of railroad dreams.

Index